Knowledge and Liberation

Tibetan Buddhist Epistemology in Support of Transformative Religious Experience

Knowledge and Liberation

Tibetan Buddhist Epistemology in Support of Transformative Religious Experience

Anne C. Klein

Snow Lion Publications
Ithaca, New York USA

Snow Lion Publications
P.O. Box 6483
Ithaca, New York 14851
USA

Printed in USA

ISBN 0-937938-23-8

Library of Congress Cataloging-in-Publication Data

Klein, Anne C., 1947–
Knowledge and liberation.

Bibliography: p.
Includes index.
1. Knowledge, Theory of (Buddhism) 2. Buddhist logic. 3. Dge-lugs-pa (Sect) — Doctrines. 4. Dignāga, 5th cent. 5. Dharmakīrti, 7th cent. I. Title.
BQ4440.K54 1986 181'.043 86-1784
ISBN 0-937938-23-8

Contents

Dedication
To my *Bakshi* and my Parents

Acknowledgements

My work on the material central to this book began in 1976 with Lati Rinbochay, shortly before his appointment as abbot of Ganden Shardzay Monastic College in Mundgod, South India. Under the instruction of this witty and rigorous scholar, born in 1923 in Eastern Tibet (Kham) and educated at Ganden near Lhasa, I studied Pur-bu-jok's *Collected Topics* (*bsDus grva*) as part of my training at the University of Virginia where Lati Rinbochay was a Visiting Lecturer in the Department of Religious Studies. In 1977, in a series of private tutorials, I went on to read the chapter on Sautrāntika from Jang-gya's *Presentation of Tenets* (*Grub mtha'i rnam bzhag*) with Lati Rinbochay, and studied it again with Denma Lochö Rinbochay in 1978 during his stay as Visiting Lecturer at Virginia. Lochö Rinbochay, born in 1927 in the Chikundo area of Kham and educated at Loseling College outside Lhasa, provided essential commentary also on sections of Den-dar-hla-ram-ba's *Presentation of Generally and Specifically Characterized Phenomena* (*Rang mtshan spyi mtshan gyi rnam gzhag*).[1]

In early 1979, I read and discussed the most detailed Gelukba analysis of this system, the Sautrāntika chapter from Jam-yang-shay-ba's *Great Exposition of Tenets* (*Grub mtha' chen mo*) with the late Geshe Gedun Lodrö who, educated at Gomang College of Drebung, Lhasa, and formerly Associate Professor at the University of Hamburg, was a scholar of unusual breadth and brilliance; his untimely death later that year at the age of 55 was a great loss to Buddhist Studies.

Work with these scholars was invaluable in allowing me to gain an overall perspective on the Gelukba presentation of Sautrāntika; with this philosophical map in mind I was able to isolate and pursue specific problems in detail. I therefore gratefully thank, not only the scholars just mentioned, but the University of Virginia Center for South Asian Studies, under whose auspices they were appointed.

The next phase in my exploration of topics discussed in this book came in India in 1980 during a year of field work funded by a Fulbright Dissertation Research Grant and carried out under the supportive advisorship of Professor K. K. Mittal of the Department of Buddhist Studies, Delhi University. During my first month in India I met daily with Loseling Geshe Belden Drakba, Head Librarian at Tibet House, New Delhi, to read the Jang-gya chapter for a third time. At this juncture I was seeking not merely clarification of the text at hand but a deeper exploration of a wide range of issues emerging from it. Geshe Belden Drakba, now in his early fifties, clarified many questions and also pointed out numerous difficult areas that he encouraged me to pursue in South India where the Tibetan monastic colleges have resettled. In February, 1980 I headed south to the new Drebung Monastic University in Karnataka State. During my four and a half months there I was fortunate in being able to consult daily with Kensur Yeshay Tupden, age 67, abbot emeritus of Drebung's Loseling College and justly famous for his ability to draw out the significance of either the smallest or most complex questions. During this period I also had numerous discussions with the excellent Gomang scholar Tsultrim Puntsok, subsequently a Professor at the University of Hamburg, who illuminated the fine points of numerous issues in Jang-gya's text.

Upon returning to the United States in early 1981, I read the Gomang College presentation of positive and negative phenomena and several sections of the Den-dar-hla-ram-ba text with the abbot emeritus of Gyumay Tantric College, Jambel Shenpen, 62, trained at Ganden Jangdzay College and subsequently in 1984 appointed as Ganden Tri Rịnbochay, the 98th successor to Tsong-ka-pa. His energetic commentary brought to life many of the essentials in these texts.

My procedure with these scholars was to elicit and tape-record their commentary on the text and then to use this as a starting point for detailed analysis of key issues — investigations which often led us to other commentators or to their Indian sources. After each session, necessarily conducted in Tibetan, I would listen to the tape, translating and summarizing its contents. Through the patience and erudition of my informants I became familiar with a wealth of contextualizing detail that would have been impossible to obtain through textual analysis alone.

In addition, I benefited much from Professor Jeffrey Hopkins, founder and head of Buddhist Studies at the University of Virginia, who went over several drafts of this book with unstinting care. Through his wide reading in Tibetan philosophical treatises he was able to lead me to numerous passages pertaining to topics under discussion and crystallize their significance. Skip Martin, Tibetan Curator and South Asia bibliographer at Virginia's Alderman Library, made available essential resources. I am also grateful for the insight of other advisors at the University of Virginia during the dissertation phase of this project: Professors Richard Barnett, Paul Groner, and David Little. Moreover, while in Asia I benefited from free-flowing and enthusiastic discussions with the Ven. Sangyay Samdrup, who recently became the first Westerner to attain a Geshe degree, with Daniel Coffman, a veteran of over ten year's study at Gelukba centers in India, and with Dr. Leonard Van der Kuijp at the Nepal Research Center in Kathmandu.

It is also my pleasure to thank Professor Masatoshi Nagatomi at the Harvard Yenching Institute. In going over several chapters of this book he was equally generous with the scarce — his time — and the plentiful — his expertise — when I was revising the manuscript while a Visiting Scholar at Harvard's Center for the Study of World Religions. It was invaluable to discuss with Professor Nagatomi the Indian sources and context for issues discussed here, especially as they pertain to one of his chief areas of interest, the work of Dignāga and Dharmakīrti. Needless to say, with such mentors whatever defects remain are entirely my own doing.

I want also to mention, as essential contributing causes to the completion of this study, the ingenious insights of my husband, Professor Harvey B. Aronson, who tirelessly thought through sticky points with me in buses and tea-stalls all over India; the kind support of my parents, Ludovic and Isabelle L. Klein, and the profound inspiration of Geshe Wangyal.

---

[1] Translation of these texts, together with the oral commentary of these scholars are included in Klein, *Knowing, Naming, and Negation* (Ithaca: Snow Lion Publications, forthcoming).

Note on Transliteration

The system of Tibetan transliteration used here was devised by Professor Turrel Wylie; it is modified slightly to capitalize the first pronounced letter in the names of persons and texts. Wylie's system gives a letter-by-letter correspondence from Tibetan to English, including letters that are unpronounced, and appears in the text italicized and enclosed in parentheses. It is given on a word's first appearance and in the glossary. For a readable phonetic rendering that maximally approximates actual Tibetan pronunciation (Lhasa dialect), an adaptation of the system created by Professor Jeffrey Hopkins[1] is used throughout the book wherever Tibetan names occur. In Hopkins' own system the line over a consonant indicates high, short, sharp pronunciation. The table below gives both the transliteration and phonetic systems, Wylie's being on the left and Hopkins' on the right.

Table 1

ka: ḡa	kha: ka	ga: ga	nga: nga
ca: j̄a	cha: cha	ja: ja	nya: nya
ta: d̄a	tha: ta	da: da	na: na
pa: b̄a	pha: pa	ba: ba	ma: ma
tsa: d̄za	tsha: tsa	dza: dza	wa: wa
zha: sha	za: sa	'a: a	ya: ya
ra: ra	la: la	sha: s̄ha	sa: s̄a
ha: ha			

In the present adaptation of the Hopkins system, lines over consonants will not appear in the text. Thus, for example, when the phonetic *ga* replaces the first column *ka* it signifies a high pronunciation; when it replaces the third column *ga* it does not. A few examples will suffice to give the gist of the system:

Table 2

B̄el-den-cho-jay (dPal-ldan-chos-byed)
D̄ak-tsang (sTag-tshang)
D̄en-dar-hla-ram-ba (bsTan-dar-lha-ram-pa)
Ḡön-chok-jik-may-wang-bo (dKon-mchog-'jigs-med-dbang-po)
Gyel-tsap (rGyal-tshab)
J̄ang-ḡya (lCang-skya)
Nga-wang-b̄el-den (Ngag-dbang-dpal-ldan)
Nga-wang-d̄ra-shi (Ngag-dbang-bkra-shis)
Pur-bu-j̄ok (Phur-bu-lcog)
Ra-d̄ö (Rva stod)
S̄ö-nam-drak-ba (bSod-nams-grags-pa)

In addition, the phonetic system substitutes *k* and *p* for the Wylie *g* and *b* in the suffix position. For those wishing to train in pronunciation, we note that when *ba* occurs as the final syllable it is *not* pronounced high due to its end position.

Regarding the pronounciation of Tibetan vowels, *a* in the phonetic system indicates the vowel sound of the English word opt; *i* the vowel sound of it or eat; *u* the vowel sound of soon; *ay* the vowel sound of 'bake'; *o* indicates the vowel sound of boat and *ö* indicates the vowel sound er.

In deference to common usage, a few exceptions to the system are permitted: the familiar Tsong-ka-pa, actually pronounced Dzong-ka-ba, is retained; also the title *Geshe*, which strictly in this system would be rendered Ge-shay. Personal names are hyphenated in phonetic transliteration except in cases where contemporary Tibetan scholars are themselves using unhyphenated renderings of their own names. However, in accordance with a growing trend and to make a visual distinction between these and other proper nouns, the names of the different religious orders of Tibet, such as Gelukba (*dGe-lugs-pa*), and monastary names such as Drebung (*'bras spungs*) are not hyphenated.

Sanskrit equivalents for Tibetan terms are given wherever possible; an asterisk beside an entry indicates reconstruction of the Sanskrit from Tibetan. Full Sanskrit and Tibetan text titles are found in the bibliography which is arranged alphabetically according to English titles of sutras and according to the phonetic rendering of the authors of Sanskrit and Tibetan works. Original-language terms and titles are found in the index, referenced with their English translation. Authors' dates, when available, also appear in the bibliography.

Introduction

SCOPE OF THE ISSUE

In Western religious and philosophical discourse, mystical experience is commonly seen as antithetical to reflective thought. This perspective has significantly affected the study of religion by undermining investigators' interest in how philosophical or symbolic expressions of a tradition relate to the mystical experiences of persons within that tradition. In short, as Steven Katz has eloquently pointed out,[1] scholars of mysticism and of religious traditions in general have not concerned themselves with how the former may shape or give rise to the latter. This has obscured questions regarding the manner in which a given mystical experience is fostered by the tradition through whose symbols and concepts it is mediated.

This point is particularly significant in the case of Tibetan Buddhism where the written and oral scholarly traditions offer an encyclopedic array of meditative techniques directed at generating specific experiences. A major category of these techniques features use of a philosophical dialectic which, in Frederick Streng's phrase, is itself a "means of knowing".[2] Implementation of this dialectic involves conceptual thinking that may on the surface seem irrevocably divorced from the "inconceivable, inexpressible" wisdom toward which the practitioner is ostensibly headed. The possibility of resolving this apparent conundrum is the major impetus and theme of this book. It has stimulated my investigation of the epistemological theory by which Gelukba — the dominant and highly scholastic order of Tibetan Buddhism — accounts for the premise that intellectual endeavor, both in preparation for and during practice of meditation, is instrumental in attaining particular forms of direct, non-conceptual or mystical experience.

The existence of such a theory, in turn, indicates how a scholastic tradition, source of the meditative dialectic, may be considered an essential formulator of a certain type of mystical experience.[3] Indeed, Gelukba scholars and meditation masters scoff at the notion that someone would study one way and meditate another. Detailed knowledge of the books is deemed useful for a scholar, but essential for a meditator.[4]

At the same time, Gelukbas must remain cognizant of the fact that inexpressibility as an epithet of the ultimate is frequently mentioned in Indian and Tibetan Buddhist texts. As generations of scholars have noted, this description has in no way impeded a massive scholastic tradition grown up in an endeavor, presumably, to be informative about ultimate truth or the nature of reality. And in the Buddhist context, as already suggested, this is not really an irony. The Dalai Lama once remarked, having cited the importance this textual material has for realizing the inexpressible ultimate, "After all, it is not *that* inexpressible." Since the inexpressibility of the ultimate is said to refer to the inability of words to convey a yogi's non-dualistic perception of ultimate reality exactly as it is experienced, there is no contradiction in words and thought leading to that experience.

The ultimate truth and the special mind which realizes or even unites with it is described in treatises and depicted in iconography, both of which serve as bases for religious practice. The extent to which ultimate reality or ultimate truth is actually revealed through verbal or symbolic expression provides significant data not only about ultimacy itself, but about the status, capacity and religious significance of symbols and words. In Mādhyamika, the latter fall into the category of conventional phenomena, also known as conventional truths. The two truths — ultimate and conventional — are variously described in different systems of Buddhist thought. In the Tibetan *siddhānta*, systemized philosophical texts, particularly, such descriptions or definitions are indexical to the overall perspective of a given system. This book explores the *expressibility* of the ultimate and how a perceived need for such expression shaped the Gelukba systemization of Sautrāntika definitions of conventional and ultimate in ways that were also important to that order's practice and theory of Mādhyamika.

In this volume I have left aside the very interesting topic of iconographic and other symbolic representations of the ultimate to focus on verbal and conceptual expressions of it.[5] My special concern is for the significance conceptual thought is seen to have in gaining experiential access to a non-conceptual understanding of the ultimate. Indeed, the possibility of harnessing the intellect in direct service of non-dualistic experience has, since Tsong-ka-pa's founding of Gelukba in the 14th century, motivated that order's famous scholasticism and shaped the practice of its exoteric and esoteric religious traditions. Exploration of this issue thus also speaks to the larger concern of a cross-cultural investigation into the relationships that may be possible between internal religious experience, that is, the intentional cultivation and achievement of specific internal states, and the particular literary or oral tradition in which such experience is embedded. Gelukba scholars would certainly agree with Steven Katz that such experience is formed "... by concepts which the practitioner brings to and which shape, his experience."[6] Indeed, Gelukbas would go a step further and maintain that their concepts are a primary method by which one gains access to the ultimate. The stages of practice begin with building up a mental image, through words and inferential reasoning, of for example the subtle disintegration that takes place in produced phenomena from one moment to the next. In this way one comes to ascertain subtle impermanence. Similarly, to gain a non-conceptual understanding of emptiness, one first builds up a mental image of the lack of substantial or inherent existence. Such mental training is considered effective in large part because the words describing momentary impermanence or the lack of inherent existence and the thought apprehending mental images of these do relate to the actual phenomena of impermanence or emptiness. Direct cognition of these is considered essential to the process of liberation. Such cognitions, ineffable and profoundly reorienting of the human psyche, are certainly forms of mystical experience. The intellect could not be claimed as a cause of such experience if Gelukba posited an unbridgeable gulf between words and thought on the one hand and reality on the other. The ways in which their epistemology frames the connection between words and actual phenomena, and the problems it encounters in doing so, is a major issue in the overall epistemological investigation appearing here.

The intellect's significance for mystical experience would also be impossible except for the assertion that the nature of awareness itself is such that conceptuality can be transformed into direct perception. The Gelukba presentation of minds and awarenesses (*bLo rig*), as well as the *Collected Topics of Logic and Epistemology* (*bsDus grva*) define mind as "that which is clear and knowing." This is the very entity, the nature, of all types of minds, conceptual and non-conceptual. Thus, conceptual thought and direct perception are not merely compatible in terms of their potential for mutual enhancement, but their very basic nature is the same. With this in mind, it is not surprising that Gelukbas maintain with such vigor the possibility of conceptual thought yielding to direct perception. This is not so much a case of making a leap over a chasm as of a shift from one mode to another.

This shift is multifaceted. Conceptual thought is not transformed of its own force into direct experience; other elements of mental training and engagement with the religious path are involved. Most significant is the gradual union of conceptual understanding with increasingly stabilized periods of concentration. The practitioner alternates between analytical meditation (*dpyad sgom*) and stabilizing meditation (*'jog sgom*). Finally, one reaches the point where instead of analysis acting as an interference to stabilization, or stabilization weakening analytical understanding, each enhances the other. This union of analytical or insight practice with a concentration developed to the point of calm abiding (*śamatha, zhi gnas*) is called special insight (*vipaśyanā, lhag mthong*). Attainment of this union of insight and concentration marks the beginning of the second of five paths or stages of practice, the path of preparation (*prayoga-mārga, sbyor lam*).

Over the four levels of this path, one's mental image of subtle impermanence or emptiness becomes increasingly representative of the actual impermanence or emptiness that will be directly or non-conceptually realized on the third path, that of seeing (*darśana-mārga, mthong lam*). Such realization is inexpressible, just as any direct experience — plunging into cold water, the taste of an orange — is inexpressible. But this is inexpressibility with a difference. Ordinary direct experience, though impossible to represent fully in words, nevertheless is organized around the same type of subject-object polarities that govern verbalization. The non-conceptual experience on the path of seeing, however, is said to be free of any such dualism. This basic paradigm — of conceptual thought leading to non-conceptual realization — is set out in the Gelukba presentation of Sautrāntika. It is significant that the same paradigm obtains in their discussion of meditative realization in Prāsaṅgika-Mādhyamika, the philosophical system Gelukbas actually practice.

Gelukba Prāsaṅgika describes a direct, non-dualistic cognition of emptiness that is like fresh water poured into fresh water. Subject and object — the mind and emptiness — are fused as if one. Is this not the very antithesis of conceptual analysis? Yet, as already indicated, Gelukbas repeatedly stress that a correct non-conceptual realization begins with a correct conceptual framework. Realizing emptiness is not a matter merely of divorcing oneself from conceptuality, but of gaining a certain type of explicit understanding. The nature of this understanding is claimed to be such that approaching it unlocks the ordinary dualistic patterning of conceptual thought.[7]

The profound compatability between intellectual activity and mystical experience is seen to arise from a coalescence of several factors — the common nature of thought and direct perception as clear and knowing, the capacity for concentration and insight to be mutually re-enforcing, and the significant ways in which the inexpressible *can* be expressed. This volume is mainly concerned with the latter, and thus with investigating the limits and capacities of knowledge as they have been analyzed in Tibetan Buddhist traditions on the basis of Indian texts, especially the works of Dignāga and Dharmakīrti. To this end it attempts a synthesis and analysis of Gelukba scholarship on Sautrāntika based on their oral and textual traditions. This perspective is further clarified by references to selected Tibetan and modern scholarship, and by tracing major themes to their Indian origins.

The result of the training or path described in Gelukba is an example of a mystical experience which, in Robert Gimello's words "is not mindless, and in [which] the intellect clearly has some role to play".[8] This experience or realization, gained through analytical meditations of the sutra path, then becomes the basis for deity yoga and all other practices of tantra.[9] Thus, to analyze Gelukba perspectives on Sautrāntika is to observe one way in which a particular religious tradition articulates its intention to mold mystical experience and its manner of doing so.

THE BUDDHIST RELIGIOUS CONTEXT

In approximately 531 B.C. a prince of the Śākya clan, Siddhārtha Gautama, sat down at dusk to meditate beneath a pipal tree on the Bodhgaya plains in northeast India. To all appearances he was an ordinary man of thirty-five; for six years he had been seeking to escape the suffering of repeated birth, aging, sickness, and death.[10] By day-break he had achieved his goal; he was liberated, a fully enlightened Buddha. This change is considered to have occurred, not through the performance of rites and rituals, nor even through the blessings of other Buddhas, but through Gautama's own attainment and cultivation of a specific type of knowledge.

During the night he had realized four truths concerning the existence of all living beings. He saw that all are subject to many types of suffering (true suffering),[11] that the cause of this suffering is ignorance (true origin), and that one can bring about a cessation of suffering (true cessation) through following the very path that he himself had just completed (true path). Moreover, in understanding true sufferings Gautama Buddha had directly realized that, despite appearances to the contrary, phenomena are impermanent and insubstantial. Due to this realization it became clear to him that the primary causes of repeated birth, aging, sickness, and death are the mistaken perceptions of phenomena as permanent and substantial whereas they actually disintegrate from one moment to the next and are insubstantial. He further observed that this misconception leads to actions of desire, hatred and the like, which impel beings into a continuous cycle of suffering that cannot be broken unless the ignorance at its source is overcome. He consequently undertook to teach others how to uproot their mistaken perceptions and thereby attain freedom from suffering.

Thus, from the time of Siddhārtha, Buddhism has been concerned with overcoming limitations and errors of ordinary perception in order to gain a liberating knowledge of reality. As Buddhist thought developed, these issues gradually came to be treated with increasing rigor. This was especially true during the Indian Gupta period when increased lay support for the clergy made possible the vigorous growth of Buddhist monastic scholarship; such scholarship was further motivated by a growing need to defeat non-Buddhists in debate. This period saw the flowering of Indian Buddhist logic: partly inspired by Vasubandhu, his disciple Dignāga,[12] the 6th-century father of Indian Buddhist logic, and Dharmakīrti, the latter's first and most important commentator[13] began to articulate principles which Gelukba scholars later took as the basis for their formulations of Buddhist epistemology.

Starting roughly with Dignāga (d. 540 B.C.),[14] Buddhist philosophers began to discuss perceptual errors — sources of suffering — in terms of direct and conceptual perception (*pratyakṣa, mngon sum; kalpanā, rtog pa*) and their objects. According to these philosophers, there are only two types of valid cognition, direct perception (*pratyakṣa-pramāṇa, mngon sum tshad ma*) and inference (*anumāṇa-pramāṇa, rjes dpag tshad ma*). Since ordinary direct perception is insufficient to generate a conscious ascertainment of subtle impermanence or selflessness, the only type of valid perception by which ordinary beings can at first know such phenomena is conceptual. Moreover, cultivation of a conceptual, inferential understanding, that is, of a correct conceptual image of impermanence or selflessness, enables one to ascertain these consciously in yogic direct perception and thereby gradually to overcome ignorance. In this way, one is said to achieve liberation from the suffering caused by ignorance.

Even if one is skeptical about the claim that study of Buddhist epistemology affords an opportunity to overcome all suffering, one can only be impressed by the rich detail of Buddhist scholarship on the topic, its internal logic, the questions it raises about the validity of human perception, and the potential for transformation it sees in the ordinary mind.

PERSPECTIVE ON THE GELUKBA FORMULATION OF SAUTRĀNTIKA

In Tibet, the four major systems of Buddhist tenets are ranked according to the subtlety with which they identify and rectify the various forms of ignorance considered to prevent liberation and omniscience. These four consist of two Hīnayāna systems — Vaibhāṣika and Sautrāntika — and two Mahāyāna systems — Cittamātra and Mādhyamika. The Gelukba order of Tibetan Buddhism, as well as the other main orders (Nyingma, Gagyu, and Sagya) each have presentations of all four systems of tenets. Almost all groups within these orders agree that Mādhyamika is the highest of the four tenet systems; it is this that the student or practitioner ultimately wishes to understand. This valuation is in contrast to the chronological development of Mahāyāna in India, where Cittamātra arose after Mādhyamika and was considered by its proponents to emend certain nihilistic tendencies in the earlier Mahāyāna system. In Tibet, the systems considered lower than Mādhyamika — the Vaibhāṣika, Sautrāntika and Cittamātra tenet systems — are studied not only for their own sake but because they aid comprehension of Mādhyamika. The study of Sautrāntika in particular accomplishes this in two ways. First, much of what is learned in the Gelukba formulation of Sautrāntika about the nature of direct perception and conceptual thought, among other topices, is carried over unchanged to Gelukba discussions of Mādhyamika. Other points of Gelukba Sautrāntika, such as its description of ultimate truths, are not carried over but are considered pedagogically essential. For, in order to realize emptiness or selflessness as explained in Gelukba presentations of Indian Mādhyamika, it is necessary to understand well the 'self' — inherent existence — which is negated. What the Gelukba Sautrāntika system presents as the meaning of an ultimate truth comes to be negated in the Mādhyamika theory of selflessness; thus, in studying Sautrāntika one begins to set up the target — the conception of self — at which Mādhyamika theory is aimed.

In Tibet, actual adherents to the four systems of tenets are not pitted against one another in the sense of one trying to gain supremacy over the other. Still, much debate goes on in the monastic colleges, with a single challenger alternately taking the positions of Vaibhāṣika, Sautrāntika, Cittamātra, or Mādhyamika. This is done for the sake of sharpening understanding with respect to the differences among the schools of tenets, not to convert the opponent to a different system.

Vaibhāṣika and Sautrāntika are the basis for the first phase of approximately twenty years of study in the Gelukba monastic curriculum. This initial phase lasts from three to six years, depending on the particular Monastic College.[15] In the educational system dominant in Tibet and presently continued at refugee Tibetan monasteries in South India, a student is introduced to the format and collected topics (*bsDus grva*) of Buddhist logic and epistemology by memorizing and debating tenets and definitions gathered from Vasubandhu's *Treasury of Knowledge* (*Abhidharmakośa*) and Dharmakīrti's Seven Treatises on Valid Cognition (see Bibliography). Vasubandhu's *Treasury of Knowledge* is considered to represent the Vaibhāṣika view but his own commentary on it is said to accord with the Sautrāntikas Following Scripture (*āgama-anusārin*), whereas

Dharmakīrti's Seven Treatises, though generally considered Cittamātrin, are studied here according to Hīnayāna interpreters who are known as Sautrāntikas Following Reasoning (*nyāya-anusārin*).

The categories of 'followers of scripture' and 'followers of reasoning' were well known in India as subdivisions of Cittamātra. Gelukbas appear to be unique in recognizing these divisions also with respect to Sautrāntika; the classification of *Sautrāntika* followers of scripture and reasoning was not wide-spread in India if it was ever used there at all.[16]

The views of Sautrāntikas Following Reasoning thus dominate the initial orientation years of study for Gelubkas. The Gelukba formulation of this system contextualizes their study of Awareness and Knowledge (*bLo rig*) as well as the topic of Signs and Reasoning (*rTags rigs*) within the first segment of their curriculum; it is also the basis for the higher Mahāyāna studies of the Perfection of Wisdom (*Phar phyin*) and the Middle Way (*Mādhyamika, dbUma*). Therefore, the system of Sautrāntikas Following Reasoning is analyzed and elaborated here. Our investigation of this Gelukba systemization of Sautrāntika is contextualized by other perspectives, Tibetan and Western, as well as by references to the major Indian roots of the system.

The Gelukba order, whose literature is the main focus of this study, was founded in the late 14th century by Tsong-ka-pa, teacher of the first Dalai Lama. Gelukbas maintained the three largest monastic universities in Tibet: Drebung (traditionally estimated at 7,700 monks), Sera (5,500) and Ganden (3,300). Each of these institutions was subdivided into several colleges; two colleges from each of the three centers have been re-established by Tibetan exiles in South India. Although each college has its own textbooks containing many points of interpretation unique to it, there is by and large consensus on the most significant issues.

In order to understand the ignorance claimed to be the root of all suffering, one must investigate several topics. Ignorance involves misperception; thus, it is necessary to analyze the objects perceived as well as the perceiving consciousnesses themselves. According to Sautrāntika, impermanent things fully appear to direct perception, and permanent phenomena fully appear to conceptual thought. In the Gelukba formulation of Sautrāntikas Following Reasoning, these two categories of phenomena are synonymous with ultimate and conventional truths respectively. The discussion of these is given in chapter one and, in chapter two, is contrasted with that of the late

15th-century Tibetan Sagya scholar, Dak-tsang, who often took issue with Gelukba views. Chapters three and four analyze Gelukba discussions of how these two types of cognition operate in relation to impermanent and permanent objects.

In the Gelukba epistemological framework, phenomena observed by direct perception are categorized according to whether or not they are cognized through the explicit elimination of another phenomenon. Such an eliminated object is known as an object of negation (*pratiṣedhya, dgag bya*). For example, a mountainless plain is conceptualized by mentally eliminating mountain. Any object, permanent or impermanent, that is cognized through such an eliminative process is considered a negative phenomenon (*pratiṣedha, dgag pa*); objects not so cognized are positive (*vidhi, grub pa*). This division, introduced in chapter five and amplified in chapters six and seven, has important ramifications for the Buddhist presentation of a path or method for development of liberating knowledge. The reality which must be cognized as an antidote to ignorance — ignorance being, in this system of Sautrāntika, the conception of self-sufficiency in persons and the objects they use — is itself a negative phenomenon. It is argued that negative phenomena can be expressed by words to a degree sufficient for helping a practitioner develop a vivid cognition of them. In order to clarify the Gelukba position on these points, other interpretations of Sautrāntika are considered. Finally, for the sake of further clarifying the description of conceptual processes, the manner in which names are originally learned and later applied to objects is discussed in chapter eight.

The topics of negation, or exclusion (*anyāpoha, gzhan sel*) and naming are considered essential for an epistemological description of how conceptual thought actually relates to and realizes external objects. Gelukba scholars such as Jang-gya and Den-dar-hla-ram-ba carefully make the point that impermanent objects cannot appear as fully to thought as they do to direct perception, but maintain that thought *does* actually cognize them and words *do* actually describe them. For this reason it is considered possible to use thought — internal images and inferential reasoning — to cultivate an actual realization of impermanence and insubstantiality. As elaborated in chapter nine, further cultivation of the path makes these realizations non-conceptual, but they and the liberation which results from their banishment of ignorance are rooted in correct conceptualization.

This analysis of Sautrāntika has three main purposes. The first is to detail Gelukba presentations of major Sautrāntika topics through analysis of the written and oral scholarly traditions. Material is drawn from a variety of Gelukba texts and utilizes oral commentary from contemporary scholars trained in four of the six existing non-Tantric Gelukba colleges; significant differences of viewpoints among the colleges are noted.

The second purpose is to establish major sources for the Gelukba presentation and to distinguish Gelukba's use of these from other systemizations of the same material. Gelukba discussions of Sautrāntika, which are primarily based on the writings of Vasubandhu, Dignāga, and Dharmakīrti, are contrasted with certain modern Western and Indian writers who, based on the same sources, also discuss the topics of valid cognition, specifically and generally characterized phenomena (*svalakṣaṇa, rang mtshan; sāmānyalakṣaṇa, spyi mtshan*), and exclusions.

It is widely recognized that the work of Dignāga and Dharmakīrti, which spans both Sautrāntika and Cittamātra, can be interpreted in many different ways.[17] It is not the purpose here to catalog, much less compare, all possible interpretations or to determine a 'true' one. My intention is to clarify the Gelukba presentation by carefully distinguishing it from non-Gelukba Tibetan writers, expecially the Sagya scholar Dak-tsang (b. 1405) and from certain dominant trends in modern scholarship. This is expected to show (a) that the Gelukba interpretation is in important aspects unique, greatly at variance with virtually all other scholarship on certain topics, and thus not a *mere* extension of Indian tradition, (b) that the unique Gelukba presentation serves as a basis for that order's explanation of and methods for realizing the Mādhyamika view, and (c) that this interpretation, though not the only one possible, is derived from and supportable by the Indian texts.

The third purpose is to assess Gelukba Sautrāntika in terms of liberative techniques. This is a central issue inasmuch as the discussion of Sautrāntika represents, for Gelukba, a method of leading the scholar or practitioner on to their presentation of the Mādhyamika view — the Middle Way school — of Nāgārjuna. To understand this school it is helpful to distinguish Sautrāntika from it. For example, modern critical literature often considers the assertion of an "inexpressible reality" to be a unique feature of Mādhyamika.

The Gelukba presentation of Sautrāntika, however, discusses in detail the ways in which 'reality' is inexpressible. Their presentation on this point is compatible with that of Mādhyamika, but distinct from it. Thus, an articulation of the ways in which a study of Sautrāntika readies one for Mādhyamika necessitates both a presentation of Sautrāntika's view of reality and a contrasting of it with Mādhyamika.

SOURCE LITERATURE

Buddhism was carried from India to Tibet over a period of about four hundred years between the seventh and twelfth centuries, A.D. Prior to this time Tibet apparently had no written language[18] but interest in the Indian Buddhist texts was such that an alphabet, precise philosophical vocabulary, and system of grammar were developed in the seventh century for the purpose of translating these works. Indian and Tibetan scholars collaborated to evolve a translation scheme capable of transmitting the sophisticated nuances of Sanskrit. After Buddhism virtually disappeared from India in the twelfth century, many Sanskrit texts were lost and are now accessible only through their Tibetan translations.

The Sanskrit 'Sautrāntika' literally means "A follower of sutra,"[19] or more colloquially, "one who belongs to the sutra tradition." However, all four Buddhist systems of tenets are based on sutras — words attributed to Śākyamuni Buddha — and thus in a sense all are followers of sutra. Still, the Sautrāntika way of following sutra is unique. Whereas the Vaibhāṣikas base their tenets on the Seven Treatises of Knowledge, which they alone among the Buddhist schools consider to be the word of Buddha, the sutras accepted by Sautrāntika are considered Buddha's word by all schools. On the other hand, whereas the upper Mahāyāna schools accept some sutras as literal and others as requiring interpretation, the Sautrāntikas accept all texts which they consider sutras to be literal.[20]

Commentarial texts written by Indian Sautrāntikas were not translated into Tibetan. Thus, the Tibetan systemization of Sautrāntika was not a case of organizing Sautrāntika assertions which were the word of Indian proponents of Sautrāntika. Rather, Sautrāntika assertions were introduced to Tibet through mention of them in texts that contained material on other systems and which were written by authors who themselves adhered to tenets other than Sautrāntika. For example, although much of the Gelukba discussion of Sautrāntika epistemology derives from Dignāga and Dharmakīrti, Gelukbas recognize that these logicians were not themselves Sautrāntikas and that, in fact, the final position of their major works is not Sautrāntika but Cittamātra.[21] Yet, Dignāga and Dharmakīrti use the Sautrāntika viewpoint extensively in their work, primarily in order to defeat the Indian realist position that external objects ultimately exist. Thus, even though their sources' final view is that of Cittamātra, the Gelukbas were able to use the texts of Dignāga and Dharmakīrti as well as other Indian Buddhist works (*see below*) to extrapolate an Indian Sautrāntika position. As already indicated, they found sufficient documentation to establish two divisions of Sautrāntikas — Followers of Scripture and Followers of Reasoning. These two divisions, patterned in accordance with similarly named divisions of the Cittamātra school, govern the uniquely Gelukba systemization (*see p. 40ff*).

According to Gelukba, the major Indian source for the position of Sautrāntikas following Scripture is Vasubandhu's *Explanation of the 'Treasury of Knowledge'*, (*Abhidharmakośabhāṣya*). Among the most frequently quoted sources for Sautrāntikas Following Reasoning is Dignāga's *Compendium on Valid Cognition* (*Pramāṇasamuccaya*), which, as Dignāga states in the opening verse, draws from his own earlier works.[22] Dharmakīrti's exposition of this text, the *Commentary on (Dignāga's) 'Compendium on Valid Cognition'* (*Pramāṇavārttikakārikā*) is another frequently quoted source, as are the remainder of his Seven Treatises on Valid Cognition (*see Bibliography*). Additional sources of significance are (1) Asaṅga's *Compendium of Knowledge* (*Abhidharmsamuccaya*) which mainly sets forth Cittamātra, (2) Bhāvaviveka's *Blaze of Reasoning, Commentary on the 'Heart of the Middle Way'* (*Madhyamakahṛdayavṛttitarkajvālā*) which primarily presents Svātantrika, and (3) Śāntarakṣita's *Compendium of Suchness* (*Tattvasaṃgraha*) and the commentary on this by his main student, Kamalaśīla, *Commentary on the Difficult Points of (Śāntarakṣita's) 'Compendium of Suchness'* (*Tattvasaṃgrahapañjikā*), both of which are also mainly Svātantrika.

PERCEPTION: ERRORS AND CAPABILITIES

Because misapprehension of phenomena, or ignorance concerning their nature, is seen as the root source of suffering, Gelukba presentations of Sautrāntika first discuss the divisions and nature of phenomena. All existent objects are divided into (1) ultimate truths, synonymous with impermanent or specifically characterized phenomena, and (2) conventional truths, synonymous with permanent or generally characterized phenomena. This presentation differs from the Vaibhāṣika system where ultimate truths are necessarily indivisible and thus not synonymous with impermanent phenomena, and from the two higher systems, Cittamātra and Mādhyamika, where ultimate truths are necessarily included among permanent phenomena. In the Gelukba formulation of Sautrāntikas Following Reasoning, impermanent phenomena (*bhāva, dngos po*) are called ultimate truths (*paramārtha-satya, don dam bden pa*) because they are capable of fully appearing to an ultimate mind, that is, to a direct perceiver such as an eye consciousness (*cakṣurvijñāna, mig gi rnam shes*) or a yogic direct perceiver (*yogi-pratyakṣa, rnal 'byor mngon sum*) which is a meditator's stabilized and penetrating consciousness that realizes, for example, subtle impermanence.[23] Permanent phenomena such as mental images (*artha-sāmānya, don spyi*) or uncaused space (*asaṃskṛta-ākāśa, 'dus ma byas kyi nam mkha'*) — the absence of obstructive contact — are conventional truths (*saṃvṛti-satya, kun rdzob bden pa*). They are designated such because, for all persons, except Buddhas, they are appearing objects (**pratibhāsa-viṣaya, snang yul*) only of a conceptual or obscured mind, that is to say, of a thought consciousness, which is a mind prevented from fully perceiving the specific characteristics of an impermanent phenomenon.[24]

The basic differences between direct perception and thought can be clarified if we focus the issue by taking a tree as the example of a perceived object. When a particular tree appears to the eye consciousness, all the characteristics of that tree which are of one undifferentiated entity with it, such as its impermanence, color, being a tree, and so forth, also appear. A tree's subtle impermanence *appears* even to the ordinary eye consciousness. However, it is emphasized that unless one cultivates a conceptual understanding of subtle impermanence, this being a subtle type of disintegration defined as a thing's inability to remain for a second moment, one cannot *ascertain* subtle impermanence as an object of the eye consciousness. Thought, on the other hand, is considered able to get at such phenomena; nevertheless thought is always subject to certain errors.

When a tree appears to a thought consciousness, that thought is obscured or prevented from clearly or unconfusedly perceiving the unique nature of a specific tree. An individual tree cannot fully appear to it. The obscuration of thought regarding the specific nature of the tree comes about because the nature of a given tree appears to thought as mixed with a general tree-nature. It is not an actual tree, a specifically characterized phenomenon, fully appearing to thought, but an image, a generally characterized phenomenon. Although generally characterized phenomena (like specifically characterized ones) *exist* such that their natures are unmixed, they cannot *appear* that way to conceptual thought. Thus, whereas direct perception is hampered by a lack of ascertainment, conceptual thought is hampered by a lack of specificity. In other words, when an image of tree, in which the natures of trees necessarily seem mixed together, appears to thought, that thought is prevented from perceiving the unmixed natures of oak, fir, pine, and other trees.

Although an image of tree enables one to identify as 'trees' all specific and ultimately established instances of actual, impermanent trees, the image itself is not ultimately established. To be ultimately established would mean that the image of mixed tree-natures corresponds to the actual situation. But this is not the case. Because an actual specifically characterized tree is not a mixture of tree-natures, thought, which necessarily apprehends such a mixed image, is mistaken.

The tendency of conceptuality to blur or generalize is considered a fault if it goes unrecognized. However, thought is by no means to be abandoned; it is for the Gelukbas an essential tool for overcoming ignorance. To give an example, one aspect of the ignorance said to bind one in a cycle of birth and death is described as the mistaken apprehension of the self as substantially existent and self-sufficient. Gelukbas emphasize that gaining a correct understanding — the knowledge that no such self exists — depends on two key tenets of Sautrāntika. The first is that system's presentation of non-affirming negatives (*prasajya-pratiṣedha, med dgag*). A non-affirming negative is a mere absence which does not suggest any other phenomenon. For example, the lack of a self-sufficient self does not suggest the existence of any positive phenomenon in its place.

Gelukbas consider Sautrāntika tenets to represent a major step toward the higher systems because of their explication of non-affirming negatives. The subtle emptiness taught in the Prāsaṅgika-Mādhyamika system is just such a negative. According to Gelukbas, it is this emptiness which must finally be cognized directly in order to overcome the subtlest and most stubborn form of ignorance. Thus, for Gelukbas it is very important to an understanding of Sautrāntika and Mādhyamika that mere absences do exist and can be cognized. This assertion, moreover, differs greatly from that of numerous modern scholars (see chapters five-seven) who report that in *all* cases of Buddhist negation or exclusion a positive phenomenon is suggested.

The second Sautrāntika tenet essential for the Gelukba presentation of a path to, or means of developing, an actual understanding of selflessness has to do with the relationship of words to reality. Before one can develop a yogic direct perception of mind and body as devoid of a substantially existent self-sufficient self, the absence of such must be understood conceptually. The philosopher-practitioner develops a mental image of selflessness until finally, through increased familiarity with that image, direct perception becomes possible. Furthermore, it is precisely because (1) words such as 'body and mind devoid of a self-sufficient self' or 'momentariness' *do express* the actual lack of such a self and the actual momentariness of phenomena and (2) thought is able to realize these features on the basis of intense reflection, that conceptual thought — or, more precisely, inferential valid cognition — is deemed part of the path to liberating knowledge.

In Gelukba interpretations, the Sautrāntika presentation of the relationship of words and thoughts to actual objects carries over to the higher systems. In those systems, cultivation of a mental image of a selflessness more subtle than that taught in Sautrantika — the lack of inherently existent persons and phenomena — can lead to direct perception of that reality. It is thus essential to have some grasp of the Sautrāntika tenet system's exposition of the relationship between concepts and reality if one wishes to understand and evaluate the tenets of Mahāyāna sutric or tantric practice.

Scholars such as D. Sharma and S. Mookerjee,[25] basing themselves on interpretations of the often cryptic Sanskrit works of Dignāga and Dharmakīrti, take the view that there is in Buddhism an unbridgeable gulf between words and reality, that names or words have no real or direct relation to external phenomena. This is partly because, in the Indian material from which they largely work, an internal image is the *only* object expressed by a statement or name. Mookerjee writes, "The Buddhist denies ... that words contain an objective reference ... words have no reference to reality in any sense."[26] This perspective, widely accepted in Western scholarship and in some aspects also present in Tibet, assumes a bridgeless chasm between words and thoughts on the one hand and actual impermanent phenomena such as trees and so forth on the other. According to Gelukba, such an interpretation precludes the possibility of the fourth of the four truths, true paths. The path to liberating knowledge requires that subtle impermanence and selflessness actually be cognized, and we have already noted that since these cannot be ascertained by an ordinary person's direct perception, the only recourse is to approach them through words and conceptual thought. To posit that words do not actually express objects or that conceptual consciousnesses cannot actually realize objects is to deny the existence of any access to objects which are presently beyond one's direct perception. By contrast, Gelukba writers like Den-dar-hla-ram-ba and Bel-den-chö-jay maintain that a phenomenon such as a table is explicitly expressed by the term 'table' and explicitly realized by the thought consciousness apprehending a table. By extension therefore, more significant cognizables such as subtle impermanence and emptiness can also be expressed by words and cognized by thought.

One important reason why some scholars consider words to have no relation with actual phenomena in Sautrāntika has to do with their interpretation of that system's presentation of specifically characterized phenomena (*svalakṣaṇa*), a term most frequently translated as 'the real.' In modern Indian and Western Buddhist scholarship 'the real' often means tiny particles or points of matter that flash into existence for only an instant. In the view of those who define the real this way, tables, chairs and so forth are not 'real' because they are gross objects that are merely superimposed onto a collection of tiny particles. Stcherbatsky (who is an important source of this view in the West) writes that "only phenomena which have no extension in space and no duration in time ... the point instant[s] of reality"[27] can be considered real or specifically characterized phenomena. In the Gelukba systemization of Sautrāntika, such tiny particles and larger impermanent phenomena are equally real. By contrast, Stcherbatsky writes that only "point instants of reality" are real and therefore "we can realize in thought and express in speech only that part of our cognition which has been constructed by imagination. We can cognize only the imagined superstructure of reality, but not reality itself."[28] Such a view strongly suggests that neither words nor conceptuality can participate meaningfully in a path or technique purportedly leading to a deeper understanding of actual phenomena or of reality itself. According to Stcherbatsky and the majority of modern scholars, words such as 'table' refer to 'unreal' objects. It is therefore argued that in general words do not relate to real phenomena and are incapable of directing conceptual thought to a cognition of them. The Gelukba interpretation, on the other hand, maintains that tables and so forth, which are aggregates of small particles, are themselves ultimate or specifically characterized phenomena. They further specify that words do indeed express these phenomena *even though* words cannot evoke as full a realization of them as occurs in direct perception.

The Gelukba assertions on impermanent or specifically characterized phenomena were not universally accepted in Tibet. In fact, Gelukbas appear unique in considering tables and so forth to be specifically characterized phenomena or ultimate truths in the Sautrāntika system. Such assertions are, for example, contradicted by the Sagya scholar Dak-tsang (b. 1405) who in part accords with modern Western and Indian scholars. Dak-tsang, unlike the Gelukbas, considers that only directionally partless 'points' or particles and temporally partless moments or 'instants' of consciousness are specifically characterized phenomena. However, unlike modern writers such as Sharma who states that "Svalakṣaṇa [a specifically characterized phenomenon] alone is real ... it alone is efficient,"[29] Dak-tsang, on the basis of his reading of Dharmakīrti, asserts that although only minute particles of matter and moments of consciousness can perform functions *ultimately*, impermanent generally characterized phenomena — collections of particles such as tables — do perform functions *conventionally*. For this reason he designates specifically and impermanent generally characterized phenomena as ultimate and conventional truths respectively (*See Table 3*).

Whether one considers gross objects — wholes — such as tables or only the particles that compose them to be ultimate depends largely on how one interprets two key assertions made by Dharmakīrti. The first is his statement that "Whatever ultimately is able to perform a function exists ultimately here [in this system]; other [phenomena, unable to do so] exist conventionally."[30] The Gelukbas define functioning in such a way as to include tables and so forth; Dak-tsang does not. In Gelukba, tables function in the sense that they hold up

Table 3

	Point Instant (partless particles and moments of consciousness) *as Real*	*Point Instant* (partless particles and moments of consciousness) *as Efficient*	*Collection* (phenomena like tables) *as Real*	*Collection as Efficient*
GELUKBA	Yes	Ultimately	Yes	Ultimately
DAK-TSANG	Yes	Ultimately	No	Conventionally
SHARMA, STCHER-BATSKY et.al.	Yes	Yes	No	No

books and so on, but even more significantly in the sense that they are capable of causing production of an ultimate consciousness — an eye consciousness, for example — that perceives a table. This is considered an ultimate consciousness here because it can fully perceive, although it might not ascertain, all the specific characteristics of its object. According to Dak-tsang, a table performs only a conventional function in holding books or dinner plates; the ultimate function of aggregating to form the table and produce the consciousness is performed only by the tiny particles; therefore, only these are *ultimately* capable of performing a function and only these are ultimate truths.

The second significant problem of interpretation comes in determining what is meant by Dharmakīrti's statement that all things by their own nature "abide in their own entities."[31] Gelukbas take this to indicate that each impermanent phenomenon has its own specific characteristics of place, time, and nature, whereas Dak-tsang argues that only partless particles can be considered "unmixed" in these ways. Therefore, for him, particles are ultimately real; gross objects are not. The arguments on both sides are cogent; moreover, there are sound pedagogical reasons for either interpretation (see chapter two). The advantage for the Gelukbas is that by equalizing the ontological status of parts and wholes at this phase of study, the student later finds it easier to grasp the Prāsaṅgika assertion that both are equally unreal. On the other hand, Dak-tsang's system helps overcome inner resistance to the concept of selflessness by making it logically and psychologically easy for the student to see wholes as merely imputed to their parts, while still retaining a sense of the parts as ultimate.

In short, the Tibetan tradition on Sautrāntika as represented by Gelukba scholars like Den-dar-hla-ram-ba, Bel-den-chö-jay, Jam-yang-shay-ba, and Pur-bu-jok and, to a lesser degree, the Sagya scholar Dak-tsang, runs counter to the view of Buddhist reality set forth in many modern Western and Indian works. Unlike them, Gelukba scholars posit a significant connection between words, thought, and actual phenomena. This in turn makes possible their assertion that inferential cognition can extend one's understanding beyond what is presently ascertained by direct perception. The tenet elaborately explored in Gelukba Sautrāntika that thought and words do relate to objects, is the basis for their asserting the ability of thought to increase understanding of things perceived by direct perception. Thought is thereby seen as an essential element of the path to the attainment of wisdom. Conceptual understanding is gradually brought to the level of direct perception through progression over a complicated series of paths. Conceptual understanding of subtle impermanence or emptiness and direct perception of it are compatible, the former being required for development into the latter. These issues are religiously significant for Buddhism because they form the basis for establishing a path from ordinary, ignorant consciousness to liberating wisdom. Thus, a discussion of them is central not only to Sautrāntika but, with minor modification, to the entire spectrum of Buddhist philosophy and psychology.

1 Gelukba Sautrāntika on the Two Truths

A presentation of the two truths is at the heart of each of the four systems of Buddhist tenets enumerated in Tibet (see chart below). All phenomena that exist — permanent or impermanent — are included in the two truths, conventional and ultimate. A system's description of ignorance and the antidotes for it revolves around what that system defines as an ultimate truth and how such can be cognized.

Table 4. *Hierarchy of Tenet Systems in Tibet* (read from bottom up)

Mahāyāna	Mādhyamika	Prāsaṅgika-Mādhyamika
		Svātantrika-Mādhyamika
	Cittamātra	Followers of Reasoning (*nyāya*)
		Followers of Scripture (*āgama*)
Hīnayāna	Sautrāntika	Followers of Reasoning
		Followers of Scripture
	Vaibhāṣika	eighteen subschools

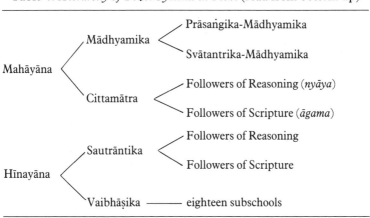

These four systems agree that all knowable phenomena are either ultimate or conventional truths. The name 'conventional truth' is given to those phenomena which, according to the tenets of a particular system, are not true for an ultimate or an analytical consciousness. In Sautrāntika, conventional truths are also known as 'truths for conceptual thought' because they are true for conceptual thought. Similarly, conventional truths are known as 'truths for the obscured' because the thought consciousness which takes them as objects is obscured from fully perceiving ultimate truths.

In all four schools, both ultimate and conventional truths are objects; but whether a given object such as a chair is an ultimate or a conventional truth depends on how these truths are defined. According to Gelukba's categorization, two groups within Sautrāntika, Followers of Scripture and of Reasoning, each have their own presentation of the two truths. This difference arose in India as a result of focusing on different texts. The Followers of Scripture emphasize the Seven Treatises of Knowledge; the Followers of Reasoning, Dharmakīrti's Seven Treatises on Valid Cognition as well as Dignāga's *Compendium on Valid Cognition.*

The Two Truths According to Sautrāntikas Following Scripture

Gelukba scholars Jang-gya and Gomang College's Gön-chok-jik-may-wang-bo write that Sautrāntikas Following Scripture define the two truths in accordance with the definitions given in the sixth chapter of Vasubandhu's *Treasury of Knowledge* (*Abhidharmakośa*, *mNgon pa'i mdzod*).[1] This text states (VI. 4):

> A conventional truth is [any phenomenon] an awareness of which no [longer] operates when [that phenomenon] is broken or mentally subdivided.[2]

For example, if a conventional truth such as a wooden chair were smashed by a hammer, the splintered boards would no longer be perceived as a chair. Similarly, if one mentally divides a chair or a table into minute portions, the mind does not perceive a whole chair or table but pays attention to the pieces only. Thus, according to Jang-gya, all gross material objects, which are aggregates of more than a single particle, and all mental continuums, which are aggregates of more than a single moment, are considered by the Sautrāntikas Following Scripture to be conventional truths. Ultimate truths for them are phenomena such as directionally partless particles of matter, temporally partless moments of consciousness, or uncaused space. Form and consciousness in general are also ultimate truths because no matter how minutely these are divided they continue to be perceived as form or consciousness respectively. Partless particles of specific material entities such as chairs or single moments of any given consciousness are also ultimate truths because, in this view, they cannot be further subdivided.

The Two Truths According to Sautrāntikas Following Reasoning

This presentation of ultimate and conventional truths is very different from the one above. Here, ultimate truths are seen as synonymous with impermanent or specifically characterized phenomena, and conventional truths are synonymous with permanent or generally characterized phenomena. These pairings are based on the explication of the two truths in Dharmakīrti's *Commentary on (Dignāga's) 'Compendium on Valid Cognition' (Pramāṇavārttika, Tshad ma rnam 'grel)* III. 3:

> Whatever ultimately is able to perform a function exists ultimately here [in this system]; other [phenomena, unable to do so] exist conventionally. These describe specifically and generally characterized [phenomena].[3]

Indeed, the Gelukba discussion of the two truths in the system of Sautrāntikas Following Reasoning derives in large part from their reading of this verse. (It will be seen in chapter two that the Sagyaba scholar Dak-tsang gives a very different presentation of the two truths in Sautrāntika based on his interpretation of this same verse.)

The Two Truths

Gelukba writers agree that in the system of Sautrāntikas Following Reasoning ultimate truth and specifically characterized phenomenon are synonymous. Some, however, consider Dharmakīrti's phrase above, "ultimately able to perform a function," to be the definition of an ultimate truth; others see this phrase as the definition of a specifically characterized phenomenon and, therefore, not the definition of an ultimate truth, because a phrase can state the acutal definition of only one defined object. Still, even those Gelukbas who take the phrase "ultimately able to perform a function" as stating the definition of a specifically characterized phenomenon agree that this refers to or describes ultimate truths inasmuch as these are synonymous with specifically characterized phenomena; whatever is one is the other. Tsong-ka-pa and his main disciples, Gyel-tsap and Kay-drub, as well as Jang-gya and the Gomang scholar Gön-chok-jik-may-wang-bo, take "ultimately able to perform a function" as stating the actual definition of a specifically characterized phenomenon whereas Jam-yang-chok-hla-ö-ser and Pur-bu-jok take it as the definition of an ultimate truth.

Another definition shared by Jang-gya and Gön-chok-jik-may-wang-bo gives a further insight into the nature of ultimate truths according to the Sautrāntika Followers of Reasoning. These scholars define an ultimate truth as "that which is able to bear reasoned analysis by way of its own mode of subsistence without depending on imputation by thought."[4] This statement is meant to include all impermanent phenomena and exclude all permanent phenomena. For, only impermanent phenomena can bear analysis in that they can appear to a sense consciousness through their own power, without having to be imputed by thought or terminology. Only phenomena that are (1) produced from causes and conditions, (2) *not* merely imputed by thought, and (3) capable of casting their own uncommon specific aspects toward the perceiving consciousness are considered able to bear analysis in this system.[5] Only such phenomena have uncommon specific characteristics that can become the vividly appearing objects of direct perception. Permanent or generally characterized phenomena cannot be appearing objects of direct perception because they have no uncommon specific characteristics whose aspects can be cast toward a direct perceiver.

For example, uncaused space — the mere lack of obstructive contact — is not produced from causes and conditions and has no specific features that can cast their aspects to a directly perceiving consciousness such as the eye consciousness. Uncaused space has only one distinguishing general characteristic not shared with other phenomena; namely, its lack of obstructiveness. This is a specific characteristic of space in the sense of being unshared with any other phenomenon; however it is the only significant characteristic of *all* instances of space. This common or general characteristic of space can fully appear to thought. Thus, although thought is obscured from fully perceiving uncommon specific characteristics it is capable of fully perceiving general ones. Therefore, uncaused space and all other generally characterized phenomena are distinguished from specifically characterized phenomena because only the latter are considered able to bear the analysis of being fully observable by direct perception, that is, by an ultimate consciousness. Generally characterized phenomena are not considered ultimate truths in the Gelukba presentation of Sautrāntika because they are not appearing objects of — that is, they cannot appear to — an ultimate mind.

The only type of consciousness to which generally characterized phenomena can appear is a conceptual consciousness. This is a conventional, not an ultimate, mind, and in this system the appearing object of a conventional mind is necessarily a conventional truth. Thus, in brief, Sautrāntika considers all impermanent phenomena — appearing objects of direct perception — to be both ultimate truths *and* specifically characterized phenomena. By contrast, permanent phenomena — appearing objects of thought — are conventional truths and generally characterized phenomena. The further implications of this division are seen below.

Identification of Specifically Characterized Phenomena

According to Gelukba writers like Pur-bu-jok and Jang-gya, phenomena such as tables and chairs are ultimate truths because, in accordance with Dharmakīrti's statement, they ultimately perform a function.[6] Specifically, they act as causal conditions (*hetu-pratyaya, rgyu rkyen*) for the generation of an ultimate or directly perceiving consciousness. An eye consciousness, for example, arises in dependence on three causal conditions: the eye sense power (*cakṣurindriya, mig gi dbang bo*) which is the empowering condition (*adhipatipratyaya, bdag rkyen*), the immediately preceding moment of consciousness — whether sensory or mental — which acts as the immediately preceding condition (*samantara-pratyaya, de ma thag skyen*), and the object perceived, the object-condition (*ālambana-pratyaya, dmigs rkyen*). No direct perceiver (*pratyakṣa, mngon sum*) can arise without all three conditions being involved. Further, only impermanent phenomena — large or small — can serve as the object-condition for such consciousnesses.

Because 'impermanent thing' and 'ultimate truth' are synonymous here any direct or conceptual consciousness is itself an ultimate truth, its function being to act as an immediately preceding condition for production of the next moment of consciousness.[7] Thus, although only directly perceiving consciousnesses are ultimate minds (*blo don dam ba*) because only they fully perceive ultimate truths, both direct and conceptual consciousnesses are themselves ultimate truths because both are impermanent. The difference is that the appearing object (**pratibhāsa-viṣaya, snang yul*) of conceptual thought is not an ultimate truth but a conventional truth or truth for an obscured mind.

The Gelukba presentation of minds and awarenesses (*blo rig*) makes a distinction between what appears to a consciousness and what is being comprehended by that consciousness. Objects of consciousness are fourfold:[8]

1. Object of operation (**pravṛtti-viṣaya, 'jug yul*)
2. Referent object (**adhyavasāya-viṣaya, zhen yul*)
3. Appearing object (**pratibhāsa-viṣaya, snang yul*)
4. Apprehended object (*grāhya-viṣaya, gzung yul*)

For example, the appearing or apprehended object of a thought consciousness conceiving of a chair is the image of a chair; what that thought realizes, however, is an actual chair, and therefore the impermanent chair is the referent object and object of operation of that thought. With respect to a direct perceiver such as an eye consciousness, the appearing object is also the object actually being comprehended. Thus, an eye consciousness observing a chair has an actual chair as its object of operation, appearing object, and apprehended object. The term 'referent object' is not used for direct perceivers.

The assertion that tables and other impermanent, functioning phenomena are ultimate truths means that they have specific characteristics which cast aspects (*ākāra, rnam pa*) toward, and act as an object-condition for, an ultimate or directly perceiving consciousness.

Only the mere table, the thing itself, not the conceptual image of it, is being called an ultimate truth, an appearing object of direct perception. Thus the Gelukbas, in maintaining that any functioning object, whatever its size, is an ultimate truth in Sautrāntika, are holding to Dignāga's principle that direct perception, which has specifically characterized phenomena for its object, is free of conceptuality (*kalpanāpoḍham, rtog pa dang bral ba*).[9]

Ontology of Specifically Characterized Phenomena

We have briefly considered the epistemology and criteria of functionality by which Gelukbas identify specifically characterized phenomena. There is also an important ontological issue involved in the designation of such directly perceived phenomena as ultimate truths. We have noted an important underlying premise here is that a table's mode of appearance to the eye consciousness accords with its final nature. That is to say, all its uncommon specific characteristics of impermanence, of being a product, a functioning thing and so forth, as well as its being a table, vividly appear to the visual sense. Hence, the eye consciousness does not see anything except characteristics that comprise the actual mode of abiding of that table. Thus, the appearance of such phenomena is not considered deceptive. To state this in the technical vocabulary of Buddhist philosophy, the table's appearance (*pratibhāsa, snang ba*) and its final mode of abiding (*paryanta-sthāna, mthar thug gyi gnas lugs*) are concordant. This is also why, as we have seen, tables and all other impermanent phenomena can function as causal conditions for an ultimate consciousness which perceives their own final nature. For this reason, also, impermanent things are said to be ultimate truths in this system.[10]

This point also pertains to our hypothesis that the Gelukbas shaped the system of Sautrāntikas Following Reasoning to serve as a pedagogical stepping-stone to their presentation of Prāsaṅgika. Before this possibility can be considered, important distinctions between the two systems must be drawn.

Unlike Sautrāntika, the Mahāyāna schools in Tibet consider direct perception can be mistaken. This tenet is also supported by an ontology quite different from the one Sautrāntika uses to support its depiction of direct perception as unmistaken. In Prāsaṅgika-Mādhyamika, even the bare appearance to direct perception of, for example, a table, is deceptive. What appears is a concretely or inherently existent table; what exists is a table which utterly lacks concrete or inherent existence. For this reason the final or actual nature of a table is not a table, though it appears to the eye consciousness to be so.[11]

For Prāsaṅgika the final nature of a table is its lack of inherent existence, also known as its emptiness.[12] The eye consciousness then, being mistaken due to the appearance of an inherently existent table, cannot be considered an ultimate mind, nor is the table an ultimate truth.

Prāsaṅgika is thus diametrically opposed to Sautrāntika on two central issues: the correctness of direct perception and the ontological status of objects. It is certainly not obvious from this how the former serves as a pedagogical stepping-stone to the latter. The details of the matter remain to be explored; we can, however, note that within Prāsaṅgika's own framework, it is considered both difficult and essential to understand that the inherently existent table to be negated is different from the mere conventionally or nominally existent table that is not negated. This distinction, moreover, can only be made on the basis of flawlessly identifying the deceptive appearance of inherent existence. This is where Sautrāntika can be helpful. For, to identify what Sautrāntikas Following Reasoning call ultimate truth is to take an important step toward identifying what Prāsaṅgika calls the deceptive appearance of inherent existence. The significance of this connection will be considered below; at this point we need only note the radically different, yet pedagogically complementary, epistemological and ontological principles that take Dignāga's framing of non-conceptual direct perception as foundational.

Both Prāsaṅgikas and the Sautrāntikas Following Reasoning maintain that ordinary objects such as tables and chairs appear to direct perception, but Prāsaṅgikas take these objects to be falsities which 'deceive' the mind that directly perceives them, whereas Sautrāntikas call these same objects ultimate truths and label as unmistaken the consciousness that knows them directly. But how did the Gelukbas come to identify these objects of direct perception as specifically characterized phenomena and to equate them with ultimate truths? Our awareness of the unique features of Gelukba literature on Sautrāntika mandates that we briefly consider the textual ambiguities and hermeneutics which, in addition to pedagogical concerns mentioned above, may have contributed to Gelukba formulating Sautrāntikas Following Reasoning as a separate system.

Gelukba Sautrāntika and Competing Definitions of Specifically Characterized Phenomena

Gelukba Sautrāntika is unique among Buddhist tenet systems in including impermanent phenomena which are aggregations of particles or moments among ultimate truths. Most modern scholarship on Indian systems offers a quite different view of what constitutes a specifically characterized phenomenon or ultimate truth in Sautrāntika.[13] Also, even within the Tibetan tradition, the scholar Dak-tsang, a Sagyaba roughly contemporaneous with Tsong-ka-pa, sharply criticized Gelukba on this issue (see next chapter). Like the Gelukba system of Sautrāntikas Following Scripture and in accordance with the *Treasury of Knowledge* (*Abhidharmakośa*), Dak-tsang maintains that only directionally partless particles of matter and irreducible moments of consciousness, and not aggregates of these, are ultimates.

How then does Gelukba come by their view that for some Sautrāntikas aggregated objects are not only ultimates but specifically characterized phenomena? What evidence can be adduced for the Gelukba position? The *Treasury* does not define ultimate truths this way, and neither Dignāga nor Dharmakīrti explicitly state that 'specifically characterized phenomena are aggregates of particles such as tables, chairs, and so forth.' On the other hand, there is also no clear statement from Dignāga or Dharmakīrti that 'specifically characterized phenomena must be partless.' Some interpretation is required. The precise parameters of this issue can be observed by taking a brief look at two classic sources for this discussion.

In the fourth verse of his *Compendium*, Dignāga states that direct perception arises due to 'many objects' (*anekārtha, anekadravya; don du ma*). This may be seen to support the Gelukba position that aggregates of particles can be objects of direct perception. Gelukba also of course concurs with Dignāga's point that in observing these objects direct perception is free of all conceptuality.[14] So far, there is no direct conflict with the Gelukba presentation.

Yet, Dignāga's text itself entertains an objection at this point: if direct perception is utterly devoid of conceptuality, then why does Vasubandhu's *Treasury* state that sense consciousnesses take as their objects aggregated phenomena? The difficulty is that according to the *Treasury* such phenomena are only conceptually construed. An essential sub-question here is whether or not, and to what extent, aggregated phenomena are conceptually imputed (*see chapter two*). The main issue at hand, however, is whether or not specifically characterized phenomena themselves can be constituted as aggregates. Regarding this, the objection entertained here goes on to note Vasubandhu's assertion that specifically characterized phenomena (*svalakṣaṇa*) are objects of sense direct perception. How is one to understand this? Here Dignāga (who himself takes *svalakṣaṇa* as an object of direct perception) clearly interprets Vasubandhu as asserting *svalakṣaṇa* to be aggregated entities:

> 4cd ... there [in the above-cited Abhidharma passages], that [direct perception], being caused by [the sense-organ through its contact with] many objects [in aggregation]

takes the whole (*sāmānya*) as its sphere of operation ...[15]

This again seems to support the Gelukba position on specifically characterized phenomena but not its equating of these with ultimate truths. The Gelukba delineation of Sautrāntikas Following Reasoning however forces the issue by making ultimate truths synonymous with impermanent or specifically characterized phenomena. This equation is an important feature of the system, and Dignāga himself here alludes to the issues involved in forging such an equation.

Dignāga's concern to note conformity with the *Treasury* is particularly interesting in light of the Gelukbas' exposition of two divisions in Sautrāntika. It seems to indicate that he was conscious of a possible tension between the *Treasury's* assertions regarding ultimate truths — such as partless particles and irreducible moments of consciousness — on the one hand and his own discussion of specifically characterized phenomena — possibly including aggregated phenomena — on the other. The *Treasury* clearly states that anything which is no longer recognizable when physically broken up or mentally subdivided is a conventional truth. This means that aggregated phenomena in general are conventional truths. If one takes the further step of considering such phenomena to be mentally or conceptually designated, there is the problem of explaining how such can be the objects of a non-conceptual direct perception.

Gelukba Systems of Sautrāntika

In effect Gelukbas took the two sides of the dilemma noted by Dignāga and developed each of them to the point that two systems of Sautrāntika were required: one in which partless particles and indivisible moments of consciousness were named ultimate truths and were not considered conceptually imputed, and the other in which all objects of direct perception — including aggregated wholes as well as their parts — were synonymous with ultimate truth and specifically characterized phenomenon. In this way they were able to justify their designation of aggregates such as tables and chairs as specifically characterized phenomena or *svalakṣaṇa* and to equate these with ultimate truths, a category here inclusive of compounded phenomena. They were able to make this case unambiguously by formulating the system known as Sautrāntikas Following Reasoning in which all impermanent things, including aggregated objects like tables and chairs, are ultimate truths and objects of direct perception.

According to virtually all scholarship outside Gelukba, Dignāga and Dharmakīrti's use of the word *svalakṣaṇa* is understood to mean indivisible portions of matter or consciousness and consequently is often translated as "particular" or "point-instant."[16] Nor could Gelukbas ignore this interpretation. They were, after all, claiming synonymity of ultimates and specifically characterized phenomena in Sautrāntikas Following Reasoning. One can speculate that they also saw fit to hold this equation in the system of Sautrāntikas Following Scripture and in doing so could hardly overlook the identification of moments of consciousness or partless particles of matter as ultimate truths in the *Treasury*. This also can be seen as providing an impetus for two presentations of the two truths in Sautrāntika.

Further Observations on Sourcing the Gelukba Perspective

We can speculate on the origins of this two-fold formulation of Sautrāntika from another vantage point, where we find that an important clue to the Gelukba's thinking on the two truths in Sautrāntika may lie with Dharmottara.

Dharmottara's commentary on Dharmakīrti's *Drop of Reasoning* (*Nyāyabindu, Rigs pa'i thigs pa*), translated by Stcherbatsky as *A Short Treatise of Logic*, seems to imply, but does not clearly indicate, the existence of external objects. Stcherbatsky himself glosses Dharmottara as referring to external objects when the latter says: "Indeed all [external] reality is vividly experienced when near and dimly apprehended at a distance."[17] If Dharmottara asserts external objects he cannot be considered a Cittamātrin; thus, the problem of how to classify him among Buddhist schools of thought could be resolved by the Gelukbas' category of Sautrāntikas Following Reasoning. We know that the division of Cittamātrins into Followers of Scripture and Reasoning is well accepted. The case of Dharmottara seems to point to an individual who does not fall into either of these categories, nor into the general category of Sautrāntika. His position could, however, be included in the system described as Sautrāntikas Following Reasoning which closely follows the thinking of Dignāga and Dharmakīrti.

Stcherbatsky himself might not disagree in principle with this classification, for he handles the difficulty thus: "Although the school[s] of Dignāga ... deny the reality of an external world corresponding to our ideas, they in their logic and epistemology investigated cognition from the empirical point of view ..."[18] That is, perception is there defined in terms that do not themselves question the existence or status of the object perceived as external. It is not clear whether the case of Dharmottara was of prime concern to Gelukbas or not. However it can certainly be argued that the Gelukbas' carving out of these two Sautrāntika systems was of primary importance in allowing them to formulate a system in which ultimate truths were co-extensive with impermanent things; this made it possible to include among ultimate truths indivisible particles as well as aggregates of these, ordinary objects such as tables and chairs. This little-noticed theoretical maneuver appears to have been essential in the formulation of Sautrāntika as it was mainly studied in the Gelukba monastic universities.

The Gelukba discussion of the two truths in the context of Sautrāntikas Following Reasoning stresses that specifically characterized phenomena are known by direct perception. This accords with Dignāga's statement above and with the bulk of Indian commentarial tradition.

The Gelukbas appear to be unique, however, in using the term '*svalakṣaṇa*' to refer to aggregates of particles — tables, chairs and the like — and, in this context, stating that such impermanent things are ultimate truths. Den-dar-hla-ram-ba, for example, etymologizes the term *svalakṣaṇa* as "specifically characterized phenomenon" (*rang mtshan*) and takes this to be synonymous with ultimate truth for Sautrāntikas Following Reasoning.[19] We will see below that the major Gelukba writers on Sautrāntika are in complete accord on this point. Moreover, we have noted that within Gelukba this view of ultimate truths is considered to derive from a careful glossing of Dignāga and Dharmakīrti's discussion of the Sautrāntika position. At the same time, in the broader picture of Indo-Tibetan commentaries on Dignāga and Dharmakīrti, in both Western and non-Gelukba Tibetan scholarship, this is unquestionably a minority position. We have noted several atypical tenets associated with this view, and will briefly give our attention to one more.

The Categories of Specifically Characterized and Existent Phenomena

Another special feature of the Gelukba presentation is that whereas it equates functioning things with specifically characterized phenomena it does not, like much of the Indian tradition, see these as concomitant with the category of existent phenomena. (*See also discussion of Ratnakīrti below, p. 181*).

In its formulation of Sautrāntikas Following Reasoning, Gelukba discussion of the two truths emphasizes that these truths are distinguished, not only by being or not being imputed by thought, but by whether it is direct perception or conceptual thought to which they fully appear. This epistemological basis for the division into generally and specifically characterized phenomena — permanent and impermanent, and conventional and ultimate truths, respectively — is itself not unusual but directly traceable to Dignāga, and through him to the *Treasury*.[20] As Hattori states it:

> Dignāga ... makes an essential distinction between *svalakṣaṇa* and *sāmānyalakṣaṇa*, the former being the particular individuality which can never be generalized and the latter being the universal which is conceptually constructed by the mind through generalizing from many individuals without regard for their particularity.[21]

The question is, what can be identified as instances or examples of such *svalakṣaṇa*, specifically characterized phenomena? Here, as we know, Gelukbas make a crucial interpretive step. In the context of Sautrāntikas Following Reasoning, they maintain that 'specifically characterized phenomenon' refers not just to indivisible particles and so forth as asserted by Sautrāntikas Following Scripture, but simply to *any* impermanent phenomenon.

This point is made even more explicit by the Gomang College debate manual in its section on generally and specifically characterized phenomena. When the opponent proposes that "Whatever is gross (*rags*) or continuous (*rgyun*) is not a specifically characterized phenomenon," the ensuing debate maintains that a pot, which is both gross and continuous over time, is a specifically characterized phenomenon because it is a functioning thing (*dngos po*).[22] This signifies that all impermanent objects, large or small, are understood to possess characteristics specific to them — that is, characteristics unshared even with other objects of the same type. It is these specific characteristics which appear to direct perception and which are generalized by conceptual thought.

Tsong-ka-pa defines a specifically characterized phenomenon as "an impermanent thing which abides unmixed in place and time."[23] His disciple Gyel-tsap writes that "whatever is a specifically characterized phenomenon abides as unmixed in place, time, and entity; this is the [definition or, more technically, the] meaning-isolate[24] (*don ldog*) of specifically characterized phenomenon."[25] Both these definitions are given by way of commentary on Dharmakīrti's statement in his *Commentary on (Dignāga's) 'Compendium on Valid Cognition'*:

> Therefore, all things by their own nature
> Abide in their very own entities.[26]

"All things" (*dngos kun*) in this verse refers to all impermanent phenomena. This much is accepted by the Indian Buddhist tradition in general and, following that, by Gelukba. However, in India and as generally interpreted by Western scholarship, impermanent phenomena are considered concomitant with whatever exists. In that view if something exists, if it is a *sattva*, it is necessarily momentary. Gelukbas on the other hand, based on Dharmakīrti's statement (III. 1) that "because there are two objects of comprehension there are two valid cognizers," (*gzhal bya gnyis phyir tshad ma gnyis*), explicitly maintain that existent phenomena (*sat, yod pa*) may be either permanent or impermanent.[27] Permanent phenomena, however, do not perform functions and are merely imputed by thought. Thus, whatever exists is not necessarily impermanent, because permanent phenomena also exist. This tenet, most explicitly set forth by Gelukbas in the context of their formulation of Sautrāntika, is also significant in the Gelukba discourse on Mādhyamika. For, once it is asserted that permanent phenomena do exist, it is possible to make the case that emptiness, which is permanent, is an existent phenomenon (*dharma, chos*) that can be realized by a wisdom consciousness. In this way Gelukbas are able to argue against the nihilistic position that a Superior's (*ārya, phags ba*) widsom has no object whatsoever, or, to put it another way, that wisdom cognizes nothing at all.

Permanent and Generally Characterized Phenomena

Examples of permanent, existent phenomena are unconditioned space (*asaṃskṛta-ākāśa, 'dus ma byas gyi nam mkha'*) and emptiness. Meaning generalities (*artha-sāmānya, don spyi*) and all generally characterized phenomena are also permanent. The Gelukba position that permanent phenomena exist thus appears to be a synthesis of assertions elaborated in Dharmakīrti's *Commentary on (Dignāga's) 'Compendium on Valid Cognition'* and Vasubandhu's *Treasury of*

Knowledge.[28] However, Gelukbas are not going as much against the stream of Indian thought as might first appear.

Whatever the earlier tradition considered impermanent, Gelukba also asserts as impermanent. Nor, in arguing for the existence of permanent phenomena, do they contradict the famous Buddhist refutation of an eternal deity.[29] 'Permanent' in their philosophical language does not necessarily mean eternal, but is defined as a 'non-momentary phenomenon' (*akṣaṇika-dharma, skad cig ma ma yin pa'i chos*). Emptiness is permanent because it does not disintegrate from one moment to the next; it is unconditioned. However, any given emptiness is not eternal; the emptiness of a table comes into existence when the table is made and goes out of existence when the table is destroyed. Such emptiness is permanent only in the sense that while it exists, it undergoes no alteration. This distinguishes it from impermanent phenomena, which the monastic textbooks define as 'momentary' (*kṣaṇika, skad cig ma*). Jang-gya explains this as the inability to remain unchanged for a second moment, that is, as the characteristic of disintegrating or approaching destruction with every passing instant. A table's impermanence therefore is its incapacity to remain unchanged for even a single moment.[30]

To consider again Dharmakīrti's verse quoted above, the Gelukba tradition, like the Indian before it, takes this to mean that all impermanent phenomena abide unmixed in place, time, and nature. The oral scholarly tradition adds that both permanent and impermanent phenomena exist in this way. In this view also, the definition of a phenomenon as "that which holds its own entity" is said to signify that it has an entity which is "unmixed in place, time, and nature."[31] Everything that exists — permanent and impermanent — can be so described. Impermanent phenomena are further distinguished by their capacity to perform functions. Moreover, and this is key, Gelukba Sautrāntika considers that the manner of abiding of impermanent phenomena — unlike that of permanent phenomena — is not merely imputed by thought.[32] (Prāsaṅgika-Mādhyamika, it will be seen, takes issue precisely with this point.)

Having thus contextualized the Gelukba interpretation of impermanent phenomena by briefly considering its discussion of permanent ones, we are ready for a closer look at Gelukba's own scholarship regarding impermanent or specifically characterized phenomena.

Gelukba Sources on Ultimate Truths in Sautrāntikas Following Reasoning

The Gelukba view that aggregates of particles are ultimate truths in the system of the Sautrāntikas Following Reasoning is widely documented in Tibet. Numerous texts of the Gelukba Monastic Colleges give evidence of this perspective. For example the *Collected Topics of Ra-dö* (*Rva stod bsdus grva*), a major source for definitions and examples used in monastic debates since the 15th century, states that impermanent things, specifically characterized phenomena, and ultimate truths are synonymous.[33] This assertion comes in the context of a debate regarding a copper pot. A copper pot, being impermanent, is given as an example of a specifically characterized phenomenon and an ultimate truth. Conversely, Ra-dö notes that permanent phenomenon, generally characterized phenomenon, and conventional truth are synonymous.[34] Pur-bu-jok, author of a major debate text used at Serajay Monastic College, gives the same list of synonyms[35] and offers a similar debate proving that a copper pot is a specifically characterized phenomenon.[36] In the course of yet another debate, Pur-bu-jok notes that "appearing object of direct perception" (*mngon sum gyi snang yul*) and "impermanent thing" are synonymous, as are "appearing object of thought" (*rtog pa'i snang yul*), and "permanent thing".[37] The Gomang College textbook makes the same point in slightly different language, noting that ultimate truth, specifically characterized phenomenon and an object explicitly comprehended by a direct valid cognizer (*mngon sum gyi tshad ma'i dngos gzhal*) are synonymous.[38]

Works that are not primarily debate texts also support this point. Gön-chok-jik-may-wang-bo, in the context of distinguishing Sautrāntikas Following Scripture from those Following Reasoning states that for the latter "the subject, a pot, is called an ultimate truth because it is a truth for an ultimate mind."[39] In the same vein, Jang-gya writes:

> [The way the Sautrāntikas Following Reasoning] assert the two truths is not the same as that explained in Vasubandhu's *Treasury of Knowledge*. This is because [in accordance with the Vaibhāṣikas and the Sautrāntikas Following Scripture] the *Treasury* posits pots and so forth as conventional truths whereas [the Sautrāntikas Following Reasoning] consider pots to be specifically characterized phenomena and ultimate truths.[40]

Thus, although Tsong-ka-pa's definition was ambiguous as to the nature of specifically characterized phenomena, it is clear that Gelukba writers came to consider this category synonymous with ultimate truth and inclusive of aggregated phenomena in the system of Sautrāntikas Following Reasoning.

It was mentioned above that the "impermanent thing which abides unmixed in place and time" of Tsong-ka-pa's definition is, in Sautrāntika, said not to be merely imputed by thought. By taking specifically characterized phenomena to be *any* impermanent thing, and not just atomic particles and the like, the Gelukba formulation of Sautrāntika emphasizes that the chief distinction between specifically and generally characterized phenomena is not, as in other interpretations, their size, or their designation as a whole or a part, but *whether or not they are merely imputed by thought*. This emphasis is essential in linking the Gelukba formulation of Sautrāntika with its view of Mādhyamika. Prāsaṅgika-Mādhyamika takes issue precisely with the contention that something can exist without being merely imputed by thought. Although Mādhyamika, like Sautrāntika, considers that things abide unmixed, the former contend that whatever exists — permanent or impermanent — is merely imputed by thought. Thus, an object such as a chair or table is an ultimate truth in this system because its mode of subsistence is its *being* a chair or a table in its own right, without depending on words or thought to impute to it the nature of a chair or table. Thus, the eye consciousness which perceives an object as a chair or table is perceiving that object's final or ultimate nature, and thus is a valid cognizer which is an ultimate consciousness. To contrast this view with that of Prāsaṅgika, Den-har-hla-ram-ba writes:

> Therefore, this is [the meaning of] the statement that what the Proponents of True Existence [such as Sautrāntikas] posit as the meaning-isolate (*don ldog*) of [being] specifically characterized, the Prāsaṅgikas assert to be the object of refutation by a reasoning consciousness analyzing the ultimate.[41]

The significance of Gelukpa assertations on ultimate and conventional truths in Sautrāntika for their overall perspective and educational system can be clarified by a further look at how the Gelukbas establish the two truths.

Status of Wholes or Aggregates

A major criterion of what constitutes a specifically characterized phenomenon or ultimate truth comes down, in this system, to what it means for a functioning thing to be unmixed in place, time, and nature.[42] According to Gelukba, whatever exists is unmixed in these three ways.

Gelukbas assert that an impermanent thing such as a table is unmixed in place because it has only one specific location; its being in the east in relation to a certain object means it is not in the west in relation to that same object, for these qualifications are contradictory and thus whatever is one cannot be the other. A table is not mixed in time because, although the continuum of the momentarily disintegrating table can exist over a long period, the previous and later portions of the continuum are not mixed; the one o'clock table, for example, is not the two o'clock table.

Finally, a table is not mixed in nature because the specific nature of a given oak table exists separately from the specific nature of a given maple table. Even though they are equally tables, the specific nature of a particular table is not shared by other tables. This assertion, therefore, is quite unlike the position of Plato and non-Buddhist Indian systems such as Nyāya-Vaiśeṣika which maintain that a single ideal or generality of, for example, table, which is substantially separate from all instances of tables, nevertheless partakes in every instance of table. Whereas Nyāya speaks of a generic tableness that applies to all individual tables, Buddhist systems do not posit a generality that exists apart from all of its instances. Therefore they can maintain that, even in terms of its nature as a table, there is no mixture with any general tableness.

When an ultimate consciousness such as an eye consciousness sees a table, it perceives this object's nature as unmixed with the nature of other tables in two ways: (1) the table itself appears separate from or unmixed with other tables and (2) the natures of the components of the table — top, legs, and so forth, do not appear mixed with each other. Thus, the table is a collection-generality (*tshogs spyi*) that encompasses its own parts, and this generality, being impermanent, is both a specifically characterized phenomenon and an ultimate truth.

Since the legs and so forth are parts of the table, their nature is mixed with the table's nature. That is to say, these parts are pervaded by the table itself. Thus, when one sees the legs or top of a table, this functions as seeing the table. However, the legs, top, and so forth are not themselves the table, and the nature of one part is not mixed with that of another; thus, the parts as well as the whole are specifically characterized phenomena according to Gelukba.

We know that the Gelukba position on the two truths in Sautrāntika was not universally held in Tibet. A major opponent to the above formulation of specifically and generally characterized phenomena was Dak-tsang, a scholar of the Sagyaba order born fourteen years prior to the death of Tsong-ka-pa. In contrast to the Gelukba presentation, Dak-tsang considers that when particles collect together to form tables or any other coarse impermanent phenomena, their very proximity constitutes a mixture of place, time, and entity or nature. Thus, a collection-generality such as table *necessarily* has a mixed nature. Moreover, its being a generality, in his system necessitates that it not be a specifically characterized phenomenon. This means that according to him anything which has parts is a generality, and Dak-tsang therefore considers only partless particles to qualify as unmixed in nature and consequently as specifically characterized phenomena. Against this view, Gelukba expositions of Cittamātra and Mādhyamika argue that there can be no such thing as a directionally partless particle; no matter how small an entity may be, there will always be a western side and an eastern side and therefore parts. For this reason, any particle however small is a collection-generality according to the higher schools as interpreted by Gelukbas. In their view generalities and minute particles are not mutually exclusive as they are for Dak-tsang.

Even in a system such as Sautrāntika, which asserts the existence of particles so small they cannot be further divided, such an indivisible entity, although not a collection-generality, would still be a generality. It would be a type-generality concomitant with all other partless particles.[43] A table is both a collection-generality that encompasses its own parts and a type-generality that is concomitant with other tables. However, that general factor (*aṃṣa, cha*) which partakes in all instances of table has no substantial existence and cannot appear to direct perception; it is merely imputed by thought and fully appears only to thought.

The assertion that there can be a generality which pervades its instances conceptually but not, as it does in Nyāya or Sāṃkhya, for example, physically, is an important feature of Buddhist philosophy that paves the way for their presentation of the selflessness of persons. In setting forth their assertions on this issue, the Buddhists were specifically arguing against the non-Buddhist Sāṃkhya school which posits a Nature (*prakṛti, rang bzhin*) that still exists even when all of its manifestations have disappeared or dissolved back into it. The Sāṃkhyas maintain that this generality (*sāmānya, spyi*) or principle (*pradhāna, gtso bo*) is partless, whereby the Buddhists force them to the position that the generality's entire, indivisible nature would then be present in each and every instance. Both Buddhists and non-Buddhists agree that this would be absured.[44] There would also be the absurdity that the nature of, for example, a golden pot would be identical with the nature of a clay pot because the same generality or nature would be fully present in both. This would make it difficult for Sāṃkhya to consider individual impermanent phenomena such as pots to have their own specific characteristics or specifically characterized nature. Moreover, just as the Sāṃkhyas are willing to uphold a generality that exists separately from its parts, they also maintain the existence of a person who exists separately from what the Buddhists consider to be its parts; namely, intellect (*buddhi, blo*) and body. The Sautrāntikas, Cittamātrins, and Mādhyamikas all deny the existence of such a substantially existent or self-sufficient person. The Buddhist philosophical systems[45] identify innate and learned tendencies to conceive of such a self of persons; these conceptions are forms of ignorance and are to be overcome by the antidote of realizing the lack or non-existence of such a substantially existent or self-sufficient self.

Substantial and Imputed Existence

All things that exist are either substantially existent (*dravya-sat, rdzas yod*) or imputedly existent (*prajñapti-sat, brtags yod*). Because these terms have various meanings the statement that 'all impermanent phenomena are substantially existent' must be made in terms of a specific interpretation of these terms. Substantial exsitence or lack thereof can be determined on the basis of three different sets of criteria:[46]

1. whether or not the object has the ability to perform a function
2. how the object is perceived
3. whether or not the object exists and can be known.

Depending on which interpretation is used, different categories of phenomena are designated as substantially or imputedly existent.

On the basis of the first interpretation above, substantially existent (*dravya-sat, rdzas yod*) is synonymous with impermanent phenomenon (*anitya, mi rtag pa*) and substantial phenomenon (*dravya-dharma, rdzas chos*).[47] From this point of view all ultimate truths posited in Sautrāntika are substantially existent; they are also necessarily susbstantial phenomena because they are (1) substantial and (2) phenomena. Similarly, in accordance with this interpretation, the following objects which lack the ability to perform a function, are considered synonymous: permanent phenomenon (*nitya, rtag pa*) which is not momentary (*akṣaṇika, skad cig ma ma yin pa*) in the sense of disintegrating from one moment to the next, imputedly existent phenomenon (*prajñapti-sat, btags yod*), and reverse or insubstantial phenomenon (*vyatireka-dharma, ldog chos*). Being this type of phenomenon excludes being an impermanent phenomenon, a substantially existent phenomenon, or a substantial phenomenon.

For example, space is a permanent phenomenon in the sense that it does not change from one moment to the next. As mentioned above, to be permanent means to be unchanging; it does not necessarily mean to be eternal. The space inside a cup is permanent in that it does not change moment by moment, but it is not eternal. It comes into existence when the cup is produced and goes out of existence when the cup is destroyed. Space is imputedly existent in the sense that it is incapable of ultimately performing a function — it cannot act as the object-condition (*ālambana-pratyaya, dmigs rkyen*) for generation of an ultimate or direct consciousness. Space is also imputedly existent in the sense that it is merely imputed by thought. It does not cast its aspect to the apprehending consciousness but is apprehended by thought through the medium of a mental image of space. Thus, although Gelukba posits that space exists, it also emphasizes that space, like other permanent phenomena, is not established by way of its own character. Further, because it does not have uncommon specific characteristics that can impinge on a consciousness, thereby acting as causal conditions for that consciousness, it cannot perform the function which, according to this first interpretation, would qualify it as a substantially existent phenomenon.

The second way of distinguishing substantially and imputedly existent phenomena is on the basis of how they are perceived by direct perception. A Gomang debate text defines a substantially existent phenomenon in this regard as "a phenomenon the ascertainment of which need not depend on valid ascertainment of another phenomenon that is not of its own entity.[48] In this context, most but not all impermanent phenomena are substantially existent. For example, an impermanent object such as a table can be directly perceived by an eye consciousness. Of course, the eye consciousness does not know the thing with legs and a top as 'table' — such naming is the work of conceptual thought — but it does fully observe this object in the sense that when an eye consciousness sees a table it does not see all the parts of the table but only those parts facing it that are not obstructed by some other object. Seeing those parts functions as seeing the table. The parts are of the same entity as the table and nothing of a different entity need be observed in order for one to perceive a table directly. Thus, a table, like most impermanent phenomena, is *substantially existent* because of how it is perceived (the second interpretation) and *a substantial existent* because of its ability to perform a function (the first interpretation).

An example of an impermanent or specifically characterized phenomenon that is substantially existent in the sense of being able to produce effects, but is not substantially existent in terms of how it is perceived, is the person. A person substantially exists in the sense of being able to perform functions. In a different sense however it is considered imputedly, rather than substantially, existent. A person cannot be cognized unless some part or aspect of mind or body is cognized. Following such cognition, conceptual thought is ready to label this object a 'person.' Thus, the person is not self-sufficient in terms of how it is perceived, for the person is an entity that is in substance neither form nor consciousness (as the table and its parts are in substance wood) but must be known through a perception of one of these. The subtle selflessness of persons is defined in the Sautrāntika system as the absence of a substantially existent self-sufficient person. The coarse selflessness of persons is a person's emptiness of being a permanent, partless, and independent self.[49]

The subtle selflessness of persons, their lack of substantial existence, should not be confused with the first meaning of a substantial existent that simply refers to the ability to perform a function. Persons do perform functions, they are impermanent and existent, but lack substantial existence and self-sufficiency in the sense that all their activities as well as the possibility of perceiving these depends on the activities and perception of form or consciousness. The person itself is simply imputed to these; thus it is imputedly existent.

In order to clarify that there are objects which, although merely imputed, do exist, a distinction can be made between a 'mere imputation' (*btags pa tsam*) and 'existing merely as an imputation' (*btags pa tsam du yod pa*). A non-existent phenomenon like the horns of a rabbit is a mere imputation in the sense that it is imagined to exist by the ignorant and is not known or established by reasoning; still, the horns of a rabbit do not exist *as* an imputation because they do not exist at all. The *image* of the horns of a rabbit, on the other hand, does exist and thus would be, like any non-functioning phenomenon, imputedly existent in the first sense.

It is only a person, not other types of phenomena such as tables, that seems to exist self-sufficiently in the sense of appearing to be an entity separate from its own parts. Sautrāntika thus maintains that only the selflessness of persons need be realized for one to attain liberation. The *denial* of such self-sufficient existence applies only to persons, not to other impermanent phenomena such as tables that perform functions and are perceived through segments of their own entities being perceived.

This lack of a self-sufficient self is thus a type of selflessness that is a quality only of persons, not other phenomena. Sautrāntika posits the direct realization of the selflessness of persons, that is, the lack of a substantially existent person, as the chief antidote to ignorance. However, phenomena other than persons also lack a self of persons in the sense of not being objects used by a substantially existent or self-sufficient person. Most phenomena other than persons do substantially exist both in the sense of performing functions and in the sense of being perceived through some portion of their own entity being perceived.

Prāsaṅgika on the Sautrāntika View of Selflessness

The above identification of the self-sufficient person is used in Gelukba to support Prāsaṅgika-Mādhyamika's claim that the selflessness realized in Sautrāntika differs from the selflessness taught in Prāsaṅgika.[50] This latter is a lack of inherent existence that is equally a quality of persons and other phenomena. Tsong-ka-pa, the supreme architect of Gelukba views on Prāsaṅgika, is emphatic on this point. In the Perfection of Wisdom section of his *Illumination of (Candrakīrti's) Thought* (*dbUma dgongs pa rab gsal*) he offers several Indian sources in support of this position. For example, the *King of Meditative Stabilizations Sutra* (*Samādhirāja-sūtra*) says:

> Just as you have known the discrimination of self
> Apply this mentally to all [phenomena].[51]

Similarly, he quotes the *Superior Sutra of the Condensed Perfection of Wisdom*:

> Understand all sentient beings as like the self,
> Understand all phenomena as like all sentient beings.[52]

According to Prāsaṅgikas, the same selflessness qualifies persons and other phenomena in exactly the same way, and is equally difficult to realize with respect to each of them, Sautrāntikas assert the selflessness which is a lack of self-sufficient or substantial existence to be a quality of persons only. The ignorance that conceives substantial existence as here defined is a misapprehension of how *persons* exist; it only indirectly relates to phenomena other than persons. In the Sautrāntika explanation of substantial existence, phenomena other than persons are perceived when their own entities are perceived and thus do not lack self-sufficiency or substantial existence in the sense that persons do. Hence it is not necessary to cultivate an understanding of this type of selflessness with respect to them.

Thus, the main meaning of 'imputedly existent' in the Gelukba discussion of Sautrāntika has to do with a phenomenon such as the person which cannot be cognized except through the cognition of some specifically characterized phenomenon — mind or body — that is a different entity from itself. Mind and body, the bases of imputation of the person, are themselves substantially existent aggregates of consciousness or matter to which the names 'mind' and 'body' can properly be imputed. More generally, however, impermanent phenomena as a class are considered substantially existent because of their ability to perform functions, as in the first interpretation above, and permanent phenomena are considered imputedly existent because of their inability to perform functions.

According to the third interpretation, 'substantial existent' is taken to mean merely 'that which is established by reasoning.' Here 'established by reasoning' simply means that a phenomenon exists and can be known. Everything that exists — whether permanent or impermanent — fulfills this meaning of a substantially existent phenomenon because all existing things can be known by some consciousness. In this context, only non-existent things are said to exist imputedly and are considered to be 'mere imputations'.

As mentioned above, in discussing the third interpretation of 'substantial existent,' the Gelukba presentation of Sautrāntika considers that anything which exists is established by reasoning and therefore able to bear some form of reasoned analysis. To bear such is a hallmark of ultimate truths in this system. Jang-gya defines an ultimate truth in Sautrāntika as "that which is able to bear reasoned analysis by way of its own mode of subsistence without depending on imputation by terminology or thought."[53] This means that ultimate truths "bear reasoned analysis" into whether they can be known through their own power in the sense of the object being able to cast an aspect toward the perceiving consciousness rather than being dependent on a thought consciousness to impute them. Jang-gya's definition refines the way in which ultimate truths bear analysis or are known; his definition is meant to eliminate permanent or generally characterized phenomena from this category. Only impermanent phenomena are considered able, through their own power, to cast an aspect toward and thereby act as a causal condition for the generation of an ultimate consciousness. Only impermanent phenomena or ultimate truths substantially exist because only they can bear reasoned analysis in this manner; in this context, therefore, permanent phenomena or conventional truths exist imputedly. All types of impermanent objects — table, music, the taste of sweetness, the odor of garlic, the touch of cold — are ultimate truths which cast their aspect to the directly perceiving sense consciousness by way of their own power. Thus, the ordinary eye, ear, nose, tongue and tactile consciousnesses[54] of ordinary people perceive ultimate truths.

This is an unusual tenet; no other Buddhist system asserts ultimate truths which can be perceived by ordinary consciousnesses. In other Buddhist systems, direct perception of an ultimate truth such as the selflessness of phenomena is cultivated with great effort. The cognition of selflessness is the antidote that overcomes the ignorant or mistaken conception of a self; thus, to cognize the ultimate truth of selflessness according to those systems is to have liberating knowledge. Of course, Sautrāntika does not say that an ordinary person's perception of ultimate truths such as trees and so forth constitutes liberating knowledge. If it did, anyone with even a single properly functioning sense consciousness would be liberated, and there would be no necessity for the careful presentation of a path to liberation. Something more than an ordinary ultimate consciousness is required.

Ordinary Perception of Ultimate Truths

Sautrāntika asserts that all four types of direct perceivers are ultimate consciousnesses: sensory direct perception (*indriya-pratyakṣa, dbang mngon*); mental direct perception (*mānasa-pratyakṣa, yid kyi mngon sum*; self-knowing direct perception (*svasaṃvedanā-pratyakṣa, rang rig mngon sum*); and yogic direct perception (*yogi-pratyakṣa, rnal 'byor mngon sum*). However, these four are not equal in every sense because yogic direct perception, unlike the others, can directly perceive and ascertain subtle impermanence and (in Mādhyamika) selflessness. Thus, only yogic direct perception is an actual instrument of liberating knowledge. Yet, it is significant that both sensory and yogic cognition are cited as instances of direct perception (*pratyakṣa, mngon sum*). This indicates that the yogic perception toward which much study and meditation is directed is itself utterly non-conceptual. Perhaps even more significantly, this classification conveys the religious message that non-conceptuality, a hallmark of liberating wisdom, is present in ordinary human experience and thus yogic perception need not be considered something entirely outside the scope of one's own experience.[55]

It has already been noted that in this formulation of Sautrāntika ordinary people do see ultimate truths, and that this is not an antidote to ignorance. To overcome ignorance it is necessary to cultivate first a conceptual and then a yogic cognition of hidden phenomena such as the momentary impermanence and subtle selflessness that are the qualities of ultimate truths such as tables and chairs. Impermanence, being capable of casting its aspect toward the consciousness, is an ultimate truth and thus can be perceived directly, but this system has the unusual assertion that selflessness — considered an ultimate truth in all other major Buddhist tenet systems — is a conventional truth, and cannot be directly perceived by any direct perception, even yogic. Rather, yogic direct perception directly perceives the aggregates of mind and body as qualified by a lack of a self-sufficient person. It realizes selflessness not directly but implicitly. This further underscores the Sautrāntika point that mere direct perception of an ultimate truth is not sufficient and does not fulfil the potential of the ordinary ultimate mind which observes these truths without properly ascertaining their characteristics and qualifications.

Features of Specifically and Generally Characterized Phenomena
Ultimate truth and specificially characterized phenomenon, synonyms in Sautrāntika, are also synonymous with ultimately established phenomenon (*paramārthasiddha-dharma, don dam par grub pa'i chos*) and appearing object of direct perception (*pratibhāsa-viṣaya, snang yul*). These are the phenomena capable of performing functions, particularly that of acting as a cause for the production of a directly perceiving consciousness. Such a direct cognizer is an ultimate mind, and because impermanent or specifically characterized phenomena are true for such minds, this system considers them to be ultimate truths.

Permanent phenomena, being static, cannot perform functions or produce effects. Thus, they do not act as a causal condition for the conceptual consciousness that perceives them. Moreover, it is a fundamental tenet of this system that permanent phenomena cannot be perceived directly. They are perceivable only by thought. Thought is a conventional mind that can fully perceive only permanent phenomena. Because a thought consciousness is prevented or obscured from vividly perceiving the uncommon specific characteristics of impermanent phenomena, it is a conventional or obscured (*saṃvṛti, kun rdzob*) mind, and the truths or phenomena which are its appearing objects are considered truths for an obscured consciousness (*saṃvṛti-satya, kun rdzob bden pa*); hence, conventional truths. Permanent phenomena, the appearing objects of thought, are synonymous with obscured or conventional truths. Because the two truths are described largely in terms of the minds which perceive them — direct perception and conceptual thought — the Sautrāntika discussion of these two types of phenomena also serves to describe the spheres and activities of direct perception and thought.

Specifically characterized phenomena or ultimate truths are distinguished from generally characterized phenomena or conventional truths in terms of four features:

1. Entity
2. Uncommon Mode of Appearance
3. Perceiving Subject
4. Activity.

Entity. Ultimate truths or specifically characterized phenomena are ultimately established because of their ability to perform the function of producing an effect. All impermanent phenomena produce the effect of their own next moment. For example, a moment of flame produces the next moment of the continuum of that flame. The last moment of a flame does not have an effect of flame; the effect it produces is smoke.

Impermanent phenomena also have the effect of partaking in the production of the consciousness that perceives them. Specifically characterized phenomena, as their name implies, appear to a direct perceiver such as the eye consciousness by way of their own uncommon specific characteristics of color, shape, and so forth appearing to that consciousness. If an impermanent object is not actually present, it cannot be fully and manifestly cognized even though the other necessary causal conditions for generating a direct cognition — an eye sense power and a previous moment of consciousness — are present. This is one reason why such objects are ultimately established.

Dharmakīrti's *Commentary on (Dignāga's) 'Compendium on Valid Cognition'* says:

> Whatever is able to perform a function
> Is asserted as [having] its own [uncommon specific]
> characteristics.[56]

This gives another reason why specifically characterized phenomena are said to ultimately exist. When such a phenomenon appears to direct perception, the mind takes as its object all the uncommon characteristics of that phenomenon. This means that when a tree, for example, appears to the eye consciousness, that consciousness vividly perceives or takes as its appearing object the tree's specific shape, color, and so forth. A specifically characterized phenomenon, then, is so called because in order for its entity to be fully realized it must be realized in this way; that is, its own specific or unique characteristics must vividly appear to the mind that takes it as an appearing object. There is no other way to directly cognize an impermanent object. Such a phenomenon, therefore, cannot be fully realized by merely hearing, uttering, or thinking of, for example, a 'tree'. Specifically characterized phenomena cannot be fully expressed by words. If they are not present, a consciousness that fully perceives them cannot be generated. This may seem so obvious as to be unworthy of mention but the Sautrāntikas, as will be seen below, drawn out extensive ramifications from this observation.

Permanent or generally characterized phenomena can be wholly perceived whether the object represented by the corresponding internal image is present or not. Such generally characterized phenomena are considered conventionally, not ultimately, established because they are permanent, lacking any capacity for producing an effect. The thought apprehending them can arise at will. Here the object is dependent on the consciousness rather than the other way around, as in direct perception. Thus, generally characterized phenomena are said to be merely imputed by thought and to lack the power to act as causal conditions for the consciousness that perceives them.[57] That consciousness, moreover, is not an ultimate (*paramārtha, don dam pa*) one; it is conventional or obscured (*saṃvṛti, kun rdzob*) because it is obscured from full perception of the specific characteristics of impermanent objects.

Moreover, unlike specifically characterized phenomena, permanent objects do not have uncommon features which can be perceived directly, that is, which can by their own power cast their aspects toward a consciousness. In other words, generally characterized phenomena do not have the ability to perform a function in the sense that their presence acts as a causal condition for the mind that apprehends them.[58]

The mind which takes a generally characterized phenomenon as its appearing object does so by taking to mind the general or common aspect of that object. For example, whereas a table is a specifically characterized phenomenon known to direct perception by way of its individual characteristics appearing to the eye consciousness, uncaused space is a generally characterized phenomenon that appears to thought by way of a generic, mental image of space. Because such an object, being an undetailed generalized phenomenon, has no specific characteristics from which thought can be obscured, thought can perceive it fully. Uncaused space has only the general characteristic of lacking obstructive contact, and the image of uncaused space that appears to thought fully conveys this characteristic; thus, uncaused space can fully appear to thought. This difference in how specifically and generally characterized phenomena are known is very significant for the Gelukba Sautrāntika discussion of the capacities and functionings of direct perception and thought (see chapters three and four).

Uncommon mode of appearance. 'Specifically characterized phenomenon' is etymologized as an object which, due to the appearance of its own uncommon specific characteristics, becomes the appearing object of a direct perceiver. An example is a table. That in another context a table is considered a generality (*sāmānya, spyi*) does not make it a generally characterized phenomenon (*sāmānya-lakṣaṇa, spyi mtshan*) and thus does not preclude its being a specifically characterized phenomenon (*svalakṣaṇa, rang mtshan*). In fact, a table is considered both a generality and a specifically characterized phenomenon. It is a generality in the sense that it encompasses its instances, such as wooden and metal tables[59] and is a specifically characterized phenomenon because of its uncommon features.

The distinction here between generalities and generally characterized phenomena is significant. It preserves the dichotomy between generally and specifically characterized phenomena originally indicated by Dignāga:

> Apart from that particular [specifically characterized phenomena] (*svalakṣaṇa*) and the universal [generally characterized phenomena] (*sāmānya-lakṣaṇa*) there is no other object to be cognized, and we shall prove that [direct] perception (*pratyakṣa*) has only the particular [specifically characterized phenomena] for its object and inference (*anumāna*) only the universal [generally characterized phenomena].[60]

The Gelukbas, like Dignāga, unequivocally bifurcate the two types of objects, specifically and generally characterized, and, correspondingly, the two types of perception.[61] On this very important point, as on others, the Gelukbas' elaboration of Sautrāntikas Following Reasoning follows a classic Indian text.

We have noted that an impermanent generality such as a table is specifically characterized because only the characteristics unique to a given table are perceived by the eye consciousness which sees that table. The common factor of being a table — or, more technically, the appearance of the general factor which is an appearance as opposite from non-table — does not appear to direct perception, but only to thought (*see chapter five on exclusions* [*apoha*]). Thus, even though the table fully appears to direct perception, the factor which pervades all instances of table does not appear to direct perception.

All the qualities of a table that come into existence or are established when the table is produced — its subtle impermanence, its four factors of momentary production, abiding, aging, and disintegration — all appear to direct perception. However, they are not necessarily *ascertained* by direct perception. The subtle impermanence of a given table is a specific characteristic of that table; subtle impermanence in general is not a specific characteristic of any table because all products are characterized as impermanent. Direct sense perceivers — eye, ear, nose, tongue, and body consciousnesses — and mental direct perceivers are known as minds of complete engagement (**vidhi-pravṛtti, sgrub 'jug*) because they operate with respect to or engage in the complete collection of features related with their object. Thus, the subtle impermanence of a table *appears* to the eye consciousness of even a common being; however, it cannot be *ascertained* by a person who has not previously cultivated an understanding of subtle impermanence to the point of yogic direct perception.

The features that appear to direct perception are said to be established from the object's own side, they are not merely dependent upon or imputed by thought. Thus, the definition of a specifically characterized phenomenon according to Pur-bu-jok, 19th-century author of an important textbook still used in the monastic curriculum, is:

> ... a phenomenon which is established from its own side without being merely imputed by thought.[62]

Generally characterized phenomena (which, as noted above, are not to be confused with generalities) are so called because they appear in a general or common manner. They do not have characteristics specific only to themselves that can appear to a direct perceiver. Thus they appear to thought by way of a general aspect. This general aspect is a mental image of an elimination or exclusion of everything that is not, for example, a table. The mind that apprehends a generally characterized phenomenon is necessarily a thought or conceptual consciousness, and necessarily not a direct perceiver. Conceptual thought can be produced just in dependencce on terms and thoughts, without the appearance of an object that is established from its own side, that is, without the object itself in any way impinging on the consciousness. Pur-bu-jok therefore defines a generally characterized phenomenon as:

> ... a phenomenon which is not established from its own side but is merely imputed by terms or thought.[63]

Such a phenomenon is an imputed existent in the sense that it (1) cannot perform a function and (2) does not exist from its own side.

Perceiving Subject and Activity. Specifically characterized phenomena or ultimate truths act as cooperative conditions (*saha-kāri-pratyaya, lhan cig byed rkyen*) for the generation of a consciousness that directly perceives them. Whereas the higher schools of tenets — Cittamātra, Svātantrika, and Prāsaṅgika — distinguish ultimate and conventional truths in terms of what does and does not appear to a Superior's wisdom of meditative equipoise, the Sautrāntikas Following Reasoning distinguish the two truths in terms of what can and cannot be known by direct perception.[64] An eye consciousness directly perceiving a table, for example, arises in dependence on three causal conditions: an actual table, a healthy eye sense (described as subtle matter shaped like a flower within the orb of the eye) and a previous moment of consciousness. Such a direct perceiver is an ultimate consciousness because it is unmistaken with regard to the object appearing to it.

A direct perceiver such as an eye consciousness apprehending a table apprehends the status and mode of being of that table; the fact that products such as tables are ultimate truths in this system means that Sautrāntika, unlike Cittamātra or Mādhyamika, does not assert that a table exists one way but appears another. A table is an ultimate truth not because ordinary cognition of it is an antidote to ignorance (as is the case with directly cognizing the ultimate truths asserted by the higher systems) but because a table itself is considered its own final nature or mode of subsistence. Thus, in directly perceiving a table one necessarily also perceives the final nature or mode of subsistence of that table. In the highest tenet system, Praśaṅgika-Mādhyamika, a table is a conventional truth precisely because the way it appears is misleading with respect to its actual nature. Although a table appears to have the nature of ultimately being a table, its final nature is actually the emptiness of being inherently existent. According to Prāsaṅgika, the generation of liberating wisdom requires that one's own conception of inherent existence be negated. This makes it important to identify inherent existence. For a table or chair to exist inherently would mean that its appearance and its actual nature were in accord. Sautrāntika, in considering tables and the like to be ultimate truths, maintains that the mark of any impermanent phenomenon is that the appearance of a table accurately represents its own final nature. It is precisely this characteristic which Prāsaṅgika analyzes and utterly negates. In this vein, Den-dar-hla-ram-ba, using almost the same words as Jang-gya uses above, says:

> ... what Proponents of True Existence [e.g., Sautrāntikas] assert as the meaning-isolate (*don ldog*) [or very meaning] of [being] specifically characterized, the Prāsaṅgikas assert to be the object of refutation by a reasoning consciousness analyzing the ultimate.[65]

The Prāsaṅgika system emphasizes that in order to negate inherent existence, one must clearly identify it. Thus, in studying the Sautrāntika position on the nature of ultimate truths, one is also, from the perspective of the highest system, engaging in the first step for overcoming the subtle ignorance identified in that system. One gains some skill in identifying the mistaken notions of the inherent existence which is to be negated.

The Sautrāntikas' unusual assertion that tables and so forth are ultimate truths comes because they do not assert that a table exists one way but appears another. In their system, the appearance to direct perception is not misleading; thus, a direct perceiver is considered an ultimate mind. Ordinary direct perception, however, is described as (1) unable to ascertain all the subtle aspects that appear to it and (2) incapable of taking permanent phenomena — most significantly, emptiness or selflessness — as an object. Thus, Sautrāntika explains that even though ordinary people see ultimate truths day in and day out, they are not thereby liberated unless they can (1) ascertain subtle qualities such as impermanence or momentary disintegration and (2) realize selflessness by understanding the directly perceived aggregates of mind and body to be devoid of a self-sufficient self and cultivate this realization repeatedly.

Conceptual thought is obscured from direct perception of ultimate truths — impermanent phenomena — because it necessarily knows an object such as a table through the medium of an image of a table. Whereas a direct perceiver is a mind that engages with the entire collection of features belonging to its objects, conceptual thought is a mind of partial or eliminative engagement. When an eye consciousness sees a table, all the particularities of that specifically characterized table appear to it. But when thought has a mental image of a table, that mental image is said to be a generally characterized phenomenon. This is not to deny the possibility of building up a richly textured mental image; indeed, much practice, especially in tantra, centers around detailed visualization. The Gelukbas simply make the point here that any mental image of a multifaceted object is necessarily a simplification or abstraction of that object. It does not have features of shape, size, and so forth that are the actual qualities of a specific object. Moreover, all mental images are said to be permanent in the sense of not deteriorating in substance from one moment to the next. (See chapter four for discussion of limitations of this position.)

Because an image does not arise in dependence on the presence of an object and can be evoked by terms or thoughts, the purview of thought is not limited to physically proximate objects as is the case with direct perception. However, it is impossible for objects to appear to thought with all the detail and clarity that a directly perceiving consciousness apprehends. Moreover, thought is always mistaken in that the image of an object appears to it to be the actual thing, even though thought does not ordinarily assent to this mistaken appearance and conceive that image to be the actual thing. One does not usually conceive the mental image of a table to be a table, but image and object are mixed in that one cannot separate out the specifically characterized phenomenon which actually appears from the generally characterized phenomenon that is the actual appearing object of thought.[66] There is however an important sense in which specifically characterized phenomena actually appear to thought; this is dealt with in the chapter on conceptual thought.

Direct perception knows its object immediately; it does not rely on an internal image and thus is not prey to the error of the internal image's seeming to be the actual object. For this and other reasons mentioned above, direct perceivers are considered ultimate awarenesses. The objects they cognize — which appear by way of their own unique characteristics being cast toward the sense or mental consciousnesses — are ultimate truths.

When juxtaposed to the ordinary person's non-ascertainment of what appears to direct perception, the very fact that these objects are called ultimate truths suggests that some type of practice or mental enhancement is necessary in order to fully realize the potential of an ultimate consciousness. Gelukba emphasizes that such practice involves using thought to develop correctly reasoned inferences about the nature of ultimate truths, so that eventually one can ascertain what appears to direct perception.

To understand the logical underpinnings of why such effort is necessary and how the development of conceptual thought is seen as leading to a richer and more correct mode of direct perception, it is necessary to examine in detail material on the functioning of direct perception and thought. This investigation occupies the next two chapters.

2 *Dak-tsang on the Two Truths*

The axiomatic thread running through Gelukba's systemization of the two truths in Sautrāntika Following Reasoning is the rigorous assertion that specifically characterized phenomenon, ultimate truth, appearing object of direct perception, and impermanent phenomenon are synonymous. These four are also dichotomous with generally characterized phenomenon, conventional truth, appearing object of thought, and permanent phenomenon, which four are also mutually synonymous.

We have seen that the category of ultimate truths includes ordinary objects such as tables, chairs, trees, and so forth, as well as the minute particles which aggregate to form these phenomena. This Gelukba tenet is based on Dharmakīrti's assertion that whatever is ultimately able to perform a function is a specifically characterized phenomenon and that other phenomena are generally characterized.[1] According to Jang-gya, and in contrast to Dak-tsang, Dharmakīrti's assertion gives an illustration (*lakṣya, mtshan gzhi*) but not a definition (*lakṣaṇa, mtshan nyid*) of the two truths. In his view, the definition of an ultimate truth is:

> That which is able to bear reasoned analysis by way of its own mode of subsistence without depending on imputation by thought or terminology.[2]

This means that objects such as tables, houses, and the like can appear to direct perception by virtue of their status as phenomena having their own mode of subsistence (*gnas lugs*); they can appear without being imputed either in the sense of having been referred to verbally or reflected upon conceptually. Accordingly, Gelukba maintains that whatever lacks its own mode of subsistence, which is to say whatever is permanent, is a conventional truth and a generally characterized phenomenon. We have noted that the categories of specifically characterized phenomenon and permanent thing, in the Gelukba presentation of Sautrāntika, are mutually exclusive; thus whatever exists must be one or the other and cannot be both.

The early 15th-century Sagyaba scholar Dak-tsang, writing a few decades after Tsong-ka-pa, presents a different interpretation of Dharmakīrti, one which brings him to quite a different understanding of the two truths in Sautrāntika. In Dak-tsang's view, Vasubandhu's explanation of the two truths in the *Treasury* and Dharmakīrti's explanation of specifically and generally characterized phenomena in his *Commentary on (Dignāga's) Compendium on Valid Cognition*, offer parallel definitions of conventional and ultimate truths. Vasubandhu says:

> A conventional truth is any phenomenon which, when broken or mentally subdivided is no longer understood as that object, like a pot or like water ...[3]

In Dak-tsang's view, Vasubandhu is here referring to the conventionally existent phenomena described by Dharmakīrti as other than those ultimately able to perform functions. Similarly, ultimate phenomena in Vasubandhu's system are ultimate truths and ultimately capable of performing functions. By contrast, in Prāsaṅgika, ultimate truths — emptinesses — are neither ultimately nor truly existent; emptiness, like all other phenomena, lacks true existence. Here however the category of ultimate phenomena refers to those things which, even when physically or conceptually subdivided, continue to be perceived as those phenomena by a factually concordant mind (*blo don mthun*) that apprehends them.

In declaring that Vasubandhu and Dharmakīrti are giving definitions of the two truths that vary in expression but not in meaning, Dak-tsang does not, like the Gelukbas, distinguish Sautrāntikas Following Reasoning from Sautrāntikas Following Scripture. The root text of Dak-tsang's *Tenets* makes no mention of this division which, as suggested above, may have been unique to the Gelukba formulation. Moreover Dak-tsang affirms that Sautrāntika, like

Vaibhāṣika, asserts as ultimate truths only indivisible particles of matter and temporally partless moments of consciousness. In this way he affirms that because of functioning conventionally, phenomena such as tables are composed of specifically characterized phenomena. At the same time he indicates that these former are aggregates by designating them *generally* characterized phenomena.[4] According to Dak-tsang, aggregates are never specifically characterized or ultimate truths. This assertion derives from his interpretation of Dharmakīrti's statement that only phenomena "ultimately able to perform a function" are specifically characterized phenomena or ultimate truths. Dak-tsang thus finds fault with the Gelukba interpretation, against which he maintains that tables, chairs and other gross impermanent things are neither ultimate truths nor specifically characterized phenomena. They are generally characterized phenomena which are impermanent things (*dngos por gyur pa'i spyi mtshan*) because they are "unable *ultimately* to perform a function." However, they are "*conventionally* able to perform the function of acting as the cause for the consciousness that apprehends it."[5]

IMPERMANENT GENERALLY CHARACTERIZED PHENOMENA

In order to include aggregated impermanent phenomena in his discussion of the two truths, Dak-tsang creates the category of 'generally characterized phenomena which are functioning things.' Thus he rejects what is considered a given in the Gelukba systemization of Sautrāntikas Following Reasoning; namely, that no single phenomenon can be both a generally characterized phenomenon and a functioning thing because these two are mutually exclusive. Dak-tsang's use of this category also means that he does not accept all impermanent things as specifically characterized; items such as pots, for example, are seen as generally characterized functioning things (*dngos por gyur pa'i spyi mtshan*).

In establishing the correctness of his own interpretation, Dak-tsang must account for Dharamkīrti's apparent acceptance of the synonymity between impermanent phenomena — those able to perform a function — and specifically characterized phenomena.

In fact, the Gelukba scholar Jam-yang-shay-ba quotes that very statement to support his position that for Dharmakīrti specifically characterized phenomena and impermanent phenomena are mutually inclusive — that whatever is one is the other and, therefore, that chairs, tables, and so forth are specifically characterized phenomena and ultimate truths:

> Whatever is able to perform a function.
> Is asserted as [having] its own [specific] characteristics.[6]

Jam-yang-shay-ba, writing more than two hundred years after Dak-tsang, even goes so far as to say that adducing this statement from Dharmakīrti (which appears to be an accurate paraphrase but not an actual quote)[7] "shortens the tongue" of Dak-tsang, meaning that the Sagyaba scholar or his adherents could not possibly give a satisfactory answer in favor of their interpretation. Dak-tsang does speak to this point, however. He cites Dharmakīrti's use of the qualification "ultimately" regarding the ability to perform a function:

> That which is ultimately able to perform a function here ultimately exists; others exist conventionally. These explain specifically characterized [phenomena] and generally characterized [phenomena].[8]

Dak-tsang maintains that for Dharmakīrti only those phenomena able to perform a function *ultimately* are specifically characterized phenomena or ultimate truths. All functioning or impermanent phenomena whatsoever are not included in this category. Dak-tsang writes:

> ... with regard to the passage [from Dharmakīrti]: "Whatever is able to perform a function ..." it is clear that the qualification 'ultimately' is required to fit this together with what appears before and after.[9]

Dak-tsang expands on this necessity, saying that it is imperative to make sense out of different statements from a given text by synthesizing their meaning:

> ... one must make an exposition having arranged all the earlier and later parts of any text; if one leaves just the explicit teaching at that particular point as it is, many internal contradictions can arise.[10]

All textual interpreters, including Gelukbas, agree on the necessity of looking at particular statements in context. Dak-tsang is thus enunciating a hermeneutical principle with which everyone can agree; it does not follow, of course, that all will arrive at identical or even similar conclusions.

Dak-tsang uses a type of textual synthesis to establish the appropriateness of qualifying Dharmakīrti's explanation of specifically characterized phenomena as those *ultimately* able to perform functions. Even though the word 'ultimately' does not appear in the first statement quoted above, it appears in the other, and Dak-tsang's way of correlating these two statements is to apply the adjective 'ultimately' to both.

To further establish his interpretation, Dak-tsang expands on the significance of the word 'ultimately.' He argues that Dharmakīrti uses this word to distinguish ultimately functioning phenomena — minute particles and so forth — from those phenomena which perform functions *conventionally* such as directly perceived tables, chairs, and all other aggregated impermanent things. The ultimate function that minute particles of matter perform is to aggregate to form impermanent phenomena — generally characterized phenomena which are functioning things. These aggregates function conventionally by holding water, supporting books, and so forth.[11]

Dak-tsang and the Gelukbas agree that specifically characterized phenomena function as object-conditions for an ultimate consciousness. One might speculate that for Dak-tsang, although individual particles which aggregate to form gross objects are not visible separately and are not themselves mixed in place, time, or nature, the gross object which they comprise does appear as such a mixture. For example, a chair represents a mixture of place because even though the left side is not the right side, both are covered by the chair. Similarly, the chair conventionally exists over a period of time stretching from yesterday to tomorrow and is permeated from top to bottom by the nature of chair. In these ways it embodies a mixture of place, time, and nature.[12] Therefore, according to Dak-tsang, chairs and all other aggregated impermanent phenomena are generally characterized phenomena which are functioning things. They do not function ultimately (if they did, they would necessarily be specifically characterized phenomena); they function only conventionally.

Gelukba scholars such as Bel-den-chö-jay, Den-dar-hla-ram-ba, Jang-gya, and Gön-chok-jik-may-wang-bo do not divide the ability to perform functions into conventional and ultimate types. They maintain that Dharmakīrti uses the word 'ultimately' in the context of a debate with Mādhyamika and for the sake of eliminating the

Mādhyamika position that things are only conventionally and not ultimately able to perform functions.[13] According to Gelukba, the Sautrāntikas seek to dissociate themselves on this issue from the Mādhyamika position by emphasizing that specifically characterized phenomena do perform functions ultimately. For example, in the *Explanation of the Meaning of Conventional and Ultimate in the Four Systems of Tenets* (*Grub mtha' bzhi'i lugs gyi kun rdzob dang don dam pa'i don rnam par bshad pa*) Bel-den-chö-jay quotes Gyel-tsap's statement in *Illumination of the Liberating Path* (*Thar lam gsal byed*) that:

> The purpose of [Dharmakīrti's] stating the qualification 'ultimately' [in III.3] is to refute the wrong conception of those [i.e., the Mādhyamikas] who assert the capacity to perform a function only conventionally.[14]

Bel-den-chö-jay himself notes another statement from Dharmakīrti which in his view counters Dak-tsang's category of generally characterized phenomena which are functioning things:

> Since it is merely an object of expression
> It is not a functioning thing.[15]

Bel-den-chö-jay sees this as evidence of Dharmakīrti's position that generally characterized phenomena do not perform functions. Thus, he echoes Gyel-tsap by concluding:

> Adding the qualification 'ultimately' to the statement "That which has the capacity to function ultimately," is done to refute the assertion by the Proponents of No Entityness [Mādhyamikas] that [things] are capable of functioning only conventionally; it is not added so that one may know that there are both ultimate and conventional capacities to function.[16]

In short, both Gelukba scholars and Dak-tsang have ways of accounting for Dharmakīrti's use of the word 'ultimately.' To Dak-tsang, it signifies that there are phenomena which function conventionally, thus justifying his implementation of the category of generally characterized phenomena which are functioning things (*dngos por gyur pa'i spyi mtshan*). The Gelukbas argue that 'ultimately' is simply used to counter Mādhyamika's position of conventional functionality.

Gelukbas also bolster their position by questioning the authenticity of the term 'ultimately' in Tibetan translations of Dharmakīrti's work. Bel-den-chö-jay quotes Kay-drup as saying that the translator Bang (*dPang*) reports most Indian editions omit the word 'ultimately.'[17] In that case, the Sanskrit simply reads:

> arthakriyāsamartham yat
> tad atra paramārthasat.

Kay-drup also cites the opinion of 14th-century Tibetan translator Lo-drö-den-ba (*blo-gros-brtan-pa*, 1276-1342) that the predicate 'ultimate' (*paramārtha*) is not found in the Sanskrit manuscript.[18] Kay-drup further notes that the expression 'ultimate ability to perform a function' (*don dam don byed nus pa*) also does not occur in any of Dharmakīrti's other works.[19]

Nevertheless, Gelukbas do not mainly rely on the problematic status of 'ultimately' to refute Dak-tsang, but rather rely on their own interpretations of this term in the context of other Dharmakīrti passages which support their position. Thus, the real point at issue becomes, not whether Dharmakīrti used the term 'ultimately' at all, but what type of phenomena could be considered 'ultimately able to perform a function' on the basis of Dharmakīrti's text.

Dak-tsang notes that Dharmakīrti uses the term 'pure things' (*vastumātra*, *dngos po dag pa ba*) to signify minute particles, for example, and to distinguish them from other impermanent phenomena that are collections of particles and thus not specifically characterized phenomena or 'pure things.'[20]

Dak-tsang also cites Devendrabuddhi, a follower of Dharmakīrti, to support his contention that Sautrāntikas adhering to Dharmakīrti's *Commentary on (Dignāga's) 'Compendium on Valid Cognition'* — like the Sautrāntikas Following Scripture — assert the two truths in accordance with Vaibhāṣika:

> Is it conventionally existent like water, milk, and so forth or
> is it ultimately existent like form, pleasure, and so forth?[21]

Dak-tsang comments that water, like pots and so forth, are conventionalities because they are unable to perform the functions of an ultimate object; namely, to act as the object-conditions (*ālambanapratyaya*, *dmigs rkyen*) of an ultimate mind. The mind observing a chair is not ultimate in Dak-tsang's system because that which is called a chair — an aggregation of particles — is simply imputed by that mind onto a collection of atoms. Only the aggregated particles, and not the chair, have functioned ultimately. Thus, such aggregated phenomena are "conventional things, mental phenomena which depend on internal factors such as appellations."[22] For Dak-tsang, wholes which are collections of particles are unreal; they are merely imputed by thought. Only the minute particles on the basis of which phenomena such as chairs and tables are imputed are ultimate truths and capable of performing an ultimate function.

Devendrabuddhi, a student of and commentator on Dharmakīrti, states that aggregated phenomena such as water and milk conventionally exist. By adducing this statement Dak-tsang intends to support his own interpretation of conventional and ultimate truths according to Dhamakīrti.[23] Jam-yang-shay-ba, who openly disputes Dak-tsang in his *Great Exposition of Tenets*, maintains that in making the statement quoted above, Devendrabuddhi was presenting the system common to Vaibhāṣikas and Sautrāntikas Following Scripture, not that of Sautrāntikas Following Reasoning.

One further statement by Dharmakīrti that is important for both Dak-tsang's and the Gelukbas' position can be considered. Dak-tsang quotes Dharmakīrti's assertions regarding the capacities of phenomena (Direct Perception Chapter (*pratyakṣa* III.5ff):

> If [it is claimed that] all specifically and generally characterized phenomena have [the capacity to produce their own effect,] it is not so [ultimately*] because it is not seen that the presence and absence of a generally characterized phenomenon [have the capacity ultimately* to produce or not an effect which is] a mind [that apprehends it] *just as an eye, a form* etc. [produce] a mind [that apprehends it.][24]
>
> *Dak-tsang's reading requires the parenthetical 'ultimately'; the Gelukba reading does not.

For Dak-tsang, the question Dharmakīrti here addresses is whether or not specifically and generally characterized phenomena — the permanent and the impermanent — perform functions *ultimately*. Dharmakīrti uses as his criterion an object's capacity to produce or give rise to a consciousness that perceives it. In saying that "it is not so" Dharmakīrti, according to Dak-tsang, indicates that generally characterized phenomena do not ultimately perform the function of producing a consciousness that can cognize it, "just as an eye, a form, etc." do not ultimately function although they do, in Dak-tsang's system, function conventionally. For Dak-tsang therefore, "an eye and form" are examples of generally characterized phenomena which are functioning things. Moreover, in the syllogystic language of Indo-Tibetan logic and debate, Dak-tsang takes these to be concordant or similar examples (*sadṛṣṭānta, mthun dpe*) of such generally characterized phenomena. For, argues Dak-tsang, if Dharmakīrti had meant to indicate something that does not function at all — not even conventionally — he would have used an unambiguously non-functional example. He could have said "just as the horns of a rabbit do not produce a mind apprehending it." Instead, Dharmakīrti used an example of conventional functionability, thereby only eliminating the ultimate functions peformed by partless particles and so forth.

The Gelukbas consider the statement "just as eye and form, etc. [produce] a mind ..." a counter example or dissimilar example (*asadṛṣṭānta, mi mthun dpe*), that is, as instances of phenomena which are *not* generally characterized. Bel-den-chö-jay writes that in fact, this statement by Dharmakīrti weakens rather than establishes Dak-tsang's position.[25] Bel-den-chö-jay maintains that when Dharmakīrti says "If [it is claimed that] all have [the capacity to produce their own effects]," he indicates that this is a mistaken assertion, inasmuch as generally characterized phenomena do not produce effects. Thus, in his view, and for the Gelukba position in general:

> [The statement] "just as an eye, a form, etc. [produced] a mind apprehending them" is a proof of the counter-pervasion [that no generally characterized phenomena perform functions] due to being stated as a *dissimilar* example.[26]

For, writes Bel-den-chö-jay, valid cognition never observes that generally characterized phenomena perform functions; thus such phenomena do *not* act as causes for a mind perceiving them.

How Impermanent Phenomena Perform Functions

Dak-tsang contends that impermanent phenomena such as chairs are not ultimate truths but are merely imputed by thought and thus unable to function ultimately. Therefore, although he and the Gelukba scholars agree on the principle that mentally imputed phenomena cannot function as a causal condition for an ultimate consciousness, Dak-tsang includes all aggregations of particles in this category whereas the Gelukbas do not.

To perform a function means to produce an effect. Impermanent phenomena produce effects in two ways: they generate the next moment of their own continuum, and they act as causal conditions for a consciousness that apprehends them. In this context Dak-tsang points out that a phenomenon which is a collection of parts cannot ultimately produce the consciousness that cognizes it because such phenomena are only mental imputations. After all, there is no whole separate from the individual particles that are the basis on which the mind imputes the existence of a whole such as a chair or a pot. The Gelukbas agree with this latter point; however, they are willing to say that the collection of parts, the whole, *is* the chair, for example, and that this collection is no more imputed by thought than the particles themselves. In their view, the collection of particles — the chair itself — casts an aspect to the eye consciousness, thereby acting as a causal condition for production of an ultimate consciousness. Thus a chair, not only its parts, is an appearing object which casts its aspect or image to an eye consciousness.

By contrast Dak-tsang emphasizes that only the particles — the indivisible components of impermanent phenomena — are appearing objects of direct perception. Only the particles, and not the imputed whole, actually cast their aspect to a consciousness. Everything else is simply fabricated by thought. In this way he emphasizes that human beings, as perceivers of wholes, live and work almost entirely in a realm that is just conceptually constructed. He contends that the Gelukbas do injustice to the subtlety of Sautrāntika by asserting that Sautrāntika considers gross objects to be ultimate truths when even the Vaibhāṣikas would not assert such. The Gelukbas can respond that the cluster of particles is all they mean by the 'chair' or 'pot' which they consider an ultimate truth in Sautrāntika. They are not referring, just as Dak-tsang does not wish to refer, to a whole which is a separate entity from the particles that are its basis of designation. For, as Bel-den-chö-jay notes in his *Annotations* to the thought of Jam-yang-shay-ba:

> [These] assertions are said to be unsuitable: that the mind which thinks 'pot' is produced from a whole which is a different substantial entity from the pot's parts, that the conceptual mind [which apprehends] the actions of picking

> up, setting down and so forth are produced from a factually separate activity which is a different substantial entity from pot and so forth.[27]

This is by way of pointing out that Gelukba does not consider the 'whole' pot to be anything *but* the collection of minute particles, for the whole is one substantial entity (*ekadravya, rdzas gcig*) with that collection. To phrase this another way, the action of, for example, a pot used in pouring water, is looked upon as an action of the collection, not of some substantially self-sufficient pot.

Although Dak-tsang and the Gelukba scholars agree that a whole is not a substantially different entity from its parts, Dak-tsang considers a whole such as a pot to be merely imputed by thought whereas these Gelukba writers do not. Thus, even though Gelukba presentations of Sautrāntikas Following Reasoning consider pots and such to be ultimate truths, they are not thereby giving these entities more ontological status than they have in Vaibhāṣika. This is because the Vaibhāṣika interpretation of conventional truths as substantially established in the sense of having their own self-sufficient entity contains all the meaning of what is, for Sautrāntikas Following Reasoning, an ultimate truth or specifically characterized phenomenon. The fact that these Sautrāntikas *call* gross impermanent phenomena such as pots ultimate truths whereas the Vaibhāṣikas call them conventional truths is thus not conclusive evidence for claiming that the Vaibhāṣika system is higher than the Sautrāntika. Beyond this, the Sautrāntikas can posit imputedly existent phenomena whereas the Vaibhāṣikas cannot. We have seen that in the Sautrāntika presentation of conventional truths, uncaused space, for example, is imputedly existent and without its own self-sufficient entity. Sautrāntika assertions on the two truths have the further subtlety of being able to encompass absences — including non-affirming negatives — which do not have their own self-sufficient entity. According to Vaibhāṣika, all conventional and ultimate truths are substantially established; therefore, even negatives are established in this way and thus Vaibhāṣika cannot posit the existence of non-affirming negatives at all because these are neither substantially established nor do they posses their own self-sufficient entity.

DAK-TSANG ON CONVENTIONAL AND ULTIMATE FUNCTIONS

According to Dak-tsang, only partless particles and so forth are ultimately able to function as causes of the consciousnesses perceiving them. Individual minute particles cannot be seen except in yogic direct perception, but collectively they have the capacity to act as a causal condition, for example, of an eye consciousness. An aggregated object such as a table is merely a conceptual artifice; nevertheless, it can perform the conventional function of holding books or dinnerware. In this way Dak-tsang distinguishes the conventional functioning of impermanent generally characterized phenomena from the ultimate functioning of ultimate truths — minute particles of matter and partless moments of consciousness. Thus, whereas in the Gelukba interpretation of Sautrāntika phenomena imputed by thought are necessarily permanent and unable to function at all, Dak-tsang has a middle ground where some phenomena imputed by thought are said to be impermanent and able to perform functions conventionally. A pitcher's holding water is a conventional function because the mind that perceives it is a conventional mind insofar as the action of holding is itself mentally imputed onto a continuum of activity that involves an aggregation of moments of time as well as of the minute particles composing the pot itself.

Gelukba scholars do not consider mentally imputed phenomena able to perform functions ultimately *or* conventionally. Only impermanent, substantially existent phenomena can function, and thus there is no need to divide functioning into categories of conventional and ultimate.

Moreover, Gelukba scholars contend that Dharmakīrti also holds that generally characterized phenomena do not perform functions at all. Here they cite Dharmakīrti's statement, noted above: "... it is not seen that the presence and absence of generally characterized phenomena [have the capacity to produce or not] a mind [apprehending them]."[28] In the Gelukba view, Dharmakīrti is here indicating that generally characterized phenomena are totally unable to perform functions. Their presence or absence does not affect sense experience; they do not appear to consciousness at all except through the medium of a meaning-generality. The Gelukba author Bel-den-chö-jay also takes this quote to indicate that since generally characterized phenomena are unable to produce minds which cognize them, such minds "operate subsequent to merely internal factors such as [internal] terminology, the exertion of motivation, and so forth."[29] Thus, Bel-den-chö-jay contends that generally characterized phenomena such as uncaused space are perceived not because an external object casts its aspect toward the perceiving consciousness, but because of an internal process of naming or being motivated to think about a certain object. Bel-den-chö-jay adds further that since the ability to produce a perceiving mind is not infallibly related with the presence or absence of a generally characterized phenomenon, such an object does not perform the function of generating a mind that perceives it. For,

> If a consciousness apprehending a generally characterized phenomenon were produced from a generality, its production would be infallibly related with the presence or absence of that generality [and it is not because one can have a consciousness fully perceiving a generally characterized phenomenon whether that object is actually present or not].[30]

Dak-tsang and Gelukba scholars agree that if a mind realizing an object necessarily comes about only on the basis of internal factors, then an external object which is the referent of that thought consciousness cannot be a causal condition for that mind. However, because of their different interpretations of generally and specifically characterized phenomena they disagree on what types of minds are produced due to internal factors.

Gelukbas maintain that chairs, for example, act as causal conditions for the production of an eye consciousness that directly perceives them. In Ḍak-tsang's view, chairs cannot perform such a function ultimately because they are merely imputed by thought. Their existence thus depends on the internal factor of conceptuality; they do not exist from their own side or under their own power.

Whereas in the Gelukba interpretation all impermanent phenomena — minute particles as well as large aggregations of them — are ultimate truths and specifically characterized phenomena, Dak-tsang considers only minute entities to be such. In this he appears to be more in the mainstream of contemporary scholarship on Dharmakīrti. Gelukba seems unique in explicitly interpreting Dharmakīrti to assert that aggregations of particles are ontologically equal to the wholes which they comprise.

Another source of this controversy[31] is Dharmakīrti's statement that specifically characterized phenomena are unmixed in place, time and nature and appear so to direct perception. According to the Gelukba thinkers, a whole such as a chair appears unmixed in place, time, and nature because its locale, chronology, and the specific fact of its being a chair appear to direct perception as unmixed with the locale, chronology, and specificity of any other chair. For Dak-tsang, however, a chair presumably appears as 'mixed' in place, time, and nature because the minute particles that comprise it are seen as aggregated together in these three ways: they exist in roughly the same place, are simultaneous, and their being together in a certain shape and so forth is what is indicated by the word 'chair.'

Dharmakīrti clearly states that only specifically characterized phenomena are ultimately able to perform functions. Thus Dak-tsang, in considering only minute entities to be specifically characterized, must and does assert that only they perform functions ultimately. Yet Dak-tsang, like Dharmakīrti and Gelukba scholars, considers all impermanent phenomena to be capable of functioning in some manner. Dak-tsang resolves this by asserting a second category of conventional functionality which he ascribes to gross impermanent phenomena. Such phenomena, being mixed in place, time, and nature in his view, are generally characterized. At the same time, they are impermanent things and thus we have seen Dak-tsang assert a sub-category of generally characterized phenomena not set forth by Gelukba; this is known as the class of generally characterized phenomena which are functioning things.

It is important to note that both Dak-tsang and the Gelukba writers categorize all existent things — objects of knowledge — in terms of specifically and generally characterized phenomena. This classification is based primarily on Dharmakīrti who, in one of the most famous lines of his *Commentary on (Dignāga's) 'Treatise on Valid Cognition'* says:

> Because there are two objects of comprehension (*gzhal bya*)
> There are two [types of] valid cognition [direct and inferential].[32]

Gyel-tsap explains that this statement is intended to eliminate misconceptions about the enumeration of valid cognizers[33] and, secondarily, to eliminate wrong views regarding the number of objects of comprehension. As noted earlier, the description of the two truths — objects of comprehension — in Sautrāntika is done in terms of the types of consciousnesses which cognize them. If the one is not definite, the other will be indefinite also.

Both the Gelukba's and Dak-tsang's presentation of Sautrāntika is formulated within the strictures of Dharmakīrti's statement quoted above that there are two types of objects and two types of valid cognizers. In the Gelukba view, specifically characterized phenomena are *appearing* objects of direct perception and *referent* objects of inferential cognition, whereas generally characterized phenomena are appearing objects of inference only, not of direct perception. Some modern scholars whose work is based on Dharmakīrti or commentaries on him report that there is only one type of phenomenon or object of comprehension.[34] They speak of a system which asserts, for example, that whatever exists is necessarily impermanent and specifically characterized. For instance the well-known Indologist Karl Potter writes that "A Buddhist is one who believes in the momentariness of everything which exists."[35] This contrasts with the Gelukba and with Dak-tsang's presentation of permanent phenomena. Similarly, Stcherbatsky: "Existence for them [that is, for followers of Dignāga and Dharmakīrti] refers to the ultimate reality of the point-instant"[36] and furthermore,

> Reality, existence, thing, are synonyms; we must not forget they are contradictorily opposed to ideality, non-existence, image, or a conception which are all different names of unreality.[37]

In these statements Potter and Stcherbatsky take specifically characterized phenomena to be synonymous with indivisible particles or partless moments of mind. Anything else, they assert, is made up by the mind and therefore unreal. As Stcherbatsky's second statement above indicates, 'non-existent' is here a synonym of the 'unreal.' Thus, in his interpretation wholes such as tables are merely imputed by thought and do not exist. Gelukbas would agree that pots are imputed on the basis of the aggregated particles which comprise them, nevertheless, they are as real as the particles themselves. They exist and perform functions. Even Dak-tsang, who does not consider tables to be ultimate truths does consider them to exist, describing them as able to perform functions conventionally. There is no question however, for either the Gelukbas or Dak-tsang, but that generally characterized and permanent phenomena do exist.

Of course, Potter's and Stcherbatsky's systemizations also derive from Dharmakīrti. Dharmakīrti indeed seems to designate only impermanent things as objects of comprehension when he says:

> Only that which has its own [specific] characteristics is an object of comprehension.[38]

However, it must be noted that the Gelukba scholar Jam-yang-shay-ba, in quoting the above line from Dharmakīrti, states that it does *not* mean that whatever is an object of comprehension — and, by implication, whatever exists — is necessarily a specifically characterized phenomenon. He maintains Dharmakīrti is here referring to the virtues a practitioner must adopt and the non-virtues she or he must discard as necessarily specifically characterized phenomena. Moreover in this system, a yogi's direct perception observes the mind and body which are empty of the self of persons; it does not explicitly realize their emptiness or selflessness. Thus, the objects explicitly comprehended by liberating wisdom are specifically characterized, not generally characterized, phenomena. Generally characterized phenomena however are also objects of comprehension. In support of this view, Jam-yang-shay-ba notes Dharmakīrti's clear statement (quoted above) that there are two objects of comprehension and comments that if generally characterized phenomena did not exist, there would necessarily be only one object of comprehension and this would contradict Dharmakīrti. Furthermore, he argues that, if all phenomena were specifically characterized, there would not be two types of valid cognizers, direct and inferential.[39] A cognizing consciousness cannot exist without an object of comprehension, and generally characterized phenomena are, in the Gelukba view, the only appearing objects of conceptual thoughts, thus they are the only possible appearing objects of an inferential valid cognizer. The 18th-century Gelukba scholar Den-dar-hla-ram-ba also takes up this point in *Beginnings of an Explanation of General Meaning of (Dharmakīrti's) "Commentary on (Dignāga's) 'Compendium on Valid Cognition'"* (*rNam 'grel spyi don rdzom 'phro*). In addition to the famous statement that because there are two types of objects there are two types of valid cognizers, he also quotes these lines from the 'Direct Perception' chapter of Dharmakīrti's text:

> Because there are [two modes of] realization by way of [taking] specifically [characterized phenomena or] the other [i.e., generally characterized phenomena] as the appearing

> object, two objects of comprehension are asserted.[40]

Thus, in order to support the position that there is only one type of object — which is tantamount to saying, as Ratnakīrti[41] and other major commentators have indicated, that only impermanent phenomena exist — one must have a way of dealing with Dharmakīrti's statements indicating that there are two types of objects. The Gelukḅa position, as we have seen, is that permanent or generally characterized phenomena exist. Direct perceivers take only specifically characterized phenomena as their appearing objects and inferential cognizers take only generally characterized phenomena, hence there are two types of objects.

Moreover, Den-dar-hla-ram-ba adduces from Dharmakīrti a powerful statement in support of two types of objects:

> There are no objects of comprehension other than
> The manifest and the hidden
> Therefore, valid cognizers are asserted as two-fold
> Due to the two objects of comprehension[42]

Dak-tsang and Gelukba scholars agree that there are two types of valid cognition and two types of objects — specifically and generally characterized phenomena. They differ, however, on what types of objects are considered specifically and generally characterized.

THE STATUS OF WHOLES AND PARTS

For both Dak-tsang and Gelukba scholars, the line between specifically and generally characterized phenomena is the line between phenomena that exist from their own side and which are merely imputed by thought. This line however is drawn in different ways. Dak-tsang considers that all wholes — conglomerates of particles or moments of time — are merely imputed by thought. The parts which are the basis of imputation are real in that they are not merely imputed. By contrast, a whole such as a chair, table, or person is merely imputed by thought onto these particles. Thus, for Dak-tsang it is not the whole which casts an aspect to the eye consciousness, it is simply the collection of particles. To conceptualize such a collection as a 'chair' or a 'table' is to superimpose onto the particles something that is not actually there.

For Gelukbas wholes and parts are equally real in Sautrāntika; both are specifically characterized phenomena and both are ultimate truths. This does not mean — as perhaps Dak-tsang thinks it does — that Gelukbas consider the whole to be an entity different from its particles and somehow spread over them, like jam over bread. The Gelukbas maintain that the collection of particles itself is the 'whole' which is called a chair. From this viewpoint their position is really not very dissimilar from Dak-tsang's; however, the fact that they are willing to call such wholes ultimate truths and thereby to put them on the same epistemological and ontological footing with the particles that compose them is quite a different perspective from that of Dak-tsang.

Dak-tsang's system has the advantages of being less prey to misunderstanding than the Gelukba presentation. In terms of providing a stepping-stone to Mādhyamika, although Dak-tsang does not consider Sautrāntika to share the Mādhyamika view that parts and wholes are of equal ontological status, his way of breaking down the reification of wholes accords with the Mādhyamika perspective. When one is trying to gain a foothold on a view in deep contradiction with ordinary perception and ordinary intuition, it can be very helpful to hear that wholes are false or mentally imputed — that there are only parts. This allows the practitioner to become aware of his or her own sense of wholes and makes it easier to negate these without plunging into utter nihilism. One may discover that, despite all reasoning to the contrary, if one's own inner sense of things is analyzed, it does *seem* that a table or a chair has an existence quite apart from its components. One may observe a sense of one's self that is as if mind and body could be placed on one side of the room and the 'I' would still exist on the other. Dak-tsang's emphasis on the fallacy of such a mode of apprehension is compatible with the Mādhyamika view that the 'I' is only imputed onto its basis of designation, the mind and body. It is also psychologically easier to allow oneself to think that there is no whole over and above the parts, or that there is no substantially existent self-sufficient 'I,' if one hears that at least the parts — the particles composing the table legs and top or the moments of mind and minute particles of the physical body — are not denied for the time being. In this way, Dak-tsang also has a pedagogically useful system that offers a pathway to Mādhyamika within making a textually supportable presentation of Sautrāntika.

In the Prāsaṅgika view as set forth in Gelukba, wholes and parts have the same status; neither exist from their own side; they are just imputed by thought. This is a subtle and difficult to understand perspective because it means negating almost everything one asserts to be characteristic of, for example, a table: its inherent power to be itself, an inherent ability to function as a table, an inherent solidity and obstructiveness. At the same time, however, one is not negating the very *existence* of a functioning table. Mādhyamika considers itself the middle way because it is a view that stands between permanence on the one hand — that is, an over-reification of persons and other phenomena — and annihilation on the other — a nihilistic view that nothing exists.

Gelukba scholars formulate Sautrāntika so as to prepare the student for the Mādhyamika perspective. One significant way in which they do this is to make wholes and parts ontologically equal. We have seen that according to Gelukba, Sautrāntika considers these to be equally real, whereas in Madhyamika they are equally unreal. But even at the level of Sautrantika, in asserting that chairs and so forth are ultimate truths, Gelukba is referring not to a sense of chair as separate from its parts but to the chair as a mere collection of particles. In this the Gelukba presentation of Sautrāntika is more subtle than Dak-tsang's because it presumes or builds from a sense of a whole that is *already* different from the ordinary, ignorant sense of a whole.

Direct perception does not see wholes and parts as separate: they only appear that way to thought. It is one of the errors of conceptuality that in reflecting, for example, on a pitcher with a handle, spout, blue bottom, and so forth, it will appear to thought that the pitcher (not the name, but the object) is different from all of its parts. This is because thought has the ability to isolate different elements within the same substantial entity. The appearance to thought of wholes and parts as different substantial entities can operate, without one being aware of it, even simultaneously with direct perception. Unless the misconception based on this false appearance is corrected, even activities involving ultimate awarenesses — direct perceivers — are tainted with error. In fact, a whole and its parts are a single entity. Moreover, although there is no 'whole' other than the collection of those parts, the untrained mind maintains a subtle sense that parts and wholes are independent of each other.

Tsong-ka-pa's system, even from the level of Sautrāntika, is directed at this rather subtle misconception. The system is almost too subtle; it is easy to misconstrue the Gelukba view of Sautrāntika as rather simple-minded in not making any distinctions between the ontological status of wholes and parts but going along with ordinary perception which accepts tangibles such as pitchers and tables as 'real'. The Gelukbas, of course, call tables and so forth ultimate truths in Sautrāntika. However they do this within holding that the actual nature of tables, although appearing to direct perception, will not be noticed or ascertained unless one has trained well in correct thought. For the Gelukba, what brings one to liberating knowledge is the ability to train in fully ascertaining ultimate truths (wholes and parts) in a process that goes from correct conceptual thought to direct perception.

One can speculate that the Gelukbas may well have a further quarrel with Dak-tsang's presentation. For, if the Sautrāntikas, as Dak-tsang claims, grant different status to minute particles and gross objects, then this itself, according to Gelukba, is a sign that they do not fully realize the extent of misconception that exists even with respect to the wholes they claim to understand as mentally imputed. In technical terms, they are not realizing the subtle object of negation — the emptiness or selflessness — that theoretically should qualify wholes as well as particles.

This is because, the Gelukbas might add, to realize any type of selflessness means to remove the mental superimpositions which act as conditions for projecting the corresponding notion of a self onto other phenomena. If these superimpositions are removed successfully with respect to one object — such as a whole — the same realization can easily, without further reasoning, be seen to apply to any other phenomena — such as parts or particles. For the practitioner, this is a way of testing her or his own realization. In Dak-tsang's system the realization gained with respect to wholes — that they are imputed to a basis of designation — does not apply to partless particles. This means, from the Gelukba perspective, that Dak-tsang is maligning the Sautrāntikas by indicating that they actually do not fully realize anything at all.

In the Gelukbas' presentation of Mādhyamika it is asserted that if one understands non-true establishment with respect to persons or other 'wholes' one will also understand this with respect to the minute particles which are *also*, in the Mādhyamika view, wholes imputed to collections of parts such as their eastern and western sides. When this sort of selflessness is understood correctly with respect to gross objects it will be understood in the same way with respect to subtler objects, since the principle at work is the same. Therefore, if Dak-tsang maintains that Sautrāntikas realize the imputed nature of wholes but not of parts, then, according to Gelukbas, he is really saying that they do not realize anything at all.

In Mādhyamika, then, one way to test realization of non-inherent existence with respect to one phenomenon is to turn the mind to another phenomenon — including to a *part* of the previous object of contemplation. One then observes whether or not this understanding carries over. If it does not, this is a sign that it was not properly understood even with respect to the former object. This, perhaps, is why the Gelukbas, unlike Dak-tsang, are unwilling to posit that the Sautrāntikas realize the non-inherent existence of gross objects but not of subtle ones and instead say that in Sautrāntika gross and subtle objects are both specifically characterized.

3 *Direct Perception*

The three higher Buddhist systems, Sautrāntika, Cittamātra, and Mādhyamika, agree that, despite its name, direct perception does not know actual phenomena nakedly but knows them through certain types of sense-data. These sense-data, moreover, are not related solely with objects but comingled with projections from the side of the subject. For Sautrāntika, to see an aspect similar to an object functions as seeing that object directly; for Cittamātra, the perceiving subject and perceived object are simultaneously produced from an internal, mental predisposition. For Cittamātra, the apparent separateness in entity of subject and object is an exaggeration of their true status. In Mādhyamika, where external and internal objects are considered valid and directly perceivable, the valid portion of perception is for ordinary persons so completely submerged in erroneous over-reification that phenomena are not perceived as they actually exist. Moreover, all three systems agree, for different reasons, that the world in which we move, the world of experience, is a complex enmeshment of objective and subjective elements.

For these systems, as for the study of phenomenalism in the West, such tenets raise difficult questions about the status of 'real' things. The challenge here is to account for common-sense experience of public, functioning, and continuous objects, and at the same time to critique this experience through analysis into the causal conditions for and machinations of perception. However important this analysis is for Buddhist thought, the primary concern is not to construct an incontestable description of mundane reality, but to articulate the limitations and deceptions of ordinary cognition in order to depict a model of mental development that purportedly leads to liberation from precisely those errors. This project is motivated in turn by a deep conviction in the alterability of the perceiving subject, and in the superior mode of behavior — ethical, serene, compassionate, and wise — that necesarily unfolds as that subject's misperceptions are dispelled.[1]

Buddhist systems have handled the issue of direct perception in different ways. Sautrāntika maintained that some image-like aspect of an object causes a perceiving sense consciousness to be generated in that object's image, much like reflections in a mirror. Thus, although a perceived object is an essential causal condition for direct perception, it is not technically that object which is perceived, but an aspect (*ākāra, rnam pa*) which is a confluence of subject and object. However, the aspect theory runs into problems, detailed below, so that the process of perception and the ontological status of objects cannot be fully explained through aspect theory. Scholars cannot fully support a claim that the aspect exists either in the perceiver, or between the perceiver and object, or solely in the object.

In Gelukba formulations of Sautrāntikas Following Reasoning, an object of direct perception is necessarily a specifically characterized phenomenon. This means it is an object whose own nature or mode of being is observed in direct perception. Dignāga and Dharmakīrti define direct perception as free of conceptuality (*kalpanāpodha, rtog pa dang bral ba*).[2] Dharmakīrti and the Gelukbas after him further qualify this as unmistaken (*abhrānta, ma 'khrul ba*). The Sanskrit term for direct perception, *pratyakṣa*, is etymologized as *prati*, meaning 'toward' and *akṣa*, meaning the sense organ which is the uncommon (*asādhāraṇa, thun mong ma yin pa*) cause of this type of consciousness.[3] A particular sense power, such as the eye, is the uncommon dominant cause (*adhipatipratyaya, bdag rkyen*) for visual direct perception; the perceived object, also a necessary cause, is known as the object condition (*ālambanapratyaya, dmigs rkyen*). A directly perceiving consciousness comes to know such an object by taking on an aspect similar to it, much like a mirror takes on the colors and shapes of objects appearing before it. A complete investigation of ultimate truths or specifically characterized phenomena in the Gelukba presentation of Sautrāntika necessitates an inquiry into how they are perceived. This in turn requires detailed analysis of how a directly perceiving consciousness takes on the aspect of its object. It is a topic on which there is a wider variety of opinion than most.

A CONSCIOUSNESS THAT FULLY PERCEIVES OBJECTS

According to Gelukba formulations of Sautrāntika Following Reasoning, specifically characterized phenomena are things which exist the way they appear. Their existence does not depend on imputation by thought or terminology, for they are established by way of their own nature and that actual nature appears to direct perception. These characteristics greatly distinguish objects of direct perception from objects of conceptual thought (*kalpanā, rtog pa*). For, the mental image (*arthasāmānya, don spyi*) of a chair that appears to thought is like a chair but not a chair. What appears to direct perception is an actual chair, not something that is merely like one. The eye consciousness observing an external chair is an ultimate mind because the features appearing to it are what they appear to be — both in the sense that the mode of being of the chair appears just as it is and because an actual, functioning chair itself is taken as the object; it is not represented by something else.

The idea that the senses perceive things 'just as they are' is traceable to Dignāga who states:

> The object of the sense (*indriya-gocara*) is the form (*rūpa*) which is to be cognized [simply] as it is (*svasaṃvedya*) and which is inexpressible (*anirdeśya*).[4]

In the following chapter's discussion of conceptual thought, we will see that Gelukba scholars went to considerable trouble to qualify the statement that objects of direct perception are inexpressible. However, the tenet that only direct perception knows objects just as they exist was systematically incorporated into the Gelukba formulation of Sautrāntika. Such cognition is possible because of the manner in which direct perceivers engage their objects.

A direct perceiver such as an eye consciousness that sees a pot is a complete engager (**vidhi-pravṛtti-buddhi, sgrub 'jug gi blo*). This means that everything which co-exists with the pot, such as its particular mouth, base, color, subtle impermanence and so forth, appears directly to that eye consciousness. All the impermanent characteristics that come into existence and go out of existence simultaneously with the pot's own momentary production and disintegration are said to be one substantial entity of establishment and abiding (*grub bde rdzas gcig*) with it. Permanent phenomena related with the pot are not one substantial entity of establishment and abiding with it. For example, the uncaused space inside a pot is a permanent phenomenon because it does not change or disintegrate from one moment to the next. Thus, as mentioned earlier, 'permanent' here means static. It does not mean eternal, for the space comes into existence when the pot is created and goes out of existence when the pot is destroyed. Even though its existence is simultaneous with that of the pot, this space is not one substantial entity of production and abiding with the pot because permanent and impermanent phenomena cannot be a single substance (**ekadravya, rdzas gcig*). Only impermanent specific characteristics, which are one substantial entity with the pot, can be explicitly realized by an eye consciousness; the permanent uncaused space is not so realized. To be explicitly realized means an object casts its own specific characteristics toward the consciousness. Uncaused space has no such specific characteristics and, as a permanent phenomenon, cannot perform the function of casting its own aspect. Therefore, it is not realized explicitly by the eye consciousness. However, the eye consciousness realizes space implicitly (*shugs rtogs*) — that is, not by means of aspects cast toward it but through observing a gap in the material of the pot.

The eye consciousness is not necessarily able to induce ascertainment of all the impermanent characteristics of pot which do actually appear (*dngos su snang*) to it. This consciousness is a complete engager in the sense that the entire collection of specific characteristics which are one substantial entity with the pot cast their aspect toward it, but not in the sense that it induces ascertainment of all of them.

A consciousness which is a complete engager is defined as a mind that engages all parts of its object.[5] This does not entail the absurdity that all particles of a table, for example, appear to a single eye consciousness in the sense that those inside it, or on the side opposite to the one facing the perceiver and so forth would appear.[6] It simply means that all parts of the object which would normally be considered within one's sphere of vision are appearing. Sautrāntikas, Cittamātrins and Svātantrikas all agree that the specific characteristics of an impermanent object must appear to direct perception.

This is because if direct perception were not valid with respect to the specific characteristics of the five types of objects (forms, sounds, odors, tastes, and tangible objects) they would not be valid with respect to specifically characterized phenomena. The eye consciousness is 'valid' with respect to specific characteristics, not in the sense that it ascertains them, but only in the sense that they appear. What the eye consciousness is able to ascertain is that the object exists by way of its own power, that is, by way of its own characterizedness, and not through being imputed by thought or terminology.

To realize the specifically characterized nature of a phenomenon means to ascertain its mode of abiding; that is, to realize everything which is one substantial entity of place, time, and nature with it: for example, production, productness, subtle impermanence, ultimate truth, form and shape, abiding and cessation.[7] Thus, even though the eye consciousness does realize a specifically characterized phenomenon and even though the aspect cast by the object accords with the nature of the object, neither the eye consciousness nor any other ultimate consciousness *ascertains* the actual specifically characterized nature of its object.

The eye consciousness of an ordinary person cannot ascertain all specific characteristics which appear. For example, it cannot ascertain an object's inability to abide for a second moment by its own power; this inability is the subtle impermanence of that object. Nor can it ascertain the subtle moment-by-moment disintegration of a product, this disintegration being the definition of a product. Thus, an ordinary person's eye consciousness cannot ascertain the specific nature of a table as a product.[8] In Sautrāntika, all these characteristics, momentary disintegration, productness and so forth, are part of the object's mode of abiding (*gnas tshul*). This is quite different from the Mādhyamika assertion that there is just one final mode of abiding (*gnas lugs mthar thug*) — an object's emptiness of inherent existence.[9]

To realize something *as* a specifically characterized phenomenon means to know that it exists from its own side, to know it as not merely imputed by thought or terminology. Even though a table, for example, is imputed to its parts in the sense that on seeing them one thinks, "This is a table," a table is not imputed by thought. According to Gelukba, for Sautrāntika to say that a thing is imputed by thought simply means that that thing is an object of thought. It is not a statement about the thing's mode of existence. Thus, although the table is imputed by thought, it is not *merely* imputed by thought. It exists from its own side, independent of thought or terminology.[10]

An eye consciousness can engage the entire collection of characteristics associated with its object because all the aspects of that object appear to or are cast toward the sense consciousness. Thus, an alternative definition of a consciousness that is a complete engager is "an awareness that operates through the power of the [functioning] thing."[11] It is the aspects cast by the object or functioning thing that appear to a direct perceiver or a mind of complete engagement. Such a perceiver observes only presently existing phenomena. The present moment's pot can be an object of the present moment's eye consciousness, but the eye can see neither the pot of the next moment, which is yet to be created, nor the pot of the previous moment which no longer exists. Only thought can reflect on past and future objects. Moreover it is thought, not direct perception, that superimposes onto presently existing phenomena a sameness extending from the past to the future.

For example, when a person observes a flowing river, what actually appears to the eye consciousness are just the minute, presently appearing particles of water as well as the impermanence and other characteristics that are one with them (i.e. one in establishment and abiding with them: *grub bde rdzas gcig*). Those present particles of water are specifically characterized phenomena. They are thus appearing objects of the eye consciousness that perceives them. The minute particles of water which have already passed and those yet to come do not appear at all to direct perception. Nevertheless, when someone whose sandal was carried off by a river earlier in the day later returns to that spot, he or she feels, "There is the river which carried away my sandal." Although the particles of water that took the item have long since passed, it appears otherwise to the mind because earlier and later parts of the water's stream appear the same for thought.[12] The person's sense of *presently* seeing the very river that previously swept away the sandal is a case of thought superimposing a mixture of former and later times onto a present object observed in direct perception. As will be discussed later, nearly all ordinary experience involves an unanalyzed mixture of conceptual thought and direct perception. This occurs to the point that what is merely imputed by thought often seems to be established by way of its own nature, just as an imputed stream stretching from morning to evening seems actually to appear to the eye consciousness which, in fact, explicitly perceives only presently existing particles of water.

How can tiny particles of water appear to the sense consciousness of an ordinary being? The individual particles are not individually ascertained and cannot serve as causal conditions for generating an eye consicousness. Nevertheless, they do *appear* to the eye consciousness. Being a complete engager, this consciousness perceives all that is one substantial entity in place, time, and nature with its object. The collection of these particles at any given time, therefore, is the specifically characterized phenomenon which is an appearing object of direct perception. Moreover, the fact that the individual particles are not ascertained and so cannot serve as an objective causal condition does not contradict the assertion that the cohesive unit which is a collection of numerous particles does appear. The same applies when larger portions of the whole are considered. For, even though one cannot see individual trees from a distance, one does not hesitate to say that the forest can be seen. Similarly, in order for a fist to appear it is necessary that the collection of five fingers appear.

Any whole, whether a pot, river, forest or fist, cannot appear to direct perception except by its components appearing; therefore, it must be said that the minute particles of matter which compose a pot, river, and so forth appear to the direct perceiver cognizing that object. Thus, in the Gelukba presentation of Sautrāntika, a whole such as a pot is not merely imputed to its parts. Just as the individual particles are specifically characterized phenomena which exist by way of their own nature without being imputed by thought or terminology, the wholes which are composites of those particles also exist by way of their own nature.

The Gelukba assertion that in Sautrāntika wholes and parts are equally established by their own nature is unusual; we have noted that other Tibetan writers such as the Sagyaba Dak-tsang and most Western scholars of Sautrāntika maintain that in this system only particles are established by their own nature whereas all wholes are merely imputed by thought. According to the Gelukba view, if the collection of particles, the whole, were not a specifically characterized phenomenon, it could not appear to direct perception. It would then be impossible for direct sense perception to ascertain that there is a table here or a bureau over there. The collection is not here considered something factually other (*don gzhan*) than or beyond the collection of particles, or a separate entity (*ngo bo gzhan*) from them.

It is *composed* of them but not *superimposed by thought* onto them. Thus, the presently existing stream of the river in the example does appear to direct perception and is a specifically characterized phenomenon. The further superimposition that occurs in this example is to see the presently existing continuum as one entity with the river continuum that existed hours earlier. Thus, the collection of presently existing particles that occupies a certain area is an ultimate truth, a specifically characterized phenomenon which exists by way of its own nature. The temporal sameness of the stream is superimposed onto presently existing particles and particles that have either ceased to exist or not yet come into existence. Past and present particles are misconstrued as one entity. This unchanging continuum is merely imputed by thought and in fact does not exist at all.

Each of the five sense consciousnesses can take only one of the five types of objects as its appearing object. That is to say, each is capable of observing, or taking on the aspects cast by, only one type of object. The eye consciousness sees only color and shape, configurations of particles; the ear consciousness hears sounds, the nose consciousness smells odors, the tongue consciousness experiences tastes, and the body consciousness feels tangible objects. Each of these consciousnesses has an explicit realization of its own particular object — a smell, taste, and so forth. This is because an explicit realization (*dngos rtogs*) can occur only when the aspect of an object is cast toward an appropriate consciousness. At that time, the eye consciousness, for example, realizes the table itself which is a collection of particles of form. This eye consciousness realizes the specifically characterized table, but it does not realize the table's own specifically characterized nature (*svalakṣaṇa, rang mtshan*). Such would involve the realization of everything that is one entity of establishment and abiding with the table, including its subtle impermanence, productness, and so forth. In other words, it would entail realizing all that, according to Sautrāntika, characterizes the mode of abiding of the table's own nature (*rang mtshan gyi gnas lugs*). To realize the specifically characterized *nature* of a phenomenon is to ascertain all its specific characteristics. Although these do appear to the eye consciousness — whereby such can be called a mind of complete engagement — these characteristics are not ascertained.[13] The fact that the eye consciousness cannot induce ascertainment of the specifically characterized nature of its objects does not mean that it is mistaken with respect to that nature. That nature does appear to it, and thus the eye consciousness is considered unmistaken with respect to the actual nature of tables and so forth and is, therefore, considered an ultimate mind. In Sautrāntika there is no contradiction between not realizing something and being unmistaken with respect to it.[14] Since phenomena cast their aspect to the consciousness in accordance with their own mode of abiding; the direct perceiver or ultimate consciousness does not perceive anything which is not the mode of abiding of the object.[15] In brief, whatever a sense consciousness — a direct perceiver — ascertains, it ascertains correctly; however, it does not ascertain all aspects of its objects.

Explicit realization of an object means that the perceiving consciousness takes on the aspect of an object, much like a mirror reflects things by taking on an image or aspect of those things. Because the eye consciousness, for example, can take on or be generated into only the aspect of color or shape, only colors and shapes can be realized directly by it. Therefore, although in general a cedar table is an object of the eye consciousness apprehending such a table, only the color and shape of that table are directly realized by that consciousness. Other factors related with the table, its odor and weight for example, are not explicitly realized by the eye consciousness. Does this undermine the Sautrāntika assertion that a direct perceivers such as the eye consciousness are complete engagers which operate with respect to everything that is of one substantial entity of establishment and abiding with its object? In this system it is suitable to say that the eye consciousness sees the table because the table itself *is* color and shape; it is also the basis of qualities such as odor and weight which are actually perceived by other senses.

Similarly, it might be asked whether or not the eye consciousness sees fire or water. Although both of these have color and shape, water is defined as "that which is damp and moistening" and fire as "that which is hot and burning."[16] In other words, these are technically defined as objects not of sight but of the body consciousness, which can experience dampness and heat. The eye consciousness experiences neither the dampness of water nor the heat of fire, yet it is considered suitable to say that water and fire appear to the eye consciousness. Does this contradict the Buddhist assertion that the eye consciousness explicitly perceives only color and shape? No, because water and fire do not appear to the eye consciousness independently as do color and shape; they appear to the eye consciousness through something else appearing first. Therefore, their appearance depends on the appearance of their color and shape to the eye consciousness. An actual object of apprehension of the eye consciousness (*mig shes kyi gzung bya*) on the other hand is something that can appear to that consciousness without depending on anything else; only color and shape fulfill this criterion, and thus only they are actual objects of apprehension for the eye consciousness. However, everything that an eye consciousness sees is not necessarily, technically speaking, its object of apprehension. For example, the impermanence of a table, its productness and so forth are not objects of apprehension of the eye consciousness, but they do appear to it through the appearance of other phenomena; namely, through the appearance of the color and shape which *are* objects of apprehension.[17] Objects of the eye consciousness, therefore, fall into two categories: (1) objects of apprehension, that is, color and shape, and (2) other phenomena such as fire which are known in dependence on color and shape.

Another measure of color and shape being objects of apprehension for the eye consciousness is that the eye consciousness, like a mirror, actually takes on the aspect of the colors and shapes it perceives. The eye consciousness does not take on the aspects of water's wetness or fire's heat. This is considered a sign that the eye consciousness is not actually seeing fire or water; it neither knows nor experiences the wetness or heat which are the distinguishing characteristics of these. However, it is suitable to say that the eye does in general see water or fire due to the fact that it sees the color and shape of these.[18] Moreover, as a direct perceiver, the eye consciousness is a mind of complete engagement that necessarily perceives all factors of its objects which are one entity of establishment and abiding in relation to place, nature, and time. It does not necessarily perceive factors that are simply one entity with its objects. With respect to seeing a table, there is thus no contradiction in the eye consciousness explicitly perceiving the table but not its tangibility as such. This is because although tangibility is in general one substantial entity with the table, that tangibility is not infallibly concomitant with the table in terms of place, time, and nature. For, whatever is one entity with a table is not necessarily one entity with a table's tangibility. For example, a table's shape is not a tangible object.[19]

Appearing Objects of Direct Perception

The table that appears to the eye consciousness is an impermanent thing. However, the appearing object (**pratibhāsa-viṣaya, snang yul*) of that eye consciousness is not just visible form — namely, color and shape. For, in the Buddhist presentation all functioning things are included within three categories: forms, consciousnesses, and non-associated compositional factors (*viprayukta-saṃskāra, ldan min 'du byed*) such as impermanence which are neither form nor consciousness.[20]

An actual or fully appearing object of apprehension of an eye consciousness cannot be included in just the category of form. This is because phenomena such as a table's productness and impermanence are not the impermanent table — and thus not form — but *are* non-associated compositional factors and appear to the eye consciousness simultaneously with the table. These are also *appearing objects* of the eye consciousness although, as in the examples of fire and water above, they are not technically *objects of apprehension* of the eye consciousness. The table is the basis of these appearances; thus, it is necessary to distinguish the appearing object of direct perception — the table or, specifically, the color and shape of the table — from the many phenomena related with it which are not the table but do also appear.[21] Everything that is one entity of establishment and abiding with table in relation to place, time, and nature is an appearing object of the collectively engaging eye consciousness that apprehends table, but all impermanent and non-associated compositional factors which are associated with table and which therefore also appear to that eye consciousness are not themselves the table.

Permanent phenomena associated with a table cannot appear to direct perception because Sautrāntika asserts that permanent phenomena, being incapable of casting an aspect, cannot be appearing objects of direct perception. Thus, the emptiness associated with a table cannot appear to direct perception even though the table itself appears and even though the table and its emptiness are a single entity. A table's emptiness here is its lack of being used or enjoyed by substantially existent persons. This can be conceptually realized but not directly perceived according to Sautrāntika. Thus, in this system emptiness — realization of which is the chief antidote to the most subtle forms of ignorance — can be realized only implicitly, not directly, by a direct perceiver. The type of valid cognition that explicitly realizes emptiness is conceptual, namely, inference (*anumāna, rjes dpag*).

The eye consciousness observing a table is non-conceptual; it does not have an articulate realization that "this is a table." Further, although it realizes the specifically characterized table, it cannot ascertain all the specific characteristics of table such as its subtle impermanence.[22] The eye consciousness does not fully realize the specifically characterized nature of the table it perceives, for such a realization would entail ascertainment of the table's subtle impermanence, productness, momentary disintegration, and so forth. It would thus have to realize the mode of abiding of the table's own nature (*rang mtshan gyi gnas lugs*). Because the eye consciousness is a complete engager, this would mean that it necessarily ascertains everything which is the nature or own-character of the table. The eye consciousness, however, is not ordinarily capable of ascertaining the subtle characteristics of its objects.[23]

Thus, even though a table is a specifically characterized phenomenon and a product, the direct perception observing a table does not ordinarily realize it as such, despite the fact that both specifically characterized phenomenon and product, which are one entity with the table, do appear to it. This point further emphasizes the limitations of ordinary direct perceivers or ultimate consciousnesses in Sautrāntika and indicates the necessity for *cultivating* an understanding of, for example, subtle impermanence, productness, and emptiness.

HOW A DIRECT PERCEIVER KNOWS OBJECTS

Buddhist philosophical systems have two ways of explaining the workings of direct perception, as non-aspected and aspected. The only proponents of non-aspected direct perception are the Vaibhāṣikas; the upper three systems of Sautrāntika, Cittamātra, and Mādhyamika all assert some type of aspected direct perception. These three systems maintain that the aspect (*ākāra, rnam pa*) of an object is cast toward or impinges on the consciousness. According to Vaibhāṣika, this is not the case. In their view, direct perception means that both the eye sense power and the eye consciousness meet the object and thereby know it. Unlike any of the upper systems, the Vaibhāṣikas maintain that both the eye sense and the eye consciousness perceive, for example, a table.[24] They argue that if, as the other systems assert, only the eye consciousness knew the object, there would be no explanation for why we do not see through walls and so forth. The eye sense is simultaneous with the object it cognizes and a different substantial entity from it.[25]

Thus, according to Vaibhāṣika, a direct valid cognizer is not necessarily a consciousness because the sense power itself — the subtle matter inside the eye organ — also cognizes its object directly. In Sautrāntika (as well as Sautrāntika-Svātantrika and Prāsaṅgika-Mādhyamika) this sense power is one of the three causal conditions of an eye consciousness and exists just prior to the eye consciousness which is its own effect. All three upper systems agree that only the eye consciousness and not the eye sense power is a direct perceiver of the object.

Because in Vaibhāṣika the eye consciousness *and* eye sense extend out to the object, there is no discussion of perception by way of an aspect, that is, of the object being reflected in the consciousness. The only aspect connected with direct perception is the objective aspect (*don rnam*) — the object itself. Furthermore, because the consciousness contacts an object with which it is simultaneous, the object is not a causal condition that affects or impinges on the consciousness.

By contrast, the upper three systems concur in asserting that an aspect of the object either appears[26] or is cast toward the consciousness; all but the Cittamātrins and Yogacāra-Svātantrikas further maintain that the object is a causal condition, specifically an object-condition (*dmigs rkyen*) of a consciousness that perceives it in the next moment. This, in the view of these systems, is the objective aspect. The proponents of non-aspected and aspected perception thereby agree on the existence of an objective aspect; there is a difference of opinion, however, even among proponents of aspected perception, as to whether this objective aspect is a cause of the perceiving consciousness or not.[27] In Sautrāntika, the subject and object of direct perception are not simultaneous as in Vaibhāṣika, but serial. Even though a directly perceiving consciousness and its object are consecutive, the consciousness does clearly perceive the object because it is one entity with the *aspect* of the object. The aspect with which it is one entity is a consciousness aspect (*shes rnam*) not an objective aspect. Thus, one reason for positing aspected direct perception is to explain how a consciousness directly perceives an object that existed in the previous moment.

For example, an eye consciousness cognizing a table knows that table by taking on, or being generated into, the aspect of table. To say that a consciousness takes on the aspect of its object does not mean that the object in any sense actually enters into the eye consciousness. This is impossible inasmuch as a consciousness cannot have any specific color or shape. Just as a glass placed over a blue cloth takes on the color blue without itself becoming blue and without blue actually entering into the glass, the eye consciousness perceiving a table takes on a likeness of table without actually becoming a table and without a table actually entering into it.[28] This means it is possible to assert that the eye consciousness takes on the aspect of a table without actually extending out and contacting the external table. In this way one can perceive a table as 'over there' but subject and object need not actually meet as they must in the Vaibhāṣika system.[29]

A direct perceiver such as an eye consciousness does not ascertain all that appears to it and therefore is not generated in the aspect of all objects before it. Being generated in the aspect of blue, for example, is the unique characteristic or uncommom positer (*thun mong ma yin pa'i 'jog byed*) of a consciousness perceiving blue. Thus, even though yellow and so forth might also appear, this eye consciousness would not be generated in the aspect of yellow and so forth because it does not take note of yellow at that time.[30]

A consciousness that does not ascertain an object is not generated in the aspect of that object. Thus if, for example, one is deeply absorbed in listening to music, various colors and shapes can appear to the eye consciousness without the consciousness necessarily ascertaining these or being generated in their aspect. Similarly, when an impermanent phenomenon such as a table appears to the eye consciousness, that consciousness takes on the aspect of table but not the aspect of the subtle impermanence of the table because one is not ascertaining subtle impermanence. Still, this subtle impermanence does appear to it. The consciousness would only be generated in that aspect however if one had previously cognized subtle impermanence directly and could therefore ascertain it.

Thus, the aspect into which the consciousness is generated, even though similar to the external object, is itself of the nature of consciousness.[31] One indication that perception is aspected is the fact that if something is placed very close to the eye you cannot see it properly. This is said to occur because the aspect cannot appear unless there is some distance between the object and perceiving consciousness.[32]

An aspect similar to the object (*yul gyi 'dra rnam*) is cast toward the eye consciousness, which then takes on or is generated in the aspect of that object. Both the objective aspect (*don rnam*) and subjective aspects (*shes rnam*) are known as apprehension aspects (*bzung rnam*). When the eye consciousness perceives a table, for example, that very consciousness — like a glass placed over a blue cloth — takes on the aspect similar to the table. This subjective apprehension aspect[33] is also known as a consciousness aspect (*jñāna-ākāra, shes rnam*). In this context, some Gelukba scholars say that the consciousness-aspect is an aspect similar to the object (*yul gyi 'dra rnam*).[34] However, this assertion is not common to all Gelukbas. Some monastic texts maintain that only objective aspects can be aspects similar to the object and that no other aspect of the object (*yul gyi rnam pa*) is involved in direct perception.[35]

In any case, the subjective and objective apprehension aspects (*bzung rnam*) are similar, like the reflection of a face in the mirror and the actual face. When it is said that the eye consciousness is generated in the aspect of the object (*dngos po'i rnam ldan du skyes pa*) the aspect referred to is the subjective apprehension aspect or consciousness aspect. To say that an eye consciousness perceiving a table, for example, is generated in the aspect of that table also means that the consciousness has become or taken on the entity of a consciousness that has table as its aspect, that is to say, which ascertains a table.

This presentation of aspected direct perception is shared by the higher systems and is a marked departure from the Vaibhāṣika view of aspectless direct perception. One significant reason why the Vaibhāṣikas do not posit aspected direct perception is that their system does not distinguish between subjective and objective apprehension aspects.[36] They therefore cannot posit a consciousness aspect or subjective apprehension aspect, for that would entail the absurdity either of the consciousness being material or of the object itself being immaterial.[37] They must argue that no aspect exists anywhere between the observing consciousness and the object itself. For, if there were something between the consciousness and its object, that something would have to be an appearance (*snang ba*) which, in their view, is none other than the object itself. For they maintain that since the appearance is not the object (the objective aspect) which appears, then it (the hypothetical subjective aspect) does not appear and there can be no proof for an object which does not appear.[38]

That which is generated in the image of the object is the consciousness aspect, also known as the subjective apprehension aspect.[39] That which is apprehended is the object — also known as the apprehension aspect existing in the object (*yul la yod pa'i gzung rnam*).[40] This apprehension aspect and the consciousness or subjective apprehension aspect are one entity, just as a mirror and the image it reflects are one entity.[41] On this point, the Sautrāntikas seem to approach the Cittamātra (Mind-Only) position that a perceiving consciousness is the same entity as the object. However, according to Sautrāntika, the aspect in the consciousness arises through the power of an external object, whereas for Cittamātrins, subject and object both arise from the same internal latency (*vāsanā*, *bag chags*).[42] Furthermore, even though the reflected aspect of an external object is one entity with the consciousness in which it is reflected and is an aspect of the external object, Sautrāntika does not assert that whatever is an aspect of the object is necessarily the object itself.[43] Thereby, Sautrāntika maintains that subject and object are different substantial entities. Unlike the Cittamātrins, the Sautrāntikas do not try to prove that the object aspect is one substantial entity with the consciousness that perceives it.[44] For, whatever is the aspect of a table, according to Sautrāntika, is not necessarily a table. The eye consciousness realizing a table, for example, takes on the aspect of the table.[45] This aspect, although similar to a table, is itself the entity of consciousness whereas the table is not. The consciousness aspect or subjective apprehension aspect has the feature of combining both the objective and subjective aspects. These aspects are 'mixed' in the sense that the apprehension aspect is common to both subject and object. The way an object becomes known is through this common aspect; as noted above however, it is not the case that the object itself becomes mixed with the consciousness.[46] In short, aspected perception means that direct perception knows an object by way of an aspect similar to that object being generated in the consciousness itself.

Cittamātra, like Sautrāntika, asserts that the consciousness is generated into or takes on the aspect of its object; however, Sautrāntika, unlike Cittamātra, asserts that the material object is external, arises from causes and conditions unrelated with the consciousness, and will continue to exist as a collection of particles even when it is no longer perceived by that particular consciousness. In brief, Sautrāntika (as well as Sautrāntika-Svātantrika-Mādhyamika and Prasaṅgika-Mādhyamika) maintains that a consciousness and its object are different substantial entities arising from different substantial causes, whereas for Cittamātra and Yogacāra-Svātantrika, subject and object are one substantial entity, arising simultaneously from a single cause, namely, a predisposition previously established in the mind.

Sautrāntika and other proponents of aspected direct perception explicitly refute the Vaibhāṣika tenet that perception is aspectless. If an object were capable of illuminating or knowing itself, no perceiving consciousness would be required, but since material objects have no such capacity, they must be known by means of a perceiving consciousness. On this much all four systems agree. The Sautrāntikas and so forth further make the case that if aspectless perception existed, the object could only be known when the consciousness actually extended out to the object. If direct perception operated in this way, says Sautrāntika, an eye consciousness, for example, should be able to see through walls and so forth, because consciousness itself is not obstructed by material objects. The Sautrāntikas reject the Vaibhāṣika explanation that the eye sense power, extending to the object along with the eye consciousness, is obstructed by walls and that therefore one cannot see through them. For, the Sautrāntikas do not consider the sense power (*indriya, dbang po*) to be a perceiver of objects. According to them, the fact that we do not see through walls is an indication that direct perception operates by way of an aspect; it is a sign that aspectless perception does not exist. Thus, the position of Sautrāntikas and the higher systems is that if there were no aspected direct perception, either objects would not be seen at all — because the consciousness would have no way of relating to them — or we should be able to see through walls because the consciousness knows objects by actually going out to them.[47]

An important Indian source for this position is a passage in Śāntarakṣita's *Ornament to the Middle Way* (*Madhyamakālaṃkāra, dbU ma rgyan*), quoted by Jam-yang-shay-ba in his *Great Exposition of Tenets*:

> Regarding the position that consciousness is aspected,
> The two [a glass and the blue cloth on which it is placed]
> are actually different;
> [Yet] because there is an image similar to the [object]
> Feeling [i.e., experience of that object] is suitable

Through the mere imputation [of seeing it in the glass].[48]

In this way, Śāntarakṣita indicated that direct perception is possible only because the perceiving consciousness can take on the aspect of its object. Jam-yang-shay-ba here also emphasizes the aspect's significance.

Location and Identification of the Aspect

The Sautrāntika discussion seems straightforward enough, but on closer examination it becomes very difficult to state precisely where the aspect arises and of what it consists. In one view, the consciousness aspect similar to the object — or the aspect into which the consciousness is generated — exists in the pupil of the eye itself. When the pupil deteriorates, one cannot see well because the proper basis for the aspect no longer exists.[49] Some Gelukba scholars assert that the objective apprehension aspect exists somewhere between the object and the perceiving consciousness. An indication in support of this view is that, as mentioned above, clear perception does not occur if the eye is too close to its object; this suggests that there is not sufficient room to allow for proper generation of the aspect.[50] In this presentation, the eye consciousness actually perceives not the object itself but the objective aspect, which is like the object but which is not the object. Seeing this similar aspect functions as seeing the object.[51] This position, although not widely asserted among present-day Gelukba scholars, is suported by a statement in Gyel-tsap's *Commentary on (Dharmakīrti's) 'Ascertainment of Valid Cognition'* where it asserts that the aspect does exist between the consciousness and its perceived object.[52]

The aspect into which the consciousness is generated is simultaneous with the directly perceiving consciousness and is itself necessarily consciousness. It cannot be either the perceived object, which is material, or the subtle matter inside the eye organ, for object and eye organ are respectively the object and uncommon dominant causal conditions of the eye consciousness. As causes, they necessarily exist prior to the consciousness which is their effect. Both have ceased when that eye consciousness begins to function. Thus, it is unsuitable for either object or sense power to be the subjective apprehension aspect.

It would also not be suitable to consider the apprehension aspect to be a non-associated compositional factor, namely, an aspect common to the three components of perception — eye consciousness, eye sense, and object. For, the actual subjective apprehension aspect, the one that mixes or is similar to subject and object aspects, can only be a consciousness.[53] Also, the apprehension aspect is not the object because the consciousness aspect, though similar to the object, is a different substantial entity from it.

From the above it is clear that the subjective apprehension aspect is not the actual object. However, it may be that this aspect *seems* to be the external object. Still, if the subjective apprehension aspect seems to be the object but is not, then direct perception would absurdly have the same type of mistake as conceptual thought. Thought's mistake is that the image seems to be the actual object it represents, but is not.[54] Thought may or may not actually misconceive the image to be the object; in most cases it does not. However, such a mistake can *never* apply to direct perception because the similar aspect (*'dra rnam*) of the table is never construed to *be* the table; the aspect merely appears as similar to table. Since it is in fact similar to table, there is no mistake involved.[55]

Some who maintain that the subjective apprehension aspect exists in the pupil of the eye say that this does not necessarily contradict the view that an apprehension aspect also exists between eye consciousness and object. This interceding apprehension aspect (*bzung rnam*) is considered an objective aspect (*don rnam*). One could assert the pupil to be the locus of the subjective apprehension aspect and consider that the aspect between subject and object is the objective aspect. However, this is difficult to uphold because the objective apprehension aspect itself is material, hence the absurdity of having to assert a material table existing between the eye consciousness and the actual table.

It makes more sense to consider the interceding 'object' as a subjective apprehension aspect. Still, this latter position seems to contradict the view that a subjective apprehension aspect exists in the eye, because there is no explicit presentation of *two* subjective apprehension aspects — although this is not explicitly refuted either. In any case, there is yet a further problem with this assertion. If the subjective apprehension aspect itself is a consciousness, why would cognition of a table require the presence of an eye consciousness? A consciousness does not need to appear to another consciousness in order to know its own object.[56] If one maintains that the subjective apprehension aspect needs to appear, does it follow that this aspect is in fact a table and not a consciousness? Some say that the perceived aspect is the table, others that it is not.[57] One way to settle it, as mentioned above, is to consider that from the viewpoint of the consciousness' perception of table, it is a consciousness or subjective apprehension aspect, and that from the viewpoint of its being the apprehended aspect itself, it is an object or objective apprehension aspect.

This is an interesting topic for further exploration, as valuable for the issues it raises as for the schematics that could be uncovered. The difficulties of making a presentation that can settle all the problems it raises without self-contradiction — for example, maintaining the existence of external objects within asserting aspected direct perception — tends to draw thought on to both the Cittamātra and Mādhyamika systems and prepares one to understand their respective positions of no external objects and no inherently existent or findable objects *or* subjects.

Assertions on Aspected Perception

There are three basic presentations of how aspected direct perception knows an object, that of the Proponents of an Equal Number of Subjects and Objects (*gZung 'dzin grang mnyam pa*), the Non-Pluralists (*sNa tshogs gnyis med pa*), and the Half-Eggists (*sGo nga phyed tshal ba*). These three presentations are in general common to the Sautrāntika and Cittamātra systems (although, as explained below, there is a disagreement among Gelukba scholars as to whether or not any Sautrāntikas assert the Half-Eggist position.)

The Proponents of an Equal Number of Subjects and Objects assert that whatever number of aspects exist as one substantial entity of establishment and abiding with, for example, a table, that number of aspects are cast to the perceiving consciousness. Some proponents of this position assert that there are as many simultaneous consciousnesses as there are appearing aspects; others, that a single consciousness is generated into as many aspects as are cast toward it.[58]

The Non-Pluralists maintain that the many aspects of a given object appear to a single consciousness simultaneously and that this consciousness itself takes on all such aspects. Some scholars assert that these aspects appear not simultaneously but serially, arising in such quick succession that they *seem* simultaneous. Holders of this position, known as Sequential Non-Pluralists (*Rim gyis pa'i sna tshogs gnyis med pa*) are said by Jam-yang-shay-ba and Jang-gya to exist among Sautrāntikas.[59]

The Half-Eggists assert that only a single aspect — for example, a general aspect similar to a table or to a mottle-colored cloth — appears to a single consciousness and that this consciousness is generated only into that aspect. One potential objection to this position is that, since direct perception is necessarily a mind of complete engagement which observes all aspects of its object, it is unsuitable to say that only the general aspect of, for example, a mottle-colored cloth is cast toward it. For, this would entail the unwanted consequence that the particular colors would not then appear. However, the Half-Eggists maintain that although only the general aspect of the mottle is cast, the consciousness is still able to see the separate colors contained in the mottle because it does not follow that only something which casts its aspect is capable of being seen. Thus, even though the entire collection of aspects appears and can be seen, the appearance of the individual colors is weak whereas that of the collection of the colors — the mottle itself — is strong. The eye consciousness which is generated in the aspect of a mere mottle is therefore a fully qualified complete engager because everything that is one entity of establishment and abiding with that mottle does appear to it.[60]

As to whether or not any Sautrāntikas assert the Half-Eggist position, Jang-gya writes that Tsong-ka-pa and his chief disciples, Gyel-tsap and Kay-grup, gave no clear opinions on this topic. However, both Jam-yang-shay-ba and Jang-gya consider it difficult to posit the Half-Egg position for Sautrāntika. This opinion is based on their interpretation of an important Indian source for the Half-Egg position, Śāntarakṣita's *Commentary on the 'Ornament to the Middle Way' (Madhyamakālaṃkāra-vṛtti, dbU ma rgyan gyi 'grel ba)*. Although mainly setting forth the Svātantrika tenet system, this text is an important source for Sautrāntika and Cittamātra discussions of the various ways in which aspected perception is asserted. In a verse frequently quoted by Gelukba scholars, this text says:

> Consciousnesses arise serially
> With respect to the white and so forth [of a mottle].
> Because they arise very quickly
> Fools think they are simultaneous.[61]

Jam-yang-shay-ba's commentator Bel-den-chö-jay considers this to be a statement of the Half-Eggist position. Jam-yang-shay-ba himself and Jang-gya do not. (This is a not-so-rare instance of Jam-yang-shay-ba's commentator disagreeing with him.) Hence, the former two maintain that there are Sautrāntika Half-Eggists, the latter that there are not. Their disagreement is due to their different interpretations of what the Half-Eggist position is. Jang-gya and Jam-yang-shay-ba consider the Half-Eggists to assert that when the aspect of a mottled design, for example, is cast, there is *no* casting of as many aspects as are one substantial entity of establishment and abiding with that design. Just the aspect of the mottle in general is cast toward the eye consciousness, not the individual aspects of red, yellow, and so forth. Because the above quote, in mentioning a serial generation of consciousnesses with respect to a single object, indicates that many different aspects are cast to the consciousness, Jam-yang-shay-ba and Jang-gya do not consider it to indicate the Half-Eggist position. Rather, they assert this quote to be an expression of the Sequential Non-Pluralist position; namely, that all aspects of the object appear serially but in such quick succession that they seem simultaneous. In other words, both sides agree on the meaning of the quote, but not on the system it represents.

Because Śāntarakṣita's *Commentary on the 'Ornament to the Middle Way'* is one of the major Indian sources for Sautrāntika,[62] those who, like Bel-den-chö-jay, consider this verse to represent the Half-Eggist position, maintain that there are Sautrāntika Half-Eggists; those who consider it to express the position of the Sequential Non-Pluralists do not. They posit the Half-Eggist position in relation to Cittamātra only, not Sautrāntika. In their view, the three Sautrāntika factions asserting aspected direct perception are the (1) Non-Pluralists, (2) Sequential Non-Pluralists and (3) Proponents of an Equal Number of Subjects and Objects.

It seems that any of these positions can be supported, depending on one's choice of quotes and interpretations. One value of investigating the merits and flaws of each position is that it draws students into critical analysis of the relevant texts. This is done within a recognition that some conclusions will be made despite the difficulties of interpretation they entail.[63] The other main value revolves around drawing one even more into examining the relationship between object and subject.

The Perceiving Consciousness as Both Subject and Object

Any perceiving consciousness is accompanied by a factor of self-knowing (*svasaṃvedanā, rang rig*) which experiences or knows that consciousness. For example, while the eye consciousness is observing a circus act, the self-knower experiencing that eye consciousness takes the eye consciousness observing the circus as its object. Although in relation to the circus the eye consciousness is a perceiving subject, in relation to the self-knower it is a perceived object. Proof that the self-knower exists is said to be the fact that when one reflects on the circus seen previously, one remembers not only the circus itself but the mind that observed it.

Sautrāntikas, Cittamātrins, and Yogacāra-Svātantrikas all assert the existence of a self-knowing consciousness such as that described by Dignāga:

> Some time after [we have perceived a certain object], there occurs [to our mind] the recollection of our cognition as well as the recollection of the object. So it stands that cognition is of two forms. Self-cognition is also [thus established]. Why?
>
> > 11d. because it [viz. recollection] is never of that which has not been [previously] experienced.
>
> It is unheard of to have a recollection of something without having experienced [it before]. For instance, the recollection of a thing of color, etc. [does not arise unless the thing of color or the like has been experienced].[64]

Those Buddhist schools which assert the existence of a self-knower maintain that this is the agent by which one remembers one's own previous cognition. Vaibhāṣikas do not assert self-knowers; they cannot, since they are unable to posit a subjective apprehension aspect that could be its object.[65] This is because the self-knower observes not merely the perceiving consciousness but the consciousness aspect which is similar to the actual object. The Sautrāntika-Svātantrika-Mādhyamikas and the Prāsaṅgika-Mādhyamikas also reject the self-knower on the basis that it would involve a confusion of agent and object.

The explicit object (*dngos yul*) of the self-knower is the perceiving consciousness that takes on the aspect of its object. Through observing this subjective apprehension aspect, the self-knower also knows the perceived object. In relation to the self-knower, all other consciousnesses are *objective* apprehension aspects (*gzung rnam*);[66] a self-knower is the only type of consciousness that is never an appearing object of any other non-conceptual consciousness in the same continuum. The consciousness which a self-knower apprehends never apprehends that self-knower.

Jam-yang-shay-ba describes the relationship between the directly perceived object, the directly perceiving consciousness, and its factor of self-knowing through the example, briefly alluded to above, of a stained glass:

> All Buddhist proponents of aspected [consciousness] assert the following: if one coats the far side of a glass with paint, then when one looks at [it] both the glass and the paint are similar in being perceived objects. [However] the glass is realized by way of its own thingness and the color by way of an image [in the glass] although there is no way of distinguishing the two, image and glass. Therefore, the master Bodhibhadra said:
>
> > When a person looks at a glass on which the color of tortoise paint has been applied, the eye apprehends both glass and paint; the glass is apprehended directly and the paint is apprehended [by way of an image]. Therefore, just as the person apprehends two objects, [direct perception involves two objects of apprehension].[67]

The two objects of apprehension indicated here are the external object perceived by the eye consciousness and the eye consciousness itself, perceived by the self-knower. The objective aspect of similar type (*'dra rnam kyi bzung rnam*) discussed above, which in some scholars' view could be posited as a third object — an objective apprehension aspect existing between the eye consciousness and an external object such as a table — is not represented in this example.

The self-knower experiences the eye consciousness directly, just as in the example the glass is seen directly. The self-knower experiences the object of the eye consciousness by way of its image, that is, through perceiving the subjective apprehension aspect into which the eye consciousness is generated, just as the blue is known indirectly by looking at it through glass. The self-knower, therefore, is aware of external objects indirectly, through the medium of the subjective apprehension aspect or the consciousness aspect. The eye consciousness knows the object directly although, as noted above, some scholars assert that what the eye consciousness actually perceives is the objective apprehension aspect and not the object itself.

Another way to express this is that in relation to the eye consciousness apprehending blue there are two aspects, apprehension and apprehending. The apprehending aspect (*grāhaka-ākāra, 'dzin rnam*) is the factor of experience, the self-knower. The apprehension aspect (*grāhya-ākāra, bzung rnam*) consists of two factors of illumination: the factor of the object which is illuminated — in this case, the color blue — and the factor of the consciousness that illuminates it.

In any case, because the self-knower is a factor of experience that is one entity with the perceiving consciousness, the difficulty remains of explaining more fully how the two factors of a single directly perceiving consciousness relate to one another. For example, it is said that the self-knower observes the subjective apprehension aspect; yet, why should one consciousness or factor of consciousness need to appear to another one? Is the self-knower itself then generated in the image of the apprehension aspect? The Prāsaṅgika system rejects the existence of a self-knower because it considers that if a self-knower had to be posited in order to explain the self-awareness of an eye consciousness, then that self-knower would also have to possess a self-knower, and so on infinitely.

The Sautrāntika system, like the higher systems, asserts aspected direct perception partly in order to avoid the faults it finds with the Vaibhāṣika assertion of aspectless direct perception. The main problem with the Vaibhāṣika presentation is that it must posit sense powers such as the eye sense as knowers of external objects; otherwise, it could not explain why consciousness do not see through walls and so forth. This means that in Vaibhāṣika the sense-power is not considered a causal condition for perception as it is in Sautrāntika, Sautrāntika-Svātantrika-Mādhyamika and Prāsaṅgika-Mādhyamika. Therefore, in Vaibhāṣika (as in Cittamātra) subject and object are simultaneous. In Sautrāntika, by contrast, the main significance of categorizing impermanent phenomena as ultimate truths is to emphasize the ability of such objects to act as causal conditions for the generation of an ultimate or directly perceiving consciousness. The entire Sautrāntika tenet system is built along the axis of distinguishing the appearing objects of direct perception (ultimate truths) from the appearing objects of thought (conventional truths) in terms of how these two types of valid cognizers know their respective objects. Thus, the presentation of aspected direct perception, a correlate of the assertion that an external object is prior to and a causal condition of the consciousness that directly perceives it, is central to the Sautrāntika system.

With certain modifications, the explanation of aspected direct perception remains valid for the higher Buddhist systems as well. Nevertheless, a presentation of aspected direct perception involves a number of difficulties, especially that of identifying exactly what the apprehension aspect is and detailing whether or not the directly perceiving consciousness knows its objects by means of a subjective apprehension aspect. The difficulties themselves are instructive: the explanation that even direct perceivers actually observe a subjective apprehension aspect leads one quite naturally to an interest in and critical appreciation of the Cittamātra system. In Cittamātra, subject and object are said to be both one entity and simultaneous, thereby avoiding certain difficulties of the Sautrāntika position (such as how to integrate the subjective and objective apprehension aspects) but encountering other problems such as how to account for shared experiences or clairvoyant knowledge of another's mind when there are no external objects which are different substantial entities from one's own mind.[68] The difficulties in Sautrāntika of pinpointing exactly where the apprehension aspects exist are also provocative. These aspects are impermanent phenomena and hence ultimate truths in this system; they are, by definition, not merely imputed by either terms or thoughts but, at least in theory, specifically located and findable. The problems associated with determining exactly where that specific location is — whether external, internal, or both — leads one to an interest in and critical appreciation of the Mādhyamika system which presents all permanent and impermanent phenomena as analytically unfindable, yet functional. This is one important way in which the Sautrāntika presentation of direct perception fulfills its long range pedagogical purpose in Gelukba of leading the scholar-practitioner on to the higher system.

4 *Conceptual Thought*

Like direct perception, conceptual thought is defined in terms of the types of phenomena that are its appearing objects, generally characterized phenomena or conventional truths, and the way in which it perceives those objects. In Gelukba presentations of Sautrāntika, objects of thought are discussed in detail for the sake of distinguishing what *appears* to thought from what a thought is actually *realizing*. For example, a thought to which an image of subtle impermanence appears is in fact realizing or concerning itself with actual subtle impermanence, not merely the image of impermanence. The overriding message of this presentation of thought and objects of thought is two-fold. First, it indicates that thought does indeed realize actual impermanent phenomena even though these cannot be appearing objects of thought. Second, the discussion of the types of images or abstractions which are appearing objects of thought indicates that, in the Buddhist view, thought itself yields vibrant, psychologically significant experience; it is not limited to a dry and meaningless mental rattle.

OBJECTS OF THOUGHT

Thought differs from direct cognition in both its objects and its mode of perception. It does not take on the aspect of specifically characterized phenomena, nor is it limited in scope to objects within sensory range. Like leading a horse on a tether, thought can bring its objects along with it.[1] Specifically characterized phenomena cannot become appearing objects of thought because all their individual characteristics cannot fully appear to thought. Thought is said to be prevented or obscured from taking ultimate truths as its appearing objects; it is obscured with respect to ultimate truths and only capable of taking conventional truths (*saṃvṛti-satya, kun rdzob bden pa*) as its appearing objects. For this reason the term 'conventional truth' is more accurately translated as 'truths for the obscured.'

Because generally characterized phenomena do not have their own uncommon specific characteristics they can fully appear to thought. Therefore, in the Sautrāntika system, appearing object of thought, permanent phenomenon, and conventional truth are all mutually inclusive. Whatever is one is all the others.

Even though impermanent phenomena do not appear fully to thought, thought is able to realize impermanent objects incontrovertibly. This is done through the medium of an image of, for example, a table. This image, for reasons to be explained below, is technically known as the "meaning-of-the-term 'table'." It differs from an actual table that appears to direct perception in several ways. An image lacks the vivid detail of a specifically characterized table and does not function as an actual table. Furthermore, the thought consciousness which has an image or meaning-generality (*artha-sāmānya, don spyi*) of table as its appearing object is said to be mistaken (*bhrānti, 'khrul ba*) with respect to it because (1) that image appears mixed with the actual specifically characterized table and (2) the place, time, and nature of all tables seems to be one with the image of the table. Because it is the nature of thought to operate in this manner, thought itself is the source for its own obscuration.

A basic tenet in the Gelukba formulation of Sautrāntika is that impermanent phenomena cannot be appearing objects of thought. Accordingly, the images which appear to thought are said to be permanent. This means that they are not momentarily changing; it does not indicate that they are eternal. Unlike impermanent phenomena such as tables which disintegrate from one moment to the next, permanent phenomena such as images do not undergo change as long as they exist, whether that be for a long or short time. The fact that past and future as well as present phenomena can appear to thought is considered a sign that the appearing objects of thought are permanent images.[2] Past and future phenomena exist *only* for thought, they cannot be perceived by ordinary direct perception, which apprehends only presently existing impermanent phenomena.

The assertion that mental images are permanent is consistent with the overall Gelukba presentation of Sautrāntika, but is not without problems of credibility. It is a matter of experience that mental images appear to undergo rapid changes. Moreover, taking to mind certain images can have an effect such as stabilizing or heightening the mind, and having an effect is supposed to be a property of impermanent phenomena only. Beyond this, the image does not appear to thought by its own power; it is imputed by thought. Because it is in this sense created, it would seem logical to consider it a product and therefore impermanent. Despite these difficulties, the Gelukbas may have pedagogical reasons for emphasizing that the image is permanent. In terms of a Buddhist path to liberating knowledge, the final purpose of practices involving mental imagery or visualization is not to create a certain type of image, but to generate a specific type of consciousness. By asserting that the image is permanent, the system emphasizes that the purpose of effort is to change the mind, not create a mental picture. For example, one seeks finally to cultivate a direct realization of subtle impermanence rather than just generate a clear image of it; nevertheless, the generation of that image — which of course does involve effort — is an integral part of the process of gaining realization.

Even if one concedes that, in terms of the wider picture of Buddhist practice, it is suitable to emphasize the cultivation of certain consciousnesses rather than of mental images, it still seems strange to insist that such images are permanent, that is, non-disintegrating. After all, as mentioned, experience strongly and easily contradicts this assertion. One way to get around this might be to say that from the viewpoint of a mental image being a functioning thing created by the mind, it is impermanent, and from the viewpoint that an image represents an elimination of what is not that object (for example, an appearance as opposite from non-pot) it is permanent.[3]

Meaning-of-the-Term

There is much to consider in the material on mental images, some of which sheds further light on the problematic assertion that these images are permanent. The image that appears to the thought consciousness apprehending table is a mental picture of table which eliminates from that thought's purview all that is not table. This non-detailed and possibly very abstract image serves as a generality which applies to or is concomitant with all instances of table. For this reason it can serve as a means of identifying all varieties of tables as tables. (*See chapter eight.*) Jang-gya calls this image the 'meaning-of-the-term' (*śabdārtha, sgra don*) because when a person familiar with the term 'table' hears that word, an image which represents the meaning of the term 'table' appears to her or his mind. Since any instance of thought is said to have such a generic image as its appearing object, Jang-gya defines thought as "a conceptual knower which apprehends a meaning-of-the-term."[4] Strictly speaking, this definition would not include young children and others unschooled in terminology. After all, someone who does not know the term 'table' cannot evoke an image of it on the basis of hearing the word 'table.' Such a person does not have table as the referent of the designation 'table.' The meaning-generality of table, which is an appearance to thought as opposite from non-table — that is, a pictorial elimination of all that is not a table — cannot be evoked by the word 'table' unless one knows to what sort of object the term 'table' refers. Jang-gya himself writes that although untrained children and animals do indeed have thought, they need not be accounted for in the definition of thought. The purpose of a definition, he contends, is to generate understanding; it need not apply to every possible situation.

In making this assertion, Jang-gya openly takes a stand against Jam-yang-shay-ba and by extension against other later Gelukbas. These scholars use a slightly lengthier definition of thought in order to include in their definition persons untrained in terminology. Jam-bel-sam-pel, author of a recent Gelukba text on Awareness and Knowledge (*bLo rig*),[5] accords with Jam-yang-shay-ba when he defines a thought consciousness as "a conceptual knower which apprehends term and meaning generalities in a manner such that they are suitable to be mixed (or associated)." In this longer definition, instead of taking the phrase 'term-meaning' (*śabdārtha, sgra don*) to refer to a single image, which Jang-gya does by reading it as 'meaning-of-the-term', Jam-yang-shay-ba takes 'term' (*śabda, sgra*) as a term-generality (*śabdasāmānya, sgra spyi*) and 'meaning' (*artha, don*) to indicate a 'meaning-generality' (*artha-sāmānya, don spyi*). The resulting definition signifies that these are *suitable* to be perceived as mixed or associated, but are not *necessarily* perceived thus.[6]

These scholars' definition is based on the commonly held view that two types of generalities can be appearing objects of thought: (1)

the term-generality which appears to a thought consciousness when for example a person who has never been to India hears the word 'India' and (2) a meaning-generality that appears when someone who has visited India hears the same word. When the name 'India' is stated to one who has been there, a mixture of term and meaning generalities appears to that person's thought. In such a case, these two generalities are not only *suitable* to be mixed, they *are* mixed. The person who has neither seen India nor realized what India is through some other means, cannot have an appearance of a meaning-generality of India. Therefore, for this person, term and meaning generalities are not actually mixed but are only suitable to be mixed or associated. A person who landed there without knowing where he was would afterwards recall only a meaning-generality unassociated with a term-generality.

In a similar way, children who have seen a bulbous thing capable of holding water but do not know that its name is 'pot' cannot take the term-generality as an appearing object of thought in the sense of associating it with its meaning. The meaning-generality or image of pot can appear to them, but the only term-generality which can appear to one untrained in language is the mere internal reverberation of the sound 'pot.' The child would not perceive this sound as having any connection with a remembered image of pot.

'Term-generality' can refer either to the mere internal reverberation of the sound of a term *or* to the image that appears to the mind of a person who has never seen the actual thing represented by that image. Gelukba scholars agree that term and meaning generalities are merely suitable to be mixed for persons untrained in language but are not actually mixed for them; in this context the former meaning of term-generality as an internal reverberation of a term is probably being used, for all agree that the term-generality which is a mere reverberation of sound appears even to children untutored in language.

If a term-generality is understood as an imagined representation of something one has never seen, then whatever is a term-generality is necessarily a meaning-generality but not the other way around. In other words, a mind that apprehends such a term-generality necessarily apprehends a meaning-generality. In this broader framework there is no problem about whether or not the definition of a thought consciousness as apprehending the meaning-of-a-term perceives a mixture of term and meaning generalities.

Term and Meaning Generalities

However, outside the context of this broader relationship between term and meaning generalities, Gelukbas assert that there can be a mind which perceives *only* a term-generality or *only* a meaning-generality, or a mixture of both.[7] In this way, there are three types of appearing objects of thought.

For example, when a person who has never seen a magnolia hears the term 'magnolia,' that person's thought has only a term-generality as its appearing object. In other words, an image corresponding merely to the sound of the term appears to the thought consciousness, but no sense of its meaning. On the other hand, when someone who does not know what a magnolia is — and who thus cannot identify it by name — happens to remember a magnolia blossom seen previously, that person does not remember it *as* a magnolia, but only recalls its shape, color and other features. The image of the flower that appears to such a person's thought consciousness is only the meaning-generality. Finally, when a person who knows what a magnolia is remembers one seen previously, that person's thought consciousness has a mixture of term and meaning generalities as its appearing object. Thus, in terms of their appearing objects, thought consciousnesses are of three types, those to which there appears (1) only a term-generality, (2) only a meaning-generality, or (3) a mixture of both.

This three-fold typology is significant for the presentation of a means for cultivating liberating knowledge. It means that even within the category of conceptual thought a considerable range of experience is possible. In the Buddhist perspective, it is possible to begin with the mere internal reverberation of sound like 'subtle impermanence' and then, through reasoning and contemplation, cultivate a sense of its meaning until the appearing object of thought is no longer a mere term-generality but a mixture of term and meaning generalities. As one cultivates an increasingly profound and deeply felt understanding of the meaning, reliance on words gradually decreases. Once one is truly well accustomed to the meaning of subtle impermanence it is possible for only the meaning-generality of subtle impermanence to appear, without depending on the term or word 'impermanence' at all.[8]

This experience is far removed from mere mental rattling of the words 'subtle impermanence.' Deeply cultivated, it can prove a life-changing experience. Nevertheless, in terms of the Gelukba presentation, this still falls within the range of conceptual thought. As long as an image of any type is involved, no matter how subtle or psychologically significant it may be, one is dwelling in conceptuality. Direct perception occurs when even the meaning-generality fades away and one is left with the actual, specifically characterized impermanence. As explained below, it is possible for conceptuality to yield to direct perception because the actual impermanence appears through the medium of an image at the time of conceptuality. When the image fades away, the actual impermanence remains as an appearing object of direct perception.

Jang-gya on the Definition of Conceptual Thought

It is significant to the Gelukba presentation of conceptuality and the path that a term or a meaning generality may become the only appearing object of a particular thought. In the case of a mind apprehending only a term or meaning generality, the two are not associated but only *suitable* to be associated. It was to take account of this that Jam-yang-shay-ba and others formulated the longer definition of a thought consciousness as a conceptual knower apprehending term and meaning generalities as suitable to be associated. In this way they claim to have a definition that accounts for the thought of persons untrained in terminology. However, Jang-gya points out that even the more extensive definition of, for example, the thought consciousness apprehending a pot as "a conceptual knower which apprehends in a manner such that the term and meaning generalities of pot are suitable to be associated" would apply only in those areas of the world where the specific term 'pot' (*bum pa* in Tibetan) is used to designate a bulbous thing capable of holding water. It does not take account of those who call such an item a *kailaś* (Hindi). Thus, Jang-gya objects that the purpose of re-casting the definition is thwarted, for there is no way to include all varieties of people and speech in a single definition.

Jang-gya notes that it is not always necessary to separate 'term-meaning' (*śabdārtha, sgra don*) into 'term and meaning generalities.' Sometimes it is appropriate to interpret this as 'meaning-of-the-term.' He cites Tsong-ka-pa to establish that the compound 'term-meaning' (*śabdārtha, sgra don*) can be interpreted as a possessive compound a genitive *tatpuruṣa*,[9] '*śabdasyārtha*' — 'the meaning-of-the-term.' On such occasions, the phrase is not interpreted as a collective compound (*dvandva*) in which case it would indicate two different types of images and be rendered in full form as 'term [generality] and meaning [generality]' (*śabdo 'rthaśca*).

Jang-gya further cites an apparent contradiction to his own thesis that 'term-meaning' need not be interpreted as 'term and meaning generalities.' He points out that Gyel-tsap, one of Tsong-ka-pa's two main disciples, refers to a child's thought consciousness as a mind for which object of expression and expression (and thus, by implication, meaning — *artha* — and term — *śabda*) are suitable to be mixed.[10] Jang-gya states that this does not signify that the 'term-meaning' (*śabdārtha*) should *always* be interpreted as term and meaning generalities; for example, it is not so interpreted when it occurs in the definition of thought as "a conceptual knower which apprehends the meaning-of-a-term". His point is that the appearing object of thought, in other words, the meaning-of-the-term, is simply the image of an object. It is not necessary that the definition specify whether this image is a term or meaning generality, or a mixture of both. Jang-gya's further point is that treating 'term-meaning' as 'meaning-of-the-term' in this definition emphasizes that the explicit object of expression of a term is an internal image. It does not indicate that it is *never* suitable to treat 'term-meaning' as referring to term and meaning generalities separately.[11] Tsong-ka-pa also points out that there are three types of appearing objects of thought as mentioned above; either one of the two generalities may appear alone or they may appear as mixed.[12] Kay-drup, the other of Tsong-ka-pa's two chief disciples, also writes:

> When someone says, "There is no pot" to a person who does not know that the term "pot" [refers to] a bulbous object, only the term-generality of a lack of pot appears, the meaning-generality does not.[13]

This clearly indicates that in certain contexts Kay-drup also finds it necessary to distinguish between term and meaning generalities. For, when an untrained person sees a flat-based bulbous thing capable of holding fluids, he does not see it as the basis of the term "pot." Only those familiar with the term see a pot this way. Thus, knowledge of the term subtly alters the type of thought induced by direct perception, and training in terminology aids the conceptual superimposition that an object is suitable to be called by a specific name. Yet, even those untrained in terminology see objects as suitable to *be* named and thus as naturally established as bases of names in general, even though such persons cannot accurately name them.

The problem of including untrained children and animals in Jang-gya's definition arises largely because the meaning-of-the-term "pot" — the image which appears as the elimination of everything except pot — is specified to be an appearance as opposite from the negative of pot (*bum pa ma yin pa las log par snang ba*). Yet, as the statement from Kay-drup above indicates, an appearance as opposite from non-pot cannot appear upon stating the term "pot" to one who does not know the term pot. Nevertheless, a child who has seen a pot can certainly think about a pot through recalling an image of it even without knowing that the name "pot" refers to it. The difficulty lies in determining what this image is. It cannot be a 'meaning-of-the-term' in the sense described above because the child does not know what the term "pot" means. If, however, the 'meaning-of-the-term "pot"' were considered to include not only the appearance as opposite from non-pot but also an appearance as opposite from non-flat-based-bulbous-thing-able-to-hold-fluid, it would be possible to include the conceptuality of those untrained in terminology in Jang-gya's definition of thought as "a conceptual knower that apprehends the meaning-of-a-term."[14] The definition could then apply to those instances when *only* a meaning-generality appears. Opposite-from-non-bulbous-thing can be remembered whether or not one knows that this is called a pot.

Analysis of a Meaning-Generality

The definition of a meaning-generality that appears to the thought consciousness apprehending pot is given by Pur-bu-jok as:

> The superimposed factor which, although not a pot, appears as like a pot to the thought consciousness apprehending a pot.[15]

We have mentioned that this meaning-generality is an appearance as opposite from non-pot. Further, although the appearance as opposite from non-pot which appears to *thought* is a meaning-generality, the opposite-from-non-pot which appears to the *eye consciousness* is not. Whereas the image is permanent and a generally characterized phenomenon, opposite-from-non-pot is a negative phenomenon known as an objective specifically characterized exclusion (*apoha, sel ba*);[16] (*See chapters on exlusions.*) Moreover, the appearance *as* opposite from non-pot is a negative but the appearance of pot to thought is a positive phenomenon.[17] From the viewpoint that this mental image is an appearance *as* opposite-from-non-pot it is a negative; from the viewpoint of the appearance itself — the mental image — it is a positive phenomenon. From either point of view, this appearance is a means by which the conceptual thought perceiving it does actually or explicitly realize a specifically characterized object.[18]

Opposite-from-non-pot is a negative phenomenon that can appear either to thought or (according to some Gelukba texts) to direct perception. However, the appearance to thought is a meaning-generality; the appearance to direct perception is not.[19]

There is some disagreement among Gelukba colleges about whether opposite-from-non-pot can appear to someone who does not know the name 'pot'. However, all colleges except Gomang agree that opposite-from-the-definition-of-pot, that is, opposite-from-non-flat-based-bulbous-thing-capable-of-holding-fluid can even appear to the thought or direct perception of persons who do not know the term 'pot' but who have seen a pot. By contrast, Gomang College, a division of Drebung Monastic University, maintains that opposite-from-non-pot *never* appears to the eye consciousness; rather, the pot which is opposite from non-pot appears. This means that the pot which is opposite from non-pot is a negative and a specifically characterized object that can appear to direct perception.

The Loseling College of Drebung asserts that opposite-from-non-pot or opposite-from-non-bulbous-thing appears to direct perception because it is one entity of establishment and abiding — that is, infallibly concomitant in place, time, and nature — with the specifically characterized pot perceived by the eye consciousness. Thus, according to Loseling, whether or not one knows the term 'pot,' both pot and opposite-from-non-pot appear to the eye consciousness apprehending a pot. Loseling therefore must find a different way than Gomang's to distinguish between what appears to those who do and do not know the term 'pot.' However, if someone does not know the term 'pot,' then for that person neither an actual pot nor the meaning-generality (*don spyi*) of a pot can be an explicit object of expression of the term 'pot.' For, if a person who does not know the term 'pot' hears this word in conversation, no meaning-generality will appear in his or her mind. The appearance as opposite-from-non-pot to a thought consciousness apprehending a pot is therefore not a meaning-generality in relation to a person who does not know the term 'pot,' even though opposite-from-non-pot does appear to the direct perception of such a person. The appearance as opposite from non-flat-based-bulbous-thing-able-to-hold-fluid, however, is a meaning-generality for such a person, because even one who does not know the name 'pot' can recall the image of a pot previously seen.

According to Loseling College, both pot and opposite-from-non-pot or opposite-from-non-bulbous-thing appears to direct perception from-non-pot is a negative phenomenon because when *thought* realizes it, it does so by way of the explicit elimination or negation of all that is not pot. Direct perception does not perceive opposite-from-non-pot by way of an explicit elimination of non-pot; it does, however, realize opposite from non-pot explicitly. When one thinks about something such as a pot that is appearing to direct perception, conceptual thought realizes pot explicitly and also realizes opposite-from-non-pot implicitly. In other words, opposite-from-non-pot is realized explicitly by direct perception at the same time that conceptual thought realizes it implicitly.

Gomang College, on the other hand, asserts that negatives such as opposite-from-non-pot are not perceived by direct perception at all. In their view, persons untrained in language recognize objects without perceiving opposite-from-non-that-object. For example, a young child recognizes water to drink or an animal recognizes its own offspring through visual and tactile cues that are impermanent, positive phenomena. Such discrimination involves thought but not words or even term-generalities. Recognition occurs through a type of reasoned correct belief or correctly assuming consciousness (**manaḥ-parikṣa, yid spyod*) on the basis of various cues appearing to the eye, ear, nose, and other directly perceiving consciousnesses.[20]

Loseling College asserts that opposite-from-non-pot appears to the direct perception even of someone who does not know the term 'pot.' However, even for Loseling the opposite-from-non-pot that is understood as pot can only appear to someone who does know the term 'pot.' Similarly, an appearance of opposite-from-non-water can only appear to *be* water to someone who knows the referent object of the term 'water.' In a similar vein, Sera College says that animals — who, of course, do not know the term 'water' — neither see nor drink water; they see and drink what is damp and moistening.[21] In this view, then, opposite-from-non-water, or, more literally, opposite from-not-being-water, does not appear to animals or to persons untrained in language. What appears to either direct perception or thought in such cases is the definition — the very entity — of water itself, that which is wet and moistening. 'Water' is simply the name given to this substance. In this context, among those trained in language, only English speakers drink water, the French drink *l'eau*, Tibetans, *chu*, and so forth.

In brief, whether or not one asserts that opposite-from-non-pot can appear only to a thought consciousness or to both the thought and direct perception of persons who know the term 'pot,' an appearance *as* opposite from non-pot to a thought consciousness cannot occur unless the term is known. For, a meaning-generality is an image which can be caused to appear when a person who knows the term 'pot' hears that word. Thus, scholars such as Jam-yang-shay-ba argue against the shorter definition of thought as "a conceptual knower which apprehends a meaning-of-the-term" because they say that a person who does not know a given term cannot apprehend the corresponding meaning. Jang-gya disputes neither this nor even the contention that sometimes it is suitable to take the phrase 'term-meaning' as referring to two distinct types of images — term-generality and meaning-generality. He simply finds it unnecessary to take all situations into account when forming a definition. For the purposes of the discussion here, however, the varying opinions on the topic serve to underscore the extent to which the learning of terminology affects conceptual and direct perception.

CONCEPTUAL ERROR

Even correct thought is mistaken in relation to the specifically characterized phenomena which are its referent objects. Its mistake is due to the fact that, whereas impermanent phenomena have their own unique characteristics, thought can perceive only general images. This point, which receives considerable attention in Gelukba, reflects a statement in verse 1007 of Śantarakṣita's *Compendium of Suchness* (*Tattvasaṃgraha, De kho na nyid bsdus pa*) that for thought an image "is erroneously taken for the particular which is excluded from dissimilar things (*vijatīya-paravṛttaṃ svalakṣaṇaṃ*."[22] Nevertheless, as elaborated below, the uncommon entity of, for example, an actual impermanent pot does appear to thought. However, it does not have the status of being an *appearing object* for thought because the complete, specifically characterized entity of the object does not appear.

The meaning of the term 'pot' that appears to thought is a generally characterized phenomenon because it is an appearance of the factor of being opposite from non-pot that applies to every instance of a specifically characterized pot. A specifically characterized pot, although it appears to thought and can be realized by thought, is not considered an appearing object of thought. If it were, the pot that appears to thought would, like any impermanent and specifically characterized pot, be capable of holding liquids and so forth. In that case anyone could have a golden pot or anything else just by thinking about it. Moreover, even if the specific pot represented by this image is smashed, the mental image remains unchanged; this of course also signifies that the impermanent pot itself is not the object appearing to thought. The fact that the image is called permanent is another way of drawing attention, not only to the obvious difference between images and objects, but to the limitations of the thought to which images appear. Although correct thought does not actually conceive that 'this image is a pot,' it is mistaken because (1) the actual pot appears as undifferentiably mixed with the image of pot and (2) the image appears to be a pot although it is not. In the *Presentation of Specifically and Generally Characterized Phenomena* Den-dar-hla-ram-ba writes:

> When a meaning-generality appears to thought the following appearances occur:
> 1. just that meaning-generality appears as if it were the entity of that object
> 2. the meaning-generality appears as if it were one with that object
> 3. the meaning-generality appears as if it were opposite from non-that-object.[23]

These are three ways of expressing the basic error of conceptual thought — that an image appearing to it seems to be the actual object it represents. Thought does not *conceive* of image and object as mixed, and thus the error is not due to a fault in reasoning or any other conscious process. It is simply in the nature of thought to operate in this manner. For example, when the image of a chair appears to thought, the image itself appears as — but is not usaully conceived to be — an actual chair. Another way of saying this is that the image appears to be one with a chair, much as a chair reflected in a mirror appears to be one with — that is, really to be — a chair.

Similarly, the image of a chair appears to be opposite from not being a chair, that is to say, to be the actually specifically characterized chair.[24]

The generalizing tendency of conceptual thought can be explained in terms of how it perceives the nature, place, and time of an object such as a tree (not a specific tree, but tree in general). Although trees are not mixed in fact, they appear mixed to a thought consciousness apprehending just tree. All the various specifically characterized instances of trees are the same in appearing as trees but are different in terms of place, time, and nature. A single 'opposite-from-not-being-a-tree' that is common to each individual tree is just something fabricated by thought.[25] Although the appearance of such exists, the natures of individual trees are not actually mixed. Because it is inevitable that thought perceive trees in this way, thought is obscured from fully knowing reality or ultimate truth as designated in the Gelukba formulation of Sautrāntika. Thought cannot perceive specifically characterized phenomena in a manner that accords with the objects' actual way of abiding. The early 19th-century scholar Bel-den-chö-jay, annotator of Jam-yang-shay-ba's *Great Exposition of Tenets*, writes in his *Annotations*:

> The appearance as opposite from non-tree imagined by a mind apprehending a tree-generality does not exist as an ultimate object. For, if it did exist ultimately, then the mind apprehending that generality would not be mistaken with respect to its appearing object. If that were the case, then since the natures of the manifestations of tree appear mixed to the mind [apprehending] the tree-generality, the natures of the manifestations of tree would have to be mixed [in actual fact]. However, the manifestations of tree are not mutually each other and abide with their natures unmixed.[26]

Thought is also obscured with respect to the individual place and time of specifically characterized phenomena. For example, a thought consciousness apprehending just 'tree' pays no attention to the difference of place that pertains to a tree at the west of one's house and another tree to the east. Or, to give a further example, whereas the eye-consciousness observing a rug correctly perceives that all its different colors occupy different areas, for the thought consciousness apprehending the rug it is *as if* all the colors and so forth are in one place — the rug. Only the general image of a rug appears to thought. This is the confusion of place. With respect to time, when the eye consciousness observes a tree, the individual moments of the tree appear serially to the eye consciousness, but for thought, these appear as mixed.[27] To a thought consciousness apprehending that tree, the tree seen yesterday seems to be the same as the one directly perceived today; in other words, although direct perception views only the present tree, the thought apprehending that tree perceives the present tree as if it were the same as the tree of yesterday. Moreover, despite the fact that the past tree is only an object of thought, direct perception experiences it as if that past tree were fused with the present object of direct perception. This is one significant way in which thought impinges on direct experience.

Although all thought consciousnesses are equally mistaken in that the image or meaning-generality which appears to them seems to be one with their referent object, all thought is not equally mistaken. For example, the inferential cognizer that correctly realizes sound to be impermanent and the superimposing consciousness which erroneously apprehends sound to be permanent are both conceptual and thus equally subject to the mistake that their appearing objects seem to be the corresponding referent object. Nevertheless, the inferential consciousness is unmistaken with respect to its referent object and is also incontrovertible in its correct conviction that sound is impermanent. The superimposing consciousness is neither correct nor incontrovertible. For, through inference one can gain access to the object of operation (*'jug yul*) or referent object (*zhen yul*) — the impermanent sound — and thus refute or controvert the thought consciousness that apprehends sound as permanent. Since permanent sound does not exist, the consciousness that superimposes such (and which probably derives from misinterpreted direct perception) does not have an existent referent object. The thought apprehending impermanent sound does have a referent object — actual impermanent sound — and is mistaken with respect to the appearing object — the image of impermanent sound — but not with respect to the referent object. The thought conceiving permanent sound, however, is not a factually concordant consciousness; it is mistaken regarding its appearing object — the image of permanent sound — and deceived with respect to its non-existent referent object — permanent sound. The difference between these two types of conceptual thought is like the difference between mistaking a jewel's light for a jewel and mistaking a candle's light for a jewel. Both conceptions are mistaken, but through following the jewel's light to its source one can get at an actual jewel; through following the candle's light, one cannot.[28]

THOUGHT AND DIRECT PERCEPTION

Conceptual thought and direct perception can operate simultaneously, but they are not established or initiated simultaneously with respect to the same object.[29] In the first moment of seeing an impermanent object such as a tree, direct perception — the eye consciousness — is active; then there is a moment of mental direct perception (*mānasa-pratyakṣa, yid kyi mngon sum*)[30] which cannot be noticed by ordinary persons. Following this, conceptuality begins to operate. Thus, in the first period there is only direct, clear perception by the eye consciousness; once conceptuality begins, it operates simultaneously with subsequent moments of direct perception. This means that while the eye consciousness, for example, is apprehending the specific characteristics of its object, the thought derived from that eye consciousness superimposes a meaning-generality onto that object.

Each consciousness has a feeling associated with it. As soon as an object is perceived, some feeling about the object as good, bad, or neutral arises. Such judgments are conceptual. Feeling arises not only on the basis of the eye consciousness, but also on the basis of thought; that is, not just on the basis of the actual presently existing object, but also on the basis of what is remembered about or imputed onto that object. In other words, one's experience of an object as good or bad, enjoyable or abhorrent, depends not only on the actual object but also on the internal image that appears to thought. However, because the meaning-generality appearing to thought is not as strong as the object perceived by direct sense perception, it is not easy to recognize that a meaning-generality is involved — one feels one is engaging in and reacting to only direct perception.[31]

In terms of Sautrāntika tenets it is difficult to establish precisely the status of such judgemental qualities as 'good,' 'bad,' 'large,' 'small' and so forth. When one sees a person one thinks of as bad, for example, the eye consciousness merely sees the color and shape; it is the conceptual mental consciousness that takes as its object the 'badness' of that person.[32] Someone else, seeing the same person, might see her or him as 'good.' In reacting to a person or thing as good or bad, one is in fact reacting largely to an image in one's own mind, even though there may be no awareness that such an image is present. From this viewpoint it can be argued that qualities such as 'good' or 'too small' or 'too large' are not specifically characterized phenomena and thus that they cannot appear to the eye consciousness. Because such qualities are not one entity of establishment and abiding with the appearing object, there is no contradiction in these not appearing to a mind of complete engagement such as the eye consciousness which must, by definition, observe all factors that are fully concomitant in terms of place, time, and nature with its appearing object. For example, the image of a good car which is an appearance as opposite from non-good car is taken as the appearing object of thought while the object itself — opposite-from-non-car — appears to the eye consciousness.

Sautrāntika however cannot categorically maintain that subjective qualities such as good and bad are *merely imputed* by thought. Such qualities must also be said to exist from their own side. Otherwise the mere assertion that something is good or bad would be enough to create goodness and badness in that object. Further, if goodness and so forth were merely imputed, they would be permanent, and this is unsuitable. Sautrāntika does not have a clear presentation of the status of such subjective qualities; to get a detailed discussion of this it is necessary to study both Cittamātra — where all objects and their qualities are said to arise from the latencies of one's mind — and especially Mādhyamika, where the person as well as any qualities of goodness and so forth are equally seen as merely imputed by thought.[33]

In the Gelukba presentation of Sautrāntika and the higher systems a false superimposition is a case of thinking that the non-existent exists. To think that there is permanence with respect to impermanent objects, or that there is a substantially existent self-sufficient person, are significant cases of superimposition by thought. 'Superimposition by thought' (*āropa, sgro btags*) is sometimes to be distinguished from 'imputation by thought' (*rtog pas btags pa*). An example of something imputed by thought that is not a superimposition is the relationship between a definition and the thing it defines (the definiendum). This relationship is said to be imputed by thought because conceptual thought realizes it in stages, considering first the definition and then the definiendum. Since that relationship does exist, it is not a mere superimposition. (Sometimes, however, no distinction is made between superimposition and imputation by thought, in which case a superimposition by thought can be either existent or non-existent.)

Phenomena imputed by thought (*rtog pas btags pa*) are necessarily permanent and are appearing objects of thought only, not of direct perception. These are not to be confused with phenomena that are imputedly existent (*prajñapti-sat, btags yod*) and which can be either permanent or impermanent. An imputedly existent phenomenon, according to the second interpretation of this term given in chapter one, cannot be seen without some other phenomenon which is not its own entity being observed. For example, there is no way to perceive a person without perceiving the head or arms and so forth, although a head or arm is not itself the person. It is also true that in order to see a table one must see its legs, top, and so forth, but this does not make a table an imputedly existent phenomenon. For, the legs and so forth of a table are parts (*cha shas*) of the table, whereas the head and so forth of a person are said to be not parts but extensions or limbs (*yan lag*) of the person.[34] Thus, in dependence on seeing head, hands and so on one imputes the existence of a person. The person itself, although impermanent and thus an ultimate truth, exists imputedly and is not an object of the eye consciousness in the same sense that tables and chairs are. From another viewpoint however, it is an object of the eye consciousness because to see a living person's form is to see that person.[35]

Another example of how thought and direct perception are intertwined in experience has to do with mistaken sense consciousnesses. The eye consciousness misperceiving a white snow mountain as blue has only the *shape* of that mountain as its appearing object. If correct direct perception is brought to bear on this, one can come to the conclusion that the blue color is just superimposed. Although both the shape of the mountain and the color blue appear to the eye consciousness, technically only the former can be posited as an actual appearing object.

A blue snow mountain does not exist but the appearance of such does exist. The difficulty in detailing exactly how this is perceived comes because, on the one hand, it seemingly does appear to the eye consciousness and yet, because it does not actually exist one might think that it is merely imputed by thought, in which case it would be a permanent phenomenon and incapable of being perceived by the eye consciousness. Some scholars assert that a mistaken eye consciousness such as the one perceiving a blue snow mountain does not have an appearing object at all.[36] The problem still remains of what exactly is appearing.

In his commentary to the *Chapter on Direct Perception* of Dharmakīrti's *Commentary on (Dignāga's) 'Compendium on Valid Cognition'* Gyel-Tsap asserts that the appearance of a blue snow mountain is an impermanent phenomenon which is of one substantial entity with the consciousness that perceives it (*shes pa dang rdzas gcig* or *shes pa'i rdzas*).[37] This appearance, being an impermanent phenomenon, is suitable to appear to direct perception. In this view, it is therefore not merely imputed by thought. Though one entity with consciousness, the appearance is not itself a consciousness.[38] It is also not a form because if it were it would have to exist out there on the mountain whereas in fact there is no blue on the snow mountain; if the form of a blue mountain did exist, the eye consciousness perceiving it would not be mistaken but affirmed as correct.[39] Thus, the appearance of a blue snow mountain is neither form nor consciousness but a third category — a non-associated compositional factor (*viprayukta-saṃskāra, ldan min 'du byed*). Any impermanent existent which is neither form nor consciousness — such as persons or impermanence — is a non-associated compositional factor.[40]

This assertion on the status of an appearance to a mistaken non-conceptional consciousness is common to Sautrāntika and Cittamātra.[41] The Cittamātrins take the further step of considering all appearances whatsoever to be one entity with the consciousness that perceives them, regardless of whether that consciousness is mistaken or non-mistaken.

Some Gelukba scholars, however, do not consider that the appearance of, for example, a blue snow mountain is one entity with the perceiving consciousness. In this view, such an appearance is merely imputed by thought and, therefore, a permanent phenomenon. The proponents of this position avoid the fault of positing that a permanent phenomenon appears to direct perception because an appearance of a double moon or a blue snow mountain is asserted to appear not to direct perception but to a consciousness that is devoid of conceptuality (*rtog 'bral gyi shes pa*). The perceiving consciousness is not a direct perceiver because it is mistaken and direct perceivers are defined in Sautrāntika as non-conceptual non-mistaken consciousnesses.[42]

The difficulty of determining exactly what types of consciousnesses and objects are involved in mistaken direct perception while still remaining within the strictures of Sautrāntika is one more indication that the line between 'actual' impermanent phenomena and phenomena imputed by thought is not always easily or clearly drawn. Yet, as we have noted, this line is the central axis of the system. The hidden premise here is that phenomena imputed by thought, or the appearing objects of thought, are always a category apart from those phenomena which are appearing objects of direct perception. The fact that this premise is sometimes difficult to maintain can be understood to indicate that a more subtle ontological theory, such as in Mādhyamika, is required. In the Buddhist context this is itself a useful insight; in the meantime, the overall purpose of contrasting the spheres of thought and direct perception is also well served. The intention behind highlighting the differences between the two types of valid cognition is to allow the informed to make maximum use of each, and this is a purpose in keeping not only with Sautrāntika but with the higher systems as well.

HOW THOUGHT REALIZES IMPERMANENT PHENOMENA

In terms of formulating a path to liberation from suffering, thought has special significance. Through training thought in the sense of developing certain conceptual images, such as that of subtle impermanence, one can ascertain truths that would otherwise never be accessible. Thought is thus seen as a vital instrument for the attainment of liberating knowledge.

This knowledge centers around developing a new understanding concerning the status of persons and other phenomena. Because the Sautrāntika system clearly states that impermanent phenomena cannot fully appear to thought, it must establish just how thought *can* get at impermanent phenomena. That it can do so is foundational to the conviction that meditative training which involves conceptual thought will in fact have a bearing on one's understanding of the actual, impermanent phenomena that *fully* appear only to direct perception. This in turn is only possible if thought does in some sense incontrovertibly and explicitly realize impermanent phenomena. The Gelukba discussion of Sautrāntika underscores that it considers such to be the case.

To take a simple example, consider the thought consciousness apprehending a pot. The appearing object of such a consciousness is an image of pot, an appearance as opposite-from-non-pot. This image or meaning-generality, the appearing object (*snang yul*) is itself permanent in the sense that (1) it does not disintegrate from one moment to the next and (2) although it comes about through the power of thought, it is not produced from thought and thus is not a product of causes and conditions.[43] Although a thought consciousness apprehending a pot does not realize it fully in the manner of direct perception, such a thought consciousness does realize pot explicitly. What does this mean? Jam-yang-shay-ba's *Presentation of Awareness and Knowledge* (*bLo rig gi rnam bzhag*) gives the following definition of an awareness that explicitly realizes an object:

> [An awareness] realizing [its object] from the viewpoint of the aspect of that object appearing to that awareness.[44]

To know an object explicitly is to know it by way of an aspect of that object appearing. An explicit realization can be either conceptual or non-conceptual. This means that both direct and conceptual consciousnesses can know their objects by way of the aspect of that object appearing. In the case of a direct perceiver, the object casts its aspect to the consciousness; in the case of a conceptual explicit awareness, the aspect appears in the sense that the meaning-generality is an appearing object of that consciousness and in the sense that when the image of a pot appears to thought, the actual specifically characterized pot itself appears.[45] Further, although thought does not realize the pot directly (*mngon sum du*), it does actually and explicitly (*dngos su*) realize pot. In other words, even though thought's appearing object is only pot's image, what thought explicitly *realizes* is the actual, specifically characterized pot.[46] In doing so, it has neither the erroneous conception that this image is a pot nor does it articulate the correct conception that "this image definitely is not pot." However, in the sense that there is no clear discrimination between the image and the actual pot, the two are confused, and for this reason thought is said to be mistaken in relation to its appearing object — namely, the appearance as being opposite from all that is non-pot or, in other words, the image's seeming to be a pot. Correct thought, however, does not conceive that this appearance *is* opposite from all that is non-pot; it simply realizes the specifically characterized pot. It does so through understanding that this is something bulbous with a flat base and capable of holding fluids. Thus, although a pot, being impermanent, cannot be an appearing object of thought inasmuch as its entity cannot fully appear to thought, it does appear by way of an image and — most important of all — thought does explicitly realize it by way of that image.

A factually concordant thought consciousness (*anvartha-kalpanā, rtog pa don mthun*) apprehending a pot is not mistaken with respect to its referent object, an acutal pot, because even though the image of, for example, a golden pot appears to be a pot, correct thought does not go so far as to conceive that 'this is a pot.' There is just the correct conception that 'a golden pot is a pot.' This is analogous to the type of conception occurring when one looks in the mirror to see if one's face is dirty: one does not think that the image is the face, but in dependence on that image one can correctly understand whether or not dirt is present. Thus, although a specifically characterized phenomenon such as a golden pot is not an actual appearing object of thought — for it appears only through the medium of its image — thought does explicitly realize specifically characterized phenomena. Thought does not, however, realize them directly. To realize a phenomenon directly, as mentioned above, means to know it by way of the object's casting an aspect toward a perceiving consciousness which is then generated in the image of that object. Because thought does not know pots and so forth through taking on their aspects, it does not know such objects directly, but it does know them explicitly. To put this yet another way, although it is only the permanent meaning-generality or mental image (a generally characterized phenomenon that is the appearing object of thought), what thought *realizes* is the referent object represented by that image. In other words, just like looking in a mirror can cause one to realize something about the reflected image, so through the image of an object thought can correctly realize something about the actual object.

There is a further reason why the thought consciousness apprehending a pot realizes a pot explicitly. Although thought is necessarily mistaken with respect to its appearing object, whatever is an appearing object of thought is not necessarily the object which is a source of that thought's mistakes or the object with respect to which the thought is mistaken. For example, uncaused space — a generally characterized phenomenon — must be an appearing object of the thought consciousness realizing uncaused space, but thought need not be mistaken with respect to it. This means that even though thought is always mistaken with respect to its appearing object, just because something is an appearing object of thought does not mean that thought is necessarily mistaken with respect to it.[47] For, in the case of factually concordant thought apprehending uncaused space, that space is both an appearing object *and* the referent object. If thought were mistaken regarding its referent object, it would be a wrong consciousness, not a factually concordant one. The import here is that correct thought apprehending space is not mistaken as to its referent object (*adhyavasāya-viṣaya, zhen yul*) — uncaused space — even though it is mistaken with respect to one of its appearing objects — the meaning-generality of uncaused space.

Just as this thought is not mistaken regarding the space that is its referent object, so the thought apprehending a pot, which is mistaken regarding the meaning-generality that is its appearing object, is not mistaken with respect to the actual pot that is its referent object. This in turn means that another type of conceptual awareness, an inferential cognizer (*anumāna, rjes dpag*) which realizes, for example, that products are impermanent, is unmistaken with respect to the impermanent products that are its referent objects.

In the Gelukba presentation it is essential that inferential cognition be asserted as unmistaken with respect to its referent objects. For, inference is a chief instrument by which mistaken conceptions are righted and, moreover, the corrective process can take place precisely because inference correctly realizes its referent objects. Inference enables one to ascertain subtle impermanence and to realize selflessness, thereby leading to liberating knowledge.

One might think that just as uncaused space is considered an appearing object of thought due to its appearing to the thought which apprehends it, the same should be true of specifically characterized phenomena because they also appear to thought. Yet, the former is an appearing object of thought, the latter is not. Why? Because (1) the pot does not appear by its own power but by the power, or through the medium of, the meaning generality[48] and (2) the complete pot with all its specific characteristics does not appear to thought. It is an emphasis special to Sautrāntika that because the complete entity of a generally characterized phenomenon fully appears to the thought apprehending it, such must be considered an appearing object of thought.[49] Thus, pot appears to thought but is not an appearing object of thought.

Most factually concordant thought consciousnesses — those

whose referent objects are actual, existent phenomena — derive from direct perception which is unmistaken regarding such objects. When an eye consciousness directly perceiving a pot arises, it establishes a predisposition for the future generation of an image of pot. When that predisposition is later activated, it will produce a thought consciousness conceiving, for instance, of a golden pot as a pot.[50] Even a thought consciousness apprehending space — a permanent phenomenon which is a lack of obstructive contact — derives from the direct perception of a tangible, obstructive object. Because of this connection between any factually concordant thought consciousness and its referent object, such thought is undeceived with respect to specifically characterized phenomena and capable of actually realizing them.[51] Not only this but, according to the early 19th-century scholar Bel-den-chö-jay, even the uncommon features of specifically characterized phenomena actually appear to thought.[52] Yet, because these features do not appear *fully* they are not appearing objects of thought. The thought apprehending pot thus has two objects: an internal image of pot and the specifically characterized pot, but only the former is its appearing object.

Specifically characterized phenomena such as pots cannot fully appear to thought because thought simplifies appearances, confusing individual characteristics. Even when one thinks of a specific golden pot, the generality of golden pot appears right along with the image of the specific golden pot, whereby thought is obscured from manifestly observing, just as they are, the specific characteristics of a particular golden pot.

Although thought does not perceive specifically characterized phenomena as vividly as do sense and mental direct perceivers, and although thought is necessarily involved in certain types of error, thought *is* able to realize such phenomena and make correct determinations regarding them. When the mistaken aspect of thought is recognized and its superimpositions identified, it is all the more possible to take advantage of thought's access to subtle objects not ordinarily ascertainable by direct perception.

For example, in order for direct perception to ascertain subtle impermanence — momentary disintegration — it is first necessary for a meaning-generality or image of subtle impermanence to appear. The images discussed above were of objects that direct perception had already seen. How can one have an image or meaning-generality of subtle impermanence when one has never consciously observed it?

The first step is to understand coarse impermanence. To do this one takes to mind a concordant example such as the end of the continuum of a candle flame. A more powerful example is the death of a person. Using this to cultivate an understanding of coarse impermanence, one would reflect on the fact that he or she is definitely going to die and that nothing can prevent this. When a doctor says, "There is nothing more that can be done for this patient," one should reflect, "So it is with me. There is nothing that can be done. I will die. My death cannot be prevented." One reflects on this deeply, for it is not easy to understand the certainty of death. This difficulty is said to result from a strong but mistaken sense of permanence to which one has been accustomed from beginningless time. This sense is further fostered by the continued appearance of objects of similar type, like a pot that sits on the shelf for years before breaking. Through reflection, one develops an image of coarse impermanence. Then, one steadily reflects that since all products are impermanent and one's own body is a product, it too must pass away. Indeed, it approaches nearer to death each moment. With such reflection one develops an image of subtle impermanence, that is, of the momentary disintegration that all products undergo. As understanding increases, the meaning-generality becomes clearer and clearer until it yields to direct realization of impermanence by yogic direct perception.[53] Formerly, the image of impermanence was mixed with actual impermanence; at the time of direct perception, the imagistic part falls away and one is left with a direct cognition of momentary disintegration.

With regard to the ability of thought to realize impermanent phenomena, Gyel-tsap, in commenting on the first chapter of Dharmakīrti's *Commentary on (Dignāga's) 'Compendium on Valid Cognition'*, writes:

> ... a factually concordant convention [that is, a conceptual mind] which is indirectly related with a functioning thing [serves as] a basis for finding or getting at [i.e., realizing] that functioning thing.[54]

The thought consciousness having an image as its appearing object is factually concordant if its image corresponds with an actual object or, more technically, if the referent object exists. Such a thought is indirectly (*brgyud nas*) related with the external specifically characterized phenomenon represented by the image because as the image becomes clearer, so does the actual object. Thus, the thought consciousness is getting at or realizing the external specifically characterized phenomenon through the medium of the image — the appearing object of that thought consciousness. It is said to be like travelling to a distant land; first it is very far off, but slowly one approaches and finally reaches it.[55] Similarly, thought approaches clarity and finally yields to the full richness of direct perception.

Thought is considered able to lead to direct perception because, from the time it initially conceives an image such as impermanence, it is not dealing solely with something imputed by thought but is correctly identifying and *explicitly realizing* the subtle impermanence that is a specifically characterized phenomenon. Thus, even while elaborating the deficiencies of conceptuality in relation to direct perception — it is less vivid, blurs specifics, and is obstructed from fully realizing ultimate truths just as they are — it is emphasized that thought is relied upon to gain access to what cannot be yet ascertained in direct perception. Valid cognition (*pramāṇa, tshad ma*) comes in only two types, direct (*pratykṣa-pramāṇa, mngon sum tshad ma*) and inferential (*anumāna-pramāṇa, rjes dpag tshad ma*), the latter necessarily being conceptual. If one wishes to ascertain something not presently accessible to direct perception, there is no other valid cognition available except for correct conceptual thought developed to the point of incontrovertible realization. In order to further clarify Gelukba views on the efficacy of thought and its significance in religious practice, the ability of thought to realize impermanent phenomena and of words to express them will be elaborated further in the discussion of negatives or exclusions in the following chapters.

5 *Discrimination Through Exclusion*

INTRODUCTION

As elaborated in the preceding discussion on Gelukba presentations of direct perception and conceptual thought in Sautrāntika, there are two ways to know or perceive objects. Either the object casts an aspect toward the directly perceiving consciousness, or the object is known conceptually through the medium of a mental image of the object. Phenomena that can give rise to an ultimate or direct consciousness are designated as ultimate truths or specifically characterized phenomena. All other existing phenomena are conventional truths or generally characterized phenomena. Thus, the two truths are defined in terms of direct and conceptual perception, and a discussion of how phenomena are divided into the two truths entails a discussion of the direct and conceptual consciousnesses that perceive them.

To understand more about how Gelukbas consider thought and words to operate in this system of Sautrāntikas Following Reasoning (*nyāya-anusārin*) and for the sake of a more complete presentation of the types of phenomena that can be known by thought or direct perception, it is necessary to investigate the Gelukba presentation of positive and negative phenomena.[1] This is a division of existent phenomena made on the basis of how objects are known by thought.

POSITIVE PHENOMENA

A positive phenomenon (*vidhi, sgrub pa*) is something thought realizes without having to explicitly negate an object of negation. For example, one can conceive of a pot without explicitly eliminating or negating anything else. By contrast, the lack of a pot can only be expressed by an explicit verbal elimination of pot and only understood by an explicit mental elimination of pot. Therefore, a pot is a positive phenomenon, and lack of pot is a negative phenomenon.

Pur-bu-jok would define a positive phenomenon as:

> A phenomenon which is not an object realized upon the explicit elimination of its own object of negation by the thought consciousness that apprehends it.[2]

When an eye consciousness sees a pot, it does not explicitly eliminate anything. Similarly, the word 'pot' expresses pot without explicitly eliminating or negating anything else. As the definition above indicates, the object being realized is a phenomenon (*dharma*, *chos*). The translation equivalent 'phenomenon' is used here because, although the word *dharma* has at least ten distinct meanings, in this context it refers to knowable objects (*jñeya*, *shes bya*) and thus accords with the non-technical Western understanding of a phenomenon as something that appears to the senses.[3] Buddhism generally maintains that both permanent and impermanent phenomena can appear or be known. Sautrāntika here holds that no permanent phenomenon can be an *appearing object* of direct perception; the higher systems agree but with one very important exception. They maintain that emptiness — the final reality — can be perceived directly. It too is a phenomenon.

Pur-bu-jok defines a phenomenon as "that which holds its own entity."[4] In other words, a phenomenon is simply anything one with itself. Anything that exists — permanent or impermanent, positive or negative, is a phenomenon. The following are all synonyms of phenomenon:

existent	(*sat*, *yod pa*)
object of knowledge	(*jñeya*, *shes bya*)
established base	(*gzhi grub*)
object	(*viṣaya*, *yul*)
object of comprehension	(*prameya*, *gzhal bya*)

All of these "hold their own entity" in the sense of *having* their own nature, though not necessarily in the sense of existing *by way of* their own nature. They are objects realized by valid cognition. They are the bases of the division into ultimate and conventional truths or specifically and generally characterized phenomena. They are also bases of the division into positive and negative phenomena. Thus, negatives are objects realized by valid cognition. Negatives are also existents, established bases, and objects of comprehension. Like positive phenomena[5] they can either be permanent or impermanent. They are distinguished from positive phenomena in terms of how they are realized by thought. Some negatives are specifically characterized phenomena and thus ultimate truths; others are generally characterized phenomena and thus conventional truths. The mere fact that a phenomenon is a negative, therefore, does not signify whether it is permanent or impermanent, functioning or not.

NEGATIVE PHENOMENA

In cognizing certain objects, thought operates by way of explicitly eliminating an object of negation (*pratiṣedhya, dgag bya*). For example, the thought consciousness realizing a mountainless plain does so by way of explicitly eliminating mountains; therefore, mountainless plain is a negative phenomenon. Gön-chok-jik-may-wang-bo defines a negative phenomenon as:

> ... an object which is realized upon the explicit elimination of an object of negation.[6]

The key word in this definition is *explicit*. Every existent phenomenon is realized by the consciousness perceiving it in the manner of that consciousness eliminating that the phenomenon is anything but itself. For example, when the eye consciousness knows a table, it implicitly eliminates that this object with four legs and so forth is anything other than a table. Thus, even the perception of positive phenomena involves *some* type of elimination but not an *explicit* elimination of an object of negation. Any given phenomenon exists exclusive of all other phenomena which are not itself; therefore, all are opposite from and eliminators of other phenomena. This, however, is not sufficient reason to assert that all phenomena are negatives. Only those phenomena which are conceptually cognized through an *explicit* elimination of some negated object are negative phenomena. For example, a realization of pot — a positive phenomenon — involves an implicit elimination of the pot's being a cow, shoe, or anything else that is not a pot. Although the consciousness observing pot does eliminate that pot is something other than pot, it does not do so explicitly but implicitly.

The difference between implicit and explicit elimination or negation is as follows. The thought consciousness that explicitly realizes the presence of money also implicitly realizes the non-existence of a lack of money. It implicitly eliminates a lack of money but this implicit elimination does not mean that money is a negative phenomenon. Money itself is a positive phenomenon and is cognized without the thought apprehending it explicitly eliminating anything. On the other hand, the lack of money can only be cognized if the mind explicitly eliminates money, the object of negation. Therefore, the lack of money is a negative phenomenon. Similarly, a mountainless plain can only be conceptualized by mentally eliminating mountains; thus, this too is a negative phenomenon.

The Gelukba presentation of negative phenomena makes clear that all negative phenomena — even those which are mere absences such as the lack of money or the absence of a substantially existent self — can be cognized. Even the subtlest type of emptiness which is a mere absence of inherent existence as presented in the Prāsaṅgika-Mādhyamika system can be cognized directly. Indeed, the possibility of cognizing negatives is essential to this presentation of the Buddhist path because the selflessness or emptiness which must be cognized in order to overcome ignorance is itself a negative phenomenon.

HISTORICAL PERSPECTIVE

In their textbook discussions of negative phenomena, Gelukba authors such as Pur-bu-jok, Ra-dö, and Jang-gya note the synonymity of negative phenomena (*pratiṣedha, dgag pa*) and exclusions (*apoha, sel ba*). Their treatment of the topic derives from Indian philosophical discourse on the nature of meaning, words, and the cognitive process, but Tibetan commentators, in taking up this discussion, incorporated and elaborated upon it in a manner appropriate to their own religious-philosophical concerns. In Gelukba, the theory of *apoha* or exclusions was brought to bear on a set of issues somewhat different from those that appear to have initially surrounded it in India. It is impossible here to consider all permutations of the theory of exclusions in Indian thought, but a few points will help to contextualize the Gelukba formulation.

The *apoha* theory in India derived from philosophical interest, not only in the ontological status attributed to an image engendered by words, but in the closely related issue of words' capacity to express objects. For instance, A.B. Keith speaks of the topic of exclusions as "The Buddhist doctrine of the negative or rather relative signification (*apoha*) of words."[7] Indeed, the Indian Buddhist discussion of *apoha* or exclusions arose in part as a refutation of the realist Mīmāṃsaka position that words are capable of fully expressing objects:

> On this [Buddhist] view, a word has not the power (*śakti*) attributed to it by the Mīmāṃsā to communicate to objects the verbal form under which we conceive them, or to express the real nature of anything: it merely serves to distinguish it from other things ...[8]

Virtually all Western scholarship on *apoha* theory to date reports the Indian tradition wherein exclusions are seen either as descriptive of a mode of cognition or, more commonly, of the words on the basis of which such a differentiation is conceptualized. The Gelukbas, however, conclude that phenomena — not just words or mental images — can be designated as negatives because of how thought cognizes them. The Gelukba presentation of the various types of negatives therefore is not a classification of terminology or mental objects, but of the all-encompassing category of objects of knowledge (*jñeya, shes bya*).

The Buddhist *apoha* theory was first presented by Dignāga in the fifth chapter of the *Compendium on Valid Cognition* (Pramāṇa-*samuccaya*), his last[9] and arguably most influential work. In formulating this theory, Dignāga was countering the then current non-Buddhist position that words directly refer to something positive.[10] Dignāga by contrast maintained that the word 'tree' for example refers not to a positive generality 'tree' but to an exclusion of non-tree, a negative phenomenon. Thus, as documented by M. Hattori, Dignāga established that words express objects which are "qualified by the exclusion of the other things [things other than itself] (*arthāntaranivṛtti, anyāpoha*).[11] This articulation of the word as positive and its expressed object as negative was a significant departure from the Brahmanical tradition which emphasized a complete identity between, for example, the word 'Brahman' and its referent, the actual Brahman.[12] In this view, to say 'Brahman' was to evoke the existence of the actual ineffable Brahman. Dignāga however maintained that words stand for only a portion (*amṣa*) of an object and not the full-bodied, multifaceted object; he also noted that such a portion is "nothing other than the product of mental construction."[13]

Nearly fifteen centuries later, this point remains central to the Gelukba discussion of verbal and cognitive processes. But the context for the argument has changed. In Dignāga's time, the assertion of a negative referent stood in contrast to the positive image (*pratibhā, pratibimba, gzugs brnyan*)[14] which both Dignāga and Bhartṛhari, by whom Dignāga was greatly influenced,[15] accepted as the referent meaning of a sentence. Thus, despite his position that the referent of *words* is negative, Dignāga echoed Bhartṛhari's assertion that a *sentence* and its meaning are indivisible, just as sound and meaning are indivisible[16] and that the meaning (*pratibhā*) of a sentence is positive.

The apparent inconsistency in Dignāga's position — holding that although the referent of words is negative, the referential meaning of a sentence composed of words is positive — was criticized by the Mīmāṃṣaka Kumārila. That criticism provided at least part of the impetus for an important modification of this viewpoint by Śāntarakṣita in the *Compendium of Suchness* (*Tattvasaṃgraha*). Śāntarakṣita resolved the incongruency as follows. He maintained, like Dignāga, that the image produced in the mind of a listener by either a word or a sentence is positive; however, he modified the theory of exclusion as found in Dignāga to assert that this image, though positive, was also an *apoha* or exclusion because it was differentiated from or, in Gelukba phraseology, served to exclude, images generated by other words or sentences.[17] In short, 'exclusion from other' referred to a *concept* formed through the mental act of excluding what was not a certain object; Śāntarakṣita thus took *apoha*, or exclusion, to be a name for the *image* directly referred to by a word.[18]

The Gelukbas made extensive use of this point. They distinguished between two levels of verbal referents in ways that allowed them to include images as well as actual objects in this category. For example, Den-dar-hla-ram-ba first states that only the mental image of impermanence is *explicitly* expressed by the term 'impermanence'. He then explains that actual impermanence *is* expressed by that term in that it is explicitly realized by the thought consciousness which arises due to hearing and reflecting on the term 'impermanence.' Bel-den-chö-jay resolves the issue in a similar fashion by making a distinction between an impermanent object's entity *fully* appearing to a consciousness and its capacity to *appear* to a thought consciousness that arises from a term. (For further discussion of Gelukba positions on this matter, see p. 195ff.). By refining the categories of 'objects of expression' and 'appearance' in this way, the latter-day Gelukbas were able to maintain that objects are explicitly expressed by words, a tenet vital to their theories of liberative technique.

In brief, it appears that Gelukba scholars made a major interpretative step in the *apoha* theory by emphasizing that (1) *apohas* or exclusions are neither words nor, exclusively mental images, but *objects* which are realized through a process of exclusion and (2) emphasizing that these objects may be either permanent or impermanent. They made this point explicit through their definition and utilization of the two categories of exclusions mentioned by Śāntarakṣita,[19] mental exclusions (*buddhyātmakānyāpoha, blo'i gzhan sel*) and objective exclusions (*arthātmaka-svālakṣaṇa-anyāpoha, don rang mtshan gyi gzhan sel*). This latter is defined by Pur-bu-jok as "That observed to be a common locus of an affirming negative and ultimately being able to perform a function."[20] Whereas mental exclusions include the type of mental image referred to by both Dignāga and Śāntarakṣita, the latter category, objective exclusions, comprises impermanent phenomena such as mountainless plain or, according to Pur-bu-jok, opposite from non-pot. Therefore, in Gelukba presentations, the category of exclusions includes *both* permanent, or non-functioning, and impermanent, or functioning, phenomena.

These two types of exclusions, mental and objective, are themselves subdivisions of the class of affirming negatives (*paryudāsa-pratiṣedha, ma yin dgag gi gzhan sel*). The Buddhist presentation, beginning at least with Śāntarakṣita,[21] gives this as one of the two major divisions of exclusions, the other being the class of non-affirming negatives (*prasajya-pratiṣedha, med dgag*). The categories of affirming and non-affirming negatives, however, predate Buddhism in India and were originally a classification of statements, not of phenomena. The Mīmāṃsakas had introduced the concepts of *paryudāsa-pratiṣedha* and *prasajya-pratiṣedha* in connection with their interpretations of moral injunctions found in the Vedas.[22] Mīmāṃsakas asserted that statements themselves were negations; an injunction such as 'One must not kill a Brahmin' was considered a non-affirming negative prohibition which did not suggest any type of activity to replace the prohibited one.

Thus, for Mīmāṃsakas, exclusions were statements. As already noted, the Buddhist presentation of exclusions has also been described, in Indian and in Western scholarship, as a theory of words. Yet Gelukbas, building on the categories established by Śāntarakṣita, classified certain *phenomena* as exclusions based on how they are known by thought or how they are expressed in words. Opposite from non-pot is known and expressed through the mental or verbal elimination of pot; this item itself — which, if instanced, cannot be anything but a pot — is considered a negative phenomenon and a functioning thing. Gelukba scholars would certainly contest the Mīmāṃsaka position that words can express objects as they actually exist and, by extension, as they appear to direct perception. But the Buddhist position was not nihilistic. They were careful to make the point that words are not entirely incapable of expressing objects, nor do they serve merely to distinguish one thing from another. How could this be?

We have already mentioned how, based on Śāntarakṣita, Gelukba scholars emphasized that exclusions could be either permanent (or non-functioning) and impermanent (or functioning) things. These latter are, in Jang-gya's words, phenomena "established by way of their own nature without being a mere mental imputation." In this way, the category of exclusions in Gelukba comes to refer, not only to mental images and verbal phrasing, but to functioning objects conceived of by explicitly excluding some other phenomenon. The details of this argument will be elaborated in the discussion below (pp. 166ff.).

The point here is that Gelukbas, drawing on the discussions and divisions of exclusions that already existed in India, emphasized certain elements of that discussion so that, whereas initially the *apoha* or exclusion theory was arguably used by Dignāga to deny an intrinsic relationship between words and their meaning, the Gelukbas came to use this theory to show the deep connection between words and meaning — the objects to which words refer — in order to establish that conceptual thought does have practical value on the religious path. Their presentation of exclusions, particularly the discussion of mental exclusions, forms an important part of their explication of how words and thought get at actual phenomena. For, as discussed above, both mental exclusions and impermanent functioning phenomena are designated as explicitly expressed by words. This in turn signifies that the unenlightened can use words to express the contents of liberating wisdom sufficiently well to use words as a means of gaining access to that understanding. It is not that, in linking words and meaning in this way, they are harkening back to the magical oneness of words and objects upheld in the Brahmanical tradition, but rather to a meaningful connection that can be used by the practitioner. It is not that through saying 'emptiness' one magically knows emptiness, or by muttering 'enlightenment' or 'compassion' one effortlessly possesses these. Rather, Gelukba scholars maintain that by cultivating familiarity with concepts pertinent to these realizations — the subtle impermanence or emptiness of phenomena, or the interrelatedness of all living beings — one begins to approach a state of direct understanding. Words then fall away. This state beyond words is also beyond attainment unless the religious aspirant discerns the proper path. For the Gelukba order, that path means a correct conceptual grasp which can then serve as the basis for immediate experience.

DIVISIONS OF NEGATIVE PHENOMENA

In order to discuss the characteristics of negative phenomena in more detail it is necessary to lay out the major divisions of these: affirming negatives and non-affirming negatives as well as their subdivisions. Briefly stated, affirming negatives are expressed by terms that, in addition to explicitly eliminating an object of negation, also suggest some other phenomenon — either another affirming negative or a positive phenomenon — in place of what is negated. Non-affirming negatives are expressed by terms that do not suggest either an affirming negative or a positive phenomenon in place of what is negated, though they might suggest another non-affirming negative. For example, the lack of money does not suggest anything positive in place of the object negated — money — but it does implicitly suggest the lack of five dollars, which absence is also a non-affirming negative.

The Indian Buddhist source for the division of negative phenomena or exclusions into affirming and non-affirming negatives is Śāntarakṣita's 8th-century *Compendium of Suchness* (*Tattvasaṃgraha*), quoted in the *Collected Topics of Ra-dö*:

> Here, exclusion has two aspects
> Non and non-existent.[23]

Then, in order to dispel the interpretation, espoused by some modern scholars noted below, that certain negatives themselves are non-existent, the Ra-dö text quotes from Kamalaśīla's 8th-century *Commentary on the Difficult Points of (Śāntarakṣita's) 'Compendium of Suchness'* (*Tattvasaṃgraha-pañjikā*):

> The phrase 'non and non-existent'
> Has the definite intention
> Of expressing affirming negatives
> And non-affirming negatives.[24]

A negative phenomenon is necessarily either an affirming or a non-affirming negative. These two categories have subdivisions but there is no third type of negative phenomenon outside of this two-fold division.

AFFIRMING NEGATIVES

The first of the two major divisions of negative phenomena, affirming negatives (*paryudāsa-pratiṣedha, ma yin dgag*), are those entities expressed by terms which explicitly eliminate an object of negation and at the same time suggest a positive phenomenon in place of what is negated. For example, the phrase 'mountainless plain' explicitly eliminates mountains, the object of negation, and also suggests the existence of a plain, a positive phenomenon. The mountainless plain itself is the negative phenomenon, not the term that expresses it.

There is both a four-fold and a two-fold division of affirming negatives; the four-fold being made on the basis of how the term expressing an affirming negative suggests a phenomenon in place of what is negated. It may make this suggestion explicitly, implicitly, both explicitly and implicitly, or contextually.

1. *Affirming negative of explicit suggestion*. Example: That expressed by the term 'mountainless plain.' This phrase explicitly eliminates an object of negation — a mountain — and explicitly suggests a plain.

2. *Affirming negative of implicit suggestion*. Example: That expressed by the phrase 'The fat Devadatta does not eat during the day.' This explicitly eliminates that Devadatta eats during the day and implicitly suggests that he eats at night.

3. *Affirming negative of both explicit and implicit suggestion*. Example: That expressed by the phrase 'The existence of a non-emaciated Devadatta who does not eat during the day.' This phrase explicitly eliminates that Devadatta eats during the day. It explicitly suggests that Devadatta exists and implicitly suggests that he is fat.

4. *Affirming negative of contextual suggestion*. Example: That ex-

pressed by the phrase 'He is not of Brahmin lineage' when this is heard by someone who has already ascertained that the person in question is either of Brahmin or Royal lineage. In this context, the phrase eliminates that the person is of Brahmin lineage and suggests that he is of Royal lineage.

The above four types of affirming negatives are designated on the basis of how the phrase expressing them suggests another phenomenon in place of what is negated. The two-fold division of affirming negatives is made on the basis of whether the negative phenomenon itself is impermanent or permanent.

1. *Functional specifically characterized exclusions.* These are impermanent and, like all impermanent phenomena, capable of performing functions and suitable to be objects of direct perception. An example is a mountainless plain.

2. *Mental exclusions.* These are affirming negatives that are merely imputed by thought. They are permanent. Examples are meaning-generalities such as the appearance to thought as opposite from non-pot. Uncaused space is also a mental exclusion.

NON-AFFIRMING NEGATIVES

Non-affirming negatives (*prasajya-pratiṣedha, med dgag*) are phenomena expressed by terms which explicitly eliminate an object of negation and do not suggest either a positive phenomenon or an affirming negative in place of what is negated. The object negated can be either existent or non-existent. A non-affirming negative expressed by a phrase that eliminates an existent object of negation is non-existence of pot. 'Non-existence of pot' negates pot without suggesting anything in its place. An example of a non-affirming negative expressed by a phrase that eliminates a non-existent object of negation in the selflessness of persons (*pudgala-nairātmya, gang zag gi bdag med*). The self of persons, something that never existed, is negated and nothing is suggested in its place. In both these examples, the non-affirming negative itself is necessarily an existent phenomenon.

In the Gelukba presentation of Sautrāntika, the self negated in the theory of selflessness of persons is a person which is substantially existent or self-sufficient (*dravya-sat, rang rkya thub pa'i rdzas yod*).[25] Although persons exist, persons qualified as substantially existent and self-sufficient do not. The lack of such existence is a non-affirming negative because no phenomenon — positive or negative — is suggested in place of what is negated. No substantially existent self exists, but the ignorance which conceives it to exist is so deeply ingrained that this misconception is considered the basis for countless actions motivated by desire, hatred, and other forms of ignorance. To realize the lack of such a self is a case of understanding the absence of something which never did exist but which is deeply conceived to exist.

In the Prāsaṅgika-Mādhyamika system of tenets, the subtle selflessness of persons and phenomena refers to their lack of inherent existence. This selflessness must be cognized in order to overcome the obstructions to liberation from cyclic existence. The lack of inherent existence is a non-affirming negative cognized by means of eliminating its object of negation — inherent existence — and not suggesting anything whatsoever in its place. Thus, meditative equipoise on such selflessness is called space-like in that uncaused space (also a non-affirming negative) is similarly a mere absence, in this case an absence of obstructive contact. During meditative equipoise, nothing appears or is implied, suggested, or indicated in place of the emptiness of inherent existence. However, the Gelukba presentation of Prāsaṅgika-Mādhyamika emphasizes over and over that this emptiness or lack of inherent existence is not mere nothingness; it is a *negative phenomenon*. Like all phenomena, emptiness is an object of knowledge. Emptiness is something to be known, first conceptually and then, according to the higher systems, directly. To pave the way for this possibility, the Gelukba presentation of negative phenomena emphasizes that negatives are objects to be realized by valid cognition. They are designated as negatives on the basis of how they are known or expressed, but negative phenomena themselves are neither thought nor words. If non-affirming negatives were not considered phenomena to be known, then the emptinesses of persons and other phenomena would similarly not be phenomena to be known. In that case the system could not assert that a meditator on the path of seeing (*darśana-mārga, mthong lam*) who directly cognizes the emptiness of inherent existence has an object of realization. If no object of realization were asserted, it would be difficult to refute those who claim that emptiness is nothingness or that persons cognizing emptiness are realizing nothing in particular. The assertion that a direct realization of emptiness is a specific realization of a specific object of knowledge plays an important part in the Gelukba presentation of Mādhyamika; the philosophical ground for this is laid in the Sautrāntika system's discussion of negative and positive phenomena.

6 *Exclusions: Affirming Negatives*

Affirming negatives are so called because the terms that express them affirm or suggest the existence of a positive phenomenon or other affirming negative in place of what is negated. Gön-chok-jik-may-wang-bo defines an affirming negative as:

> A negative [expressed by a phrase which] suggests some other phenomenon, either a positive phenomenon or another affirming negative, or both, in place of its own object of negation.[1]

For example, the phrase, "The corpulent Devadatta does not eat during the day" suggests that he eats at night due to the fact that it mentions his corpulence. This statement (1) explicitly eliminates that Devadatta eats during the day and (2) in place of this, implicitly suggests that he eats at night. The suggested positive phenomenon, eating at night, *replaces* what is negated, eating during the day, in much the same way as one person might sit down in a chair vacated by another.[2] This feature of the suggested item replacing what is negated is a significant characteristic of affirming negatives. For example, the statement "Brahmins do not drink beer" explicitly suggests Brahmins, who are positive phenomena; however, because Brahmins are not being suggested *in place of* what is negated, the drinking of beer, this statement does not express an affirming negative. Rather, it expresses a non-affirming negative because an alternative activity to the drinking of beer is not suggested. This feature of replacement, not specifically mentioned in the short definition given above, is included in the *Collected Topics by a Spiritual Son of Jam-yang-shay-ba* (*Sras bsdus grva*), a text used by Gomang College:

> An affirming negative is a negative [phenomenon] that is expressed by a phrase which indicates another phenomenon — either a positive phenomenon or an affirming negative — in place of its own object of negation.[3]

Thus, it is not that *any* phenomenon expressed by a term suggesting either an affirming negative or a positive phenomenon is a negative. If it were, then even the word 'product' would express a negative because this word implicitly suggests causes and conditions, which are positive phenomena. However, product is not realized by way of explicitly eliminating non-product and, therefore, the implied causes and conditions are not suggested in place of anything; hence, 'product' indicates a positive, not a negative, phenomenon.

The 19th-century Gelukba scholar Pur-bu-jok gives a definition of affirming negatives which, though somewhat more complex than that of Gön-chok-jik-may-wang-bo above, is concordant with it:

> [An affirming negative is] that which is observed as a common locus of (1) *being* a negative phenomenon and (2) *having* a common locus of (a) being an object of comprehension for the thought consciousness apprehending it which is suggested in place of its own object of negation by the phrase expressing it and (b) being a positive phenomenon.[4]

This is another way of saying that an affirming negative is a negative — that is, a phenomenon realized by way of the thought which realizes it eliminating the appropriate object of negation. An affirming negative has the two features of being something suggested in place of the object negated and that something itself being a positive phenomenon. For example, the corpulent Devadatta's not eating during the day is a negative phenomenon and the phrase that expresses it suggests a positive phenomenon, namely Devadatta's eating at night, to the thought consciousness that, on the basis of the phrase "The corpulent Devadatta does not eat during the day," takes this negative — not eating during the day — as an object of comprehension.

This longer definition, although several centuries later, is not substantially different from the shorter ones quoted above. It is, however, notable that the Gomang *Collected Topics* and the Gomang scholar Gön-chok-jik-may-wang-bo specify that the suggested phenomenon replacing the negated one can be *either* a positive phenomenon *or* another affirming negative. Pur-bu-jok, and the Ra-dö text transcribed by Jam-yang-chok-hla-ö-ser, as well as Jang-gya (who defines an affirming negative concisely as "an exclusion that suggests another positive phenomenon")[5] all mention only positive phenomena as suggestible by a phrase expressing an affirming negative.

There is a reason why Gomang modified these scholars' position to specify that either a positive phenomenon or an affirming negative may be suggested. Gomang, unlike the other Gelukba colleges, considers that impermanence is an affirming negative, not a positive phenomenon. However, the term 'impermanence' does not suggest a positive phenomenon, only another affirming negative. For, the only thing it suggests in place of the permanence it negates is itself — namely, impermanence — and this is an affirming negative. Hence they see the need to include in their definition of affirming negatives the possibility of suggesting an affirming negative in place of what is negated.[6]

The Gomang assertion that the term 'impermanent' or 'impermanence' expresses an affirming negative has other ramifications. For 'impermanent sound' is then also asserted to be a negative, whereas other colleges consider it a positive phenomenon. Gomang reasons that the phrase 'impermanent sound' explicitly eliminates 'permanent sound' and thus expresses a negative. The other colleges point to the fact that the definition of an impermanent thing is stated as 'a momentary thing.' Since this is a positive phenomenon, 'impermanent thing,' despite the fact that the phrase expressing it involves a negative term ('im'), must itself be a positive phenomenon.

In terms of the Buddhist presentation of a path to liberating knowledge, the fact that conceptual thought realizes subtle impermanence is significant. Indeed, this conceptual understanding of the momentary nature of phenomena is the first step toward (1) ascertaining the subtle impermanence that appears to but usually goes unnoticed by direct perception and (2) developing a very steady heightened mind that can cognize impermanence directly. This special mind is known as a yogic direct perceiver (*yogi pratyakṣa, rnal 'byor mngon sum*).

Gomang's assertion that impermanent sound is a negative phenomenon has interesting ramifications for that college's presentation of the yogic direct perceiver which realizes impermanence. Because this mind is a directly perceiving consciousness, it is necessarily a mind of complete engagement. This means that a yogic direct perceiver knows impermanence fully. Thus, although in general it is suitable to say that negative phenomena are cognized by way of eliminating some object of negation, it would not be suitable to assert that yogic direct perception cognizes impermanence in this way. All Gelukbas agree that direct perception of subtle impermanence is a special ability attained by advanced practitioners on the path of seeing (*darśana-mārga, mthong lam*), the third in a series of five stages culminating in liberation from cyclic existence. Therefore, yogic direct perception, like all direct perception, cognizes an object in the manner of taking on aspects similar to it, not merely through eliminating something which is not that object. Unlike other types of direct perception, however, yogic cognition does not *depend* on the aspect of its object. The base that it depends on is not a sense-power such as the eye, but a special type of mind possessing a union of calm abiding (*śamatha, zhi gnas*) and special insight (*vipaśyanā, lhag mthong*). Because of this special base, yogic direct perception is superior to other types of direct perception which must depend on the aspect of an object being cast to them.

Neither yogic nor any other type of direct perception can be posited as a partial engager. This is because a hallmark of direct valid cognition is that it perceives the complete array of characteristics associated with its object. Gomang's position that impermanence is a negative phenomenon, however, obliges its scholars to assert that even yogic direct perception of impermanence cognizes its object through an explicit elimination of the negated object, permanence. At the same time, Gomang must also uphold that yogic direct perception is a mind of complete engagement, and thus that the fact of its explicitly eliminating an object of negation does not make it a mind of partial engagement. The college therefore maintains that yogic direct perception is a mind of complete engagement because its *main* activity is to prove the object to be established — impermanence — and not to eliminate the object of negation. Since the positive factor is dominant, Gomang considers it suitable to posit yogic direct perception as a mind of complete engagement.[7]

The assertion of a single consciousness having both positive and negative elements is unique to Gomang. The other colleges maintain that impermanence is a positive phenomenon. Both sides agreee however that permanence is eliminated for a direct cognizer of impermanence; they disagree on whether this elimination is explicit or not. If the negation is not explicit, the part of the definition of a negative which specifies that it be a phenomenon realized by a thought consciousness which explicitly eliminates an object of negation is not fulfilled, and thus the object so cognized is not a negative. Therefore, with the exception of Gomang, Gelukbas consider that a direct perceiver of impermanence does not explicitly eliminate permanence; rather, the appearing object of such a consciousness is momentary disintegration, a positive phenomenon. Thus, they do not have to assert that the yogic direct perception realizing impermanence has characteristics of both complete and partial engagement.[8]

Because Gomang considers impermanence to be a negative phenomenon, it must define affirming negatives as expressed by terms which can suggest either a positive phenomenon or another affirming negative in place of what is negated. As explained above, this in turn leads them to a unique explanation of how yogic direct perception works. However, except for consequently asserting that an affirming-negative can be suggested in place of what is negated, the Gomang presentation of the four-fold and two-fold divisions of affirming negatives accords with the presentations of other Gelukba colleges.

THE FOUR-FOLD DIVISION OF AFFIRMING NEGATIVES

We have seen that, based on the way in which the phrase expressing an affirming negative suggests another phenomenon, affirming negatives are divided into four types: those expressed by terms that suggest another phenomenon (1) explicitly, (2) implicitly, (3) both explicitly and implicitly, and (4) contextually. These four, briefly outlined in the previous chapter, are more fully discussed below.

Affirming Negative of Explicit Suggestion

Pur-bu-jok's definition of this type of affirming negative is:

> An affirming negative expressed by a phrase which explicitly suggests another positive phenomenon that is its own suggested object.[9]

An example of a negative phenomenon expressed by a term of

explicit suggestion is a mountainless plain. For, the words "mountainless plain" explicitly suggest or mention a plain, a positive phenomenon. This particular plain is described or understood through an explicit verbal or mental elimination of mountains, the object of negation. The explicitly suggested plain is indicated in its place.

Another example of a negative phenomenon expressed by a term of explicit suggestion is "the existence of non-production from self" (*bdag las ma skyes pa yod*).[10] Hence, the existence of production from self is the object negated, and the existence of non-production from self is suggested in its place. The existence of non-production from self is an affirming negative since it is known through the explicit elimination of its object of negation. The statement "non-production from self" (*bdag las ma skyes pa*), however, expresses a non-affirming negative because it merely eliminates production from self without suggesting any positive thing in its place. The statement itself, in all cases above, is a positive phenomenon.

The Gomang text gives a slightly longer definition of an affirming negative of explicit suggestion:

> A negative [phenomenon] expressed by a phrase that explicitly suggests another phenomenon which is either a positive phenomenon or an affirming negative upon the verbally explicit negation of its own object of negation.[11]

The example given here is the existence of a pot's lack of a self of persons, meaning a pot's not being an object of use by a substantially existent person. The definition makes clear what the previous definition merely implied, namely that the explicitly suggested phenomenon is suggested by way of a verbally explicit elimination of the object of negation. Thus, the phrase "the existence of a pot's lack of a self of persons" makes its suggestion that such a lack exists through expressing a verbally explicit elimination of the object of negation, a pot's self of persons.[12]

It is an essential tenet of the Gelukba presentation of negative phenomena or exclusions that these can be cognized by valid cognition (*pramāṇa, tshad ma*). A mountainless plain is cognized by the eye consciousness as well as by thought. The existence of a pot which lacks a self of persons and, more significantly, the actual selflessness of persons, can be validly cognized conceptually according to Sautrāntika (and directly according to the higher systems). Although all these negatives are realized through the elimination of their own objects of negation, they are suitable to be objects of valid perception themselves. They are objects of knowledge (*jñeya, shes bya*), objects to be known. This assertion, vital to the Gelukba presentation of a path which involves direct cognition of selflessness, stands in marked contrast to the position reported by a modern scholar writing on the theory of exclusions (*apoha, gzhan sel*), C.L. Tripathi:

> In the process of negation the cognition of an object does not take place ... Hence it may be said that the essence of negation lies in an experience that does not take place.[13]

It is essential to the Gelukba presentation of the path that cognition of a negative such as the emptiness of persons is a specific experience which *does* take place at an advanced level of practice. If such a cognition could not be posited, the entire structure of this presentation of a method for overcoming ignorance would collapse. The antidote or means by which subtle misconceptions are overcome is none other than a cognition of selflessness or emptiness, and this selflessness is a negative phenomenon.

For this reason, the various Gelukba definitions make clear that the negative is an object; it is something expressed by a phrase but not the phrase itself. This contrasts with the to-date more well known Indian tradition that has been discussed by a number of contemporary scholars. In this view, the division into positive and negative refers not to objects but to types of verbal and conceptual functioning. It is true that the Gelukba Sautrāntika discussion of exclusions or negatives presents in some detail the manner in which words relate to external objects; nevertheless, the Tibetan literature on *apoha* is primarily a discussion of what constitutes a negative phenomenon. Thus, the Gelukba position does not accord with Dhirendra Sharma's statement that

> ... in dealing with *apoha* the problems we meet are essentially concerned with the propositional attitude, the logical nature of *meaning* ... The Buddhist logicians here seem to be dealing with propositions rather than with entities.[14]

The presentation of negative and positive phenomena does involve the relation of words and names to objects; moreover, phenomena are designated as negative or positive in dependence on how they are cognized by thought or expressed in words. Nevertheless, it is important to note that according to the Gelukba presentation it is the negative entities themselves — not the phrases which express them — that are being defined.

Implicit Suggestion

An affirming negative of implicit suggestion is defined by Pur-bu-jok as:

> An affirming negative expressed by a term which implicitly suggests another positive phenomenon that is its own suggested object.[15]

Pur-bu-jok's example is opposite-from-non-pot. This is an affirming negative of implicit suggestion because the term "opposite-from-non-pot" (*bum pa ma yin pa las log pa*) implicitly suggests pot, which is a positive phenomenon. Here a negative phenomenon is expressed and understood by way of explicitly eliminating all that is non-pot.

In accordance with the definition of affirming negatives in general, pot is implicitly suggested *in place of* the non-pot which is eliminated. The term 'non-pot' refers to everything that is not a pot, and therefore the only things that are not non-pot or, to put it more traditionally, which are opposite from non-pot, are pots. If someone says "Show me something that is opposite from non-pot," the *only* thing one can point to is a pot.

The assertion that pot itself, a positive phenomenon, *is* opposite from non-pot, a negative phenomenon, and the assertion that these comprise a single entity, indicates that the division into positive and negative phenomena is epistemologically and not ontologically based. In other words, something is designated as positive or negative in dependence on how it is known conceptually and, for the most part, on how the term that expresses it operates. If the process of knowledge or expression proceeds through the explicit elimination of an object of negation, then the object known — not merely the statement — is a negative. Thus, opposite-from-non-pot is a negative phenomenon, and yet, if someone asks, "What *is* opposite-from-non-pot?" it is nothing other than pot.

Opposite-from-non-pot and pot — negative and positive phenomena respectively — are one entity, but because they appear differently to thought it is not seen as erroneous to posit one as positive and the other as negative. The various instances of pots — gold, silver, clay, and so forth — are also different instances of opposite-from-non-pot. Therefore, although the division into positive and negative is a dichotomy in the sense that whatever exists must be one or the other and cannot from the same point of view be both, positive and negative phenomena do exist within the same entity. Just as pot and opposite-from-non-pot are one entity, a table, which is a positive phenomenon, and its emptiness, a negative phenomenon, are also one entity. Similarly, a person and its emptiness — its lack of being substantially existent — are also one entity. There is no paradox here if it is recalled that according to their definitions, positive and negative phenomena are designated on the basis of how thought cognizes them. Thus, to those who argue that Buddhism is nihilistic, the Gelukbas can answer that when a person directly cognizes emptiness there is no falling to nihilism; one is simply cognizing an attribute of existing phenomena which, like other attributes, is the very same entity as the phenomenon it qualifies.

This is a different perspective from that evinced, for example, in A.B. Keith's interpretation of negatives; Keith writes that negatives are asserted "on the basis of the relationship between subject [in this case, a pot] and predicate [in this case, 'non']."[16] Nor does the Gelukba view accord with Sharma's statement that "in the negative judgement we reject the property of *being present* as belonging to the expected or suggested thing at a certain time and place."[17] The lack or absence of a pot is a negative phenomenon but, in the Gelukba presentation, this itself does not determine whether the pot is positive or negative. How the object in question is cognized is the sole determining factor. For example, a pot in another room is a positive phenomenon, a pot not in this room is a negative phenomenon. On the other hand, to realize the existence or presence of opposite-from-non-pot is to observe a negative phenomenon. Any absence is a negative phenomenon but all phenomena that are absent are not. Moreover, uncaused space, which is a lack of obstructive contact, is a case of a certain type of absence that occurs when space itself is present. Thus, uncaused space is a negative phenomenon by virtue of its own entity, not in dependence on whether it is present or not.

The Gomang text defines an affirming negative of implicit suggestion as:

> A negative expressed by a phrase that implicitly suggests another phenomenon which is either an affirming negative or a positive phenomenon upon a verbally explicit negation of its own object of negation.[18]

The example here, as in Jang-gya, is the corpulent Devadatta's not eating during the day. As mentioned in the general discussion on affirming negatives above, the statement "The fat Devadatta does not eat during the day" (1) explicitly and literally refutes its own object of negation — that Devadatta eats during the day — and (2) implicitly suggests in its place that Devadatta eats at night, a positive phenomenon. If the statement did not specify that Devadatta is fat, it would not *necessarily* implicitly suggest that he eats at night, it would simply deny that he eats during the day and thus would be a non-affirming negative. Whether or not another phenomenon is suggested by a phrase depends on what is understood by the person hearing the words expressing that phenomenon. For example, if Devadatta is sick and someone says at sundown "He didn't eat today" or even "Fat Devadatta didn't eat today" this does not suggest that he eats or will eat at night.[19] This is not an affirming negative at all but a non-affirming negative because nothing is suggested in place of Devadatta's not eating in the day-time.

There is a limit to the suggestive power of a phrase, its capacity for suggestion being based on what would normally appear to the mind as a result of hearing or thinking it. Thus, a phrase which suggests the existence of something need not explicitly negate the non-existence of that thing. For example, to say "My wallet is not empty" would, in most contexts, suggest that one has some money. It does not explicitly negate that one is poor, or that one is too poor to buy a pizza, although it might suggest either of these had this been a question in the mind of someone involved in the conversation.

If it were otherwise, if to explicitly suggest the existence of a thing were to explicitly negate its non-existence, then the thought consciousness which explicitly realizes that pot exists would also have to explicitly negate what was opposite from the non-existence of pot — i.e., would have to eliminate that pot does not exist — whereas it actually negates this only implictly. This is a significant distinction, its most important ramification having to do with the inferential thought consciousness realizing, for example, impermanent sound. We have seen that realization of impermanence is an important part of the path and that conceptual or inferential realization must precede direct cognition. If to explicitly realize impermanent sound were to explicitly refute permanent sound, it would be impossible to focus fully on the necessary explicit realization of impermanence.[20]

Both Explicit and Implicit Suggestion

Pur-bu-jok defines this type of affirming negative as:

> An affirming negative expressed by a phrase which both explicitly and implicitly suggests another positive phenomenon that is its own suggested object.[21]

Jang-gya's definition is almost identical; the Gomang text too offers a similar definition:

> That which is expressed by a phrase that both explicitly and implicitly suggests another phenomenon which is either a positive phenomenon or an affirming negative upon the verbally explicit negation of its own object of negation.[22]

All three sources give the same example for this type of negative: The existence of a non-emaciated Devadatta who does not eat *food*[23] during the day. 'Non-emaciated' implicitly suggests that Devadatta is fat, and the existence of Devadatta is the explicitly suggested positive phenomenon. Thus, this phrase has both implicit and explicit modes of suggestion.

The two modes of implicit and explicit suggestion are not simultaneous but serial inasmuch as the respective suggestive phrases are consecutive. We can consider that as each part of the phrase is spoken, the corresponding meaning-generality appears to the thought consciousness of the listener. But it can also be asserted that all the words in combination give rise to a single meaning-generality or image that includes all the characteristics described. (Compare with Dignāga's discussion of words and sentences, p. 146ff.) Both systems of explanation — the consecutive generation of images and the existence of a single, complete image, are found among Gelukba thinkers.[24]

Contextual Negative

Pur-bu-jok and Jang-gya define a contextual negative as:

> An affirming negative expressed by a phrase which contextually suggests another positive phenomenon.[25]

The definition in the Gomang text is slightly more detailed and, as in the previous Gomang definitions, specifies that either a positive phenomenon or another affirming negative may be suggested:

> A negative expressed by a phrase that contextually suggests another phenomenon which is either a positive phenomenon or an affirming negative upon the verbally explicit negation of its own object of negation.[26]

To "contextually suggest" means that in a certain context a phrase has implications it might not have otherwise. For example, if one knows that a certain person is a teacher either of English or history and then hears that this person is not an English teacher, through having eliminated the latter possibility one understands this person to be a teacher of history. In other circumstances, however, learning that someone does not teach English would not suggest the teaching of history. Similarly, Jang-gya gives the following example of a statement expressing a contextual affirming negative:

> Having ascertained that a person is either of royal lineage or Brahmin lineage, and not yet having ascertained the particular lineage, [being told that] he is not of Brahmin lineage.[27]

In other words, after ascertaining that a person is either of these two lineages, a statement eliminating one of them suggests he is the other. This is much like the manner of realization through implicit suggestion, except that in this case the suggestion results from the circumstances in which one hears the statement rather than the words of the statement itself. For, the statement, "The corpulent Devadatta does not eat during the day," implicitly suggests that he eats at night because the word 'corpulent' makes it clear that Devadatta is accustomed to eating and the phrase as a whole eliminates what we know to be one of the two possible times for him to do so. No special context is necessary for this phrase to suggest that Devadatta eats at night.

Any realization of a negative phenomenon that comes about through one of the above four types of suggestion is an example of cognition through a negative route. In each case the elimination of the object negated brings another object to mind. The revolving set in a theater is roughly analagous to this type of cognition, for the same revolving motion that eliminates one scene reveals another. The audience experiences the second scene as becoming visible through removal of the first. Someone who walks in after the set has turned — much like someone who simply cogznies pot directly and not through a conceptual elimination of non-pot — does not observe the second scene through the elimination of anything, but sees only a positive phenomenon. The object apprehended is the same in both cases, the mode of arriving at it is different.

The major Indian source for the four-fold division of affirming negatives is a passage from Avalokitavrata's *Commentary on (Bhāvaviveka's) "Lamp for (Nāgārjuna's) 'Wisdom'"*:

> Negative [phenomena] which [are expressed by terms that] indicate [a positive phenomenon] implicitly,
> Which with one phrase [explicitly] establish [a positive phenomenon and eliminate an object of negation],
> Which involve [both of] those [implicit and explicit suggestions,]
> And the words of which do not indicate [a positive phenomenon except through context] are affirming negatives.[28]

Jang-gya and the Ra-dö text clearly interpret this quote as indicating the four types of affirming negatives outlined above.[29] Jang-gya even matches the ordering of his own presentation of these four to Avalokitavrata, putting affirming negatives of implicit suggestion first. He also describes affirming negatives expressed by phrases which both explicitly and implicitly suggest another phenomenon as establishing these two types of suggestion "with one phrase." A radically different interpretation of this passage is given by Kajiyama who states:

> Negation having the following characteristics must be regarded as *paryudāsa* [affirming negative]: (1) It states implication (*arthāpatti*) (2) by a single sentence (3) affirms a positive entity (too) having (the characteristics of) implication and the affirmation of a positive entity, (4) does not use the very word (of the entity) as when one, meaning a *kṣatriya* [warrior] uses not the word *kṣatriya* but the word *abrāmaṇa* [non-Brahmin].[30]

The main discrepancy between this statement and the Gelukba position is that Kajiyama takes this list to represent four qualities of a single affirming negative rather than four distinct types of affirming negatives as discussed above. Kajiyama also, like a number of other scholars, here maintains that the statements themselves are affirming negatives. In the Gelukba presentation, words are positive phenomena and it is the object expressed by a phrase which suggests a positive phenomenon (or affirming negative) in place of what it explicitly negates which is the affirming negative.

Beyond this, for the Gelukbas, a suggestion as such is not 'stated'; rather, a certain object is suggested by the statement which expresses an affirming negative. Further, the Gelukba presentation offers many exceptions to Kajiyama's fourth point that negation does not use the very word of the entity. In the examples given above, 'opposite from non-table' or 'mountainless plain' both contain the names of the objects to which they refer; namely, table and plain. In this presentation, the example of the word 'non-Brahmin' suggesting a warrior pertains only to the fourth type, contextually suggesting non-affirming negative.

THE TWO-FOLD DIVISION OF AFFIRMING NEGATIVES

Affirming negative phenomena can be either permanent or impermanent. Meaning-generalities or mental images are considered permanent; within the two-fold division of affirming negatives they are known as mental exclusions (*buddhyātmakānyāpoha, blo'i gzhan sel*). Impermanent negatives such as mountainless plains are objective specifically characterized phenomena (*arthātmaka-svalakṣaṇānyāpoha, don rang mtshan gyi gzhan sel*). Like all impermanent phenomena in this system, they are ultimate truths and capable of acting as a causal condition for the production of an ultimate mind, a direct perceiver.

Objective Specifically Characterized Phenomena

Jang-gya defines this type of negative as:

> An exclusion that is an affirming negative established by way of its own nature without being a mere mental imputation.[31]

For example, a mountainless plain is an affirming negative because of how it is known by thought or expressed in words. Both modes involve an explicit negation of 'mountain' and an explicit suggestion of 'plain.' Such a plain is established from its own side inasmuch as it does not depend on being imputed by thought. Like all impermanent phenomena, objective specifically characterized exclusions are functioning things, as Pur-bu-jok makes clear in his definition of this type of negative:

> That which is observed as a common locus of an affirming negative and being ultimately able to perform a function.[32]

All impermanent phenomena are specifically characterized and able to perform functions, but this does not make all impermanent things negatives. Only those impermanent phenomena which are conceptually cognized by means of an explicit elimination of some object of negation are affirming negatives. A chair is a positive phenomenon, but opposite-from-non-chair is a negative phenomenon because the latter is only cognized by way of explicitly eliminating non-chair. Thus, although chair and opposite-from-non-chair are a single entity, from the viewpoint of how they are cognized they are designated as positive and negative phenomena, respectively. Moreover, although all phenomena exclude — that is to say, they are not — phenomena other than themselves, anything that excludes other objects is not necessarily an exclusion. Even positive phenomena such as pots and chairs exclude all other phenomena. A negative however, in addition to excluding what is not itself, is conceptually realized by way of an explicit elimination of its object of negation. As Jang-gya states:

> All things [permanent and impermanent] abide without being mixed with other entities; therefore, they abide as opposite from all other [phenomena of] similar and dissimilar types.[33]

For example, pot is opposite from things of similar type — other forms — such as pillar and even golden pot. It is also opposite to or different from objects of dissimilar type such as uncaused space. Jang-gya mentions this by way of elaborating on Dharmakīrti's statement that:

> Because all things naturally abide in their own entity,
> They possess dependence on reversal from other things.[34]

All phenomena whatsoever have the quality of "abiding in their own entity." This means that they are not mixed with the entities of other phenomena. However, although a pot and opposite-from-non-pot are equally unmixed with other phenomena and equally specifically characterized, they are different for thought. Pot is a positive phenomenon because conceptual thought realizes 'pot' without explicitly negating anything else; opposite-from-non-pot is a negative phenomenon because it is conceptually realized through making an explicit elimination of non-pot. The two are one entity and, according to the Gelukba presentation (with the exception of Gomang College), both are seen by direct perception. Direct perception does not perceive opposite-from-non-pot in the manner of explicitly negating non-pot but there is no contradiction here because opposite-from-non-pot is not designated as a negative in dependence on how direct perception perceives it, but on the basis of how it is cognized conceptually.[35]

We have observed in some detail that in this Sautrāntika system, specifically characterized phenomenon (*svalakṣaṇa, rang mtshan*), functioning thing (*bhāva, dngos po*), and appearing object of direct perception (**pratyakṣa-pratibhāsa-viṣaya, mngon sum gyi snang yul*) are synonymous. Therefore, objective specifically characterized exclusions such as a mountainless plain or opposite-from-non-pot are, like positive specifically characterized phenomena, appearing objects of direct perception.[36] All impermanent phenomena are highest truths in this system, but they cannot categorically be referred to as positive or negative without making reference to the way in which they are conceptually cognized. Whereas ultimate and conventional truths are so posited because of the *type* of mind for which they serve as appearing objects — direct perception or conceptual thought — positive and negative phenomena are designated in accordance with *how* they are known by the conceptual mind that perceives them.

Further, any phenomenon, permanent or impermanent, is one entity with a negative phenomenon — its own emptiness — but this does not mean all phenomena are negatives. The description of positive and negative phenomena tells as much or more about the minds that cognize them as it does about the objects themselves. Nevertheless, the focus of the discussion is not on words or thought but on phenomena. This focus, and the Gelukba assertion that ultimate truths or impermanent phenomena can be negatives, contrasts with Tripathi's statement that "[A negation] is not real like a cow or a deer."[37] This could not account for the category of objective specifically characterized phenomena and assumes, in Gelukba terms, that all negatives are either mental exclusions or non-affirming negatives. The Gelukba presentation is not limited to these categories; rather, as the definitions by Jang-gya and Pur-bu-jok above indicate, an affirming negative such as a mountainless plain is a specifically characterized phenomenon and thus an ultimate truth of the same ontological status as a cow or a deer.

Mental Exclusions

Pur-bu-jok defines this type of negative as:

> A common locus of being [1] an exclusion which is an affirming negative and [2] which is also being imputed by thought.[38]

Jang-gya says the same thing a bit more succinctly:

> An affirming negative exclusion with the status of a mere imputation by thought.[39]

The appearance to thought of the mental image representing that which is opposite from all which is non-pot is the appearance as opposite from non-pot. This appearance is a mental image and a mental exclusion. It fulfills the definition of a mental exclusion because it is an affirming negative in that it is realized through the explicit elimination of non-pot, and it is a superimposition or mere imputation by thought because of being a permanent phenomenon which does not exist from its own side but is entirely dependent on thought or terminology. Mental exclusions are permanent and thus are generally characterized phenomena and conventional truths in the Sautrāntika system. Although impermanent phenomena can be *objects* of thought (*rtog pa'i yul*) they cannot be *appearing objects* of thought (*rtog pa'i snang yul*). Mental images, however, are fully knowable by thought and therefore can be asserted as appearing objects of thought.

The appearance as opposite from non-pot to the thought consciousness apprehending pot eliminates all that is non-pot, whereby pot appears to thought. This appearance is an affirming negative. Its object of negation is all that is non-pot and the explicitly suggested phenomenon is itself, the opposite from all that is non-pot.

A mental exclusion is necessarily involved in the process of conceptually realizing an objective specifically characterized exclusion. For, in order to conceive of opposite from non-pot, for example, the meaning-generality or mental exclusion which is an appearance to thought as opposite from non-pot must appear to thought. The actual object being realized is the specifically characterized opposite-from-non-pot, but the appearing object of thought is a mental exclusion or image of this. All meaning-generalities, however, are not necessarily mental exclusions, except in Gomang's presentation which considers all permanent phenomena to be negatives. Other colleges would consider that an appearance *as pot*, which is not expressed by a term that explicitly eliminates non-pot, is a positive phenomenon.[40] In any case this appearance to the thought consciousness apprehending pot does not differ 'visually' from the appearance as opposite from non-pot. Still, because an appearance as pot is neither described nor conceived of by means of eliminating an object of negation, it is not a negative and thus not a mental exclusion. Yet, like the appearance as opposite from non-pot, the appearance as pot serves to exclude from thought all that is not pot.[41]

The reason thought is mistaken with respect to impermanent specifically characterized phenomena is that it erroneously apprehends a fusion of the actual object and its image — whether that image be positive or negative. The image or meaning generality of a pot is defined as:

> That imputation (*sgro btags*) by thought which although not a pot, appears as like a pot to the thought consciousness apprehending pot.[42]

The Tibetan word for mental imputation is etymologized by the present Ganden Tri Rinboche, Jambel Shenpen Rinboche, as 'mentally fused phenomenon.' The term has two parts: *sgro*, which in the colloquial language refers to a pair of appendages such as the wings of a bird, the fins of a fish, or the oars of a boat, and *btags*, which means to attach or bring these two together. In the case of thought, there is an attaching or fusion of the two 'appendages' — the image and the actual object.[43]

When a person who knows the conventionality or name 'pot' hears or reads the word 'pot,' an image which is the explicit object of expression (*dngos kyi brjod bya*) of that word can appear to the mind. This image is typically instanced in texts as the appearance as opposite from non-pot. It at the most entails an implicit elimination of non-pot. Similarly, a person who wishes to understand impermanence cultivates a mental image of it by conceptually negating or eliminating increasingly subtle types of permanence. For example, one first eliminates the idea that one will live forever and thereby understands the coarse impermanence of life. Then one might eliminate the sense that the body remains unaltered for a period of ten years, a single year, a month, a day, an hour, or a minute. Finally, one develops a mental image of momentary impermanence. Once the meditator has gained sufficient familiarity with an understanding of impermanence, it is no longer necessary to make effort at eliminating some type of permanence; an image of momentary disintegration will simply appear to the mind.

Some Gelukba scholars say that if the image is arrived at through an explicit elimination of coarse or subtle permanence, it is a negative phenomenon, a mental exclusion, but if the image of momentary disintegration simply appears without any explicit elimination, it is a positive phenomenon (except for Gomang which considers all permanent phenomena, including mental images, to be negatives). Gelukba scholars who assert such mental images (expressed by phrases that arguably do explicitly eliminate permanence) to be positive phenomena do so with a sense that this opinion is somewhat controversial.[44] Nevertheless, they are also aware that this conveys well the very uncontroversial point that through becoming familiar with impermanence the effort of proceeding by means of first excluding permanence gives way to a more automatic type of understanding. In any case, whether the image is described as a negative — that is, as an appearance as opposite from non-impermanence — or as a positive — that is, an appearance as impermanent or an appearance as momentarily disintegrating — the understanding it yields for the thought consciousness to which it appears is the same. It is more accurate, however, to understand the image to be an appearance as opposite from non-impermanence because this wording clearly reflects what actually is taking place. Something is being excluded and something is being included for the apprehending thought consciousness.

Any mental image or meaning-generality is a generality that is common to both the thought conceiving the object represented and the object itself. For example, the appearance as opposite from non-pot is a generality that is common to the thought conceiving a pot and the actual pot. The image is of the nature (*bdag nyid*) of the thought consciousness — that is, it is imputed or made up by thought — and it is similar in aspect to the pot itself.[45] Moreover, the appearance as opposite from non-pot is the factor that applies to the various instances of pots — silver, gold, copper and so forth. The various types of pots are the field (*sa*) to which the meaning-generality applies.[46] (*See 'Naming' chapter for a discussion of how such an image serves to identify phenomena of the same type.*)

Other Views on Negatives

In this presentation of Sautrāntika, objective specifically characterized exclusions are ultimate truths, and mental exclusions are conventional truths. Their common denominator as negatives is not due to a shared ontological status but to how they are known conceptually. Perhaps because the two types of affirming negatives — objective and mental — are so different, some scholars have classified only one type as a negative and thus, from the Gelukba perspective, overlook the other. For example, Barlingay writes that the *apoha* theory "states that an entity is the negation of its opposite."[47] In the Gelukba context, this would account for an objective exclusion such as opposite-from-non-pot which is, in Barlingay's words, "an entity that is the negation of its opposite." However, as already indicated, the mere fact that something is a negation of its opposite does not make it a negative phenomenon because all existent objects exclude what is opposite from or other than themselves. Beyond this, Barlingay's description seems to refer only to objective specifically characterized phenomena, not to mental exclusions. Although a generic image is opposite from non-generic image, just as a pot is opposite from non-pot, the significance of its being designated as a negative is that it is an *appearance as*, for example, opposite from non-pot. Such an image merely appears to be a pot, it is not an actual elimination of what is opposite to that which it represents. Thus, if one follows the implications of Barlingay's statement, one would have to conclude that mental images — not being included among negatives — would necessarily be positive phenomena.

Other modern commentators have interpreted 'exclusions' to refer only to mental images. For example C.L. Tripathi states that "*apoha* [exclusions] are regarded as mental constructions and unreal."[48] Thus, Tripathi's system would not consider objects of direct perception such as opposite-from-non-pot to be negatives or exclusions, inasmuch as opposite-from-non-pot is not a mental construction but a functioning thing. With the exception of Gomang, Gelukbas consider that when the eye consciousness sees a pot, it also sees opposite-from-non-pot. Direct perception does not cognize opposite-from-non-pot by way of explicitly eliminating pot, for only thought operates in this manner. Still, when a pot is cognized through a negative route, one realizes opposite-from-non-pot, a negative phenomenon. Because opposite-from-non-pot is an impermanent thing, it can also be an appearing object of direct perception. Gomang College, however, does not consider opposite-from-non-pot to be a functional exclusion but a permanent thing; therefore, they do not posit it as appearing to direct perception.[49]

The idea that affirming negatives are necessarily mental exclusions is not new. Some Tibetan scholars prior to Ra-dö's time (approximately the 16th century) apparently also held this view. This assertion occurs in a verse from an early 13th-century work, the *Treasury of Reasoning* (*Tshad ma rigs pa' i gter*) by the renowned Sagyaba scholar Sagya Paṇḍita. The Ra-dö text quotes this verse but does not agree with it:

> Exclusion is the [conceptual] mind's mode of operation.
> Material objects are without exclusion.
> If exclusions existed in objects,
> Even [mental] appearances would exist as material
> objects.[50]

Indeed Sagya Paṇḍita — like Tripathi — considers that an exclusion cannot be material. He argues that exclusions do not exist in material objects such as chairs and tables. He reasons that because exclusions appear to thought, if they also existed in material objects then there would be the absurd consequence that mental images would be material or that material objects themselves would be imbued with mental images. It is a potent argument. Still, as we know, the Gelukbas have quite a different view. They agree that *certain* exclusions — mental exclusions — are appearing objects of thought. They also have no quarrel with Sagya Paṇḍita's statement that "Exclusion is the [conceptual] mind's mode of operation," only with taking this to be descriptive of all negative phenomena. However, Ra-dö, like other Gelukba scholars such as Jang-gya and Jam-yang-shay-ba, does assert the existence of material exclusions — objective specifically characterized exclusions. These impermanent phenomena are considered negatives because they are conceptually cognized by means of an explicit elimination of their object of negation. For example, opposite-from-non-pot is conceptually cognized through an explicit elimination of non-pot; however, opposite-from-non-pot itself is not an appearing object of thought, but an appearing object of direct perception. Thought must get at objective specifically characterized exclusions through the medium of an image — in this case, an appearance as opposite from opposite-from-non-pot just as it must get at all impermanent phenomena through the medium of an image.

AFFIRMING NEGATIVES AND THE GELUKBA PATH

The Ra-dö text expresses a quintessential of the Gelukba perspective when it states that the chief purpose in making a presentation of negative phenomena or exclusions is to facilitate an understanding of non-affirming negatives. Specifically, it emphasizes an understanding of the selflessness of persons and phenomena which, in terms of the Buddhist path, are the most significant non-affirming negatives.[51] In analyzing the various types of affirming negatives discussed in the four-fold division of explicitly, implicitly, both explicitly and implicitly, and contextually suggestive statements, those exclusions which are *not* non-affirming negatives are identified. The most salient characteristic of affirming negatives is that they are expressed by terms which in some manner suggest another phenomenon — either a positive one or another affirming negative — in place of the object negated. Such suggestion is not a characteristic of non-affirming negatives. By clearly understanding what it means for something to be suggested in place of a negated object, one can better understand the significance of the assertion that the term 'selflessness of persons' or 'emptiness of persons' does not suggest anything whatsoever in place of the object negated. Sautrāntika, Cittamātra, and Mādhyamika have different ways of identifying the self which is negated in the theory of selflessness; they do agree, however, that the selflessness or emptiness which is a mere absence of such a self is a non-affirming negative.

Thus, the presentation of non-affirming negatives is an important step in gaining an understanding of emptiness. All non-affirming negatives are not emptinesses however, and therefore it is necessary to consider non-affirming negatives as a class before focussing on the most important member of that class. The explanation of non-affirming negatives, the topic of the next chapter, both completes the presentation of negative phenomena and forms an integral part of the Buddhist presentation of a path to liberating knowledge.

7 *Exclusions: Non-Affirming Negatives*

Non-affirming negatives (*prasajya-pratiṣedha, med dgag*) are expressed by terms that do not suggest any positive phenomenon or affirming negative in place of what is negated. The presentation of non-affirming negatives supports depiction of selflessness or emptiness as a phenomenon, not only in Sautrāntika but in the higher systems of Cittamātra, Mādhyamika, and in Tantra as well.

The simplest definition of a non-affirming negative is given by Jang-gya:

> An exclusion which does not suggest another positive phenomenon.[1]

The Gomang text's longer definition makes clear that a non-affirming negative is a phenomenon, not an expressive term:

> [A non-affirming negative is] a negative phenomenon expressed by a term that does not implictly suggest another phenomenon, either a positive phenomenon or an affirming negative, upon the verbally explicit negation of its own object of negation.[2]

We have already seen an example of this, the negative expressed by the statement, "Brahmins do not drink beer." As noted earlier, this phrase does suggest Brahmins, who are positive phenomena, but does not suggest them through the explicit refutation of the object negated, the drinking of beer, nor are Brahmins suggested in place of what is negated.

We noted too that the earliest usage of the concept of negation (*pratiṣedha, dgag pa*) in general, and non-affirming negation in particular, occurred in the non-Buddhist Mīmāṃsā teachings on Vedic injunctions. There, an injunction such as "Brahmins should not drink beer" or "He shall not eat" is given in the Sanskrit optative mode. In Mīmāṃsā, such statements function as prohibitions that merely enjoin against some type of behavior without suggesting any other type.[3] In the Buddhist usage, the concept of negatives, and here specifically of non-affirming negatives, does not have a prohibitive cast but refers to a simple negation of some phenomenon without any value judgment being involved. Thus, the Buddhists do not use the statement 'Brahmins do not drink beer' as an example of a moral obligation but as a statement expressing an absence of Brahmins' drinking beer without at the same time suggesting either implictly or explicitly anything that they do drink.

Pur-bu-jok defines a non-affirming negative as:

> That which is observed to be a common locus of [1] being a negative and [2] there not occurring a common locus of [a] being an object of comprehension for the thought consciousness apprehending it that is suggested in place of its own object of negation by the term that expresses it and [b] being a positive phenomenon.[4]

This is a more technically complex way of stating the same thing. Brahmins' non-drinking of beer is a negative phenomenon, and the term expressing it does not suggest any positive phenomenon in place of its object of negation.

Although the term expressing a non-affirming negative does not suggest an affirming negative or positive phenomenon, it may suggest another non-affirming negative. Thus, the statement "Brahmins do not drink beer" implies that Brahmins do not drink Budweiser.[5]

The statement expressing a non-affirming negative can mention positive phenomena without suggesting these in place of what is negated. For example, the statement 'Snow is not black' indicates a non-affirming negative because though it suggests snow, it does not do so in place of an object of negation. However, 'non-black-snow' does explicitly suggest snow in place of the object of negation and thus is an affirming negative. However, 'non-green horns of a rabbit' is a non-affirming negative because the horns of a rabbit do not exist and thus to mention them is not to suggest either a positive phenomenon or an affirming negative, but a non-existent.

All non-affirming negatives are permanent and therefore are appearing objects only for thought. In this respect the category of non-affirming negatives differs from that of affirming negatives. The latter category has both permanent and impermanent instances, and impermanent affirming negatives can be appearing objects of direct perception. Non-affirming negatives exist through their being imputed by thought, but because they do exist they must be carefully distinguished from non-existents like the horns of a rabbit. This is again to underscore the point that emptiness, a non-affirming negative, although imputed by thought, does exist; it is not *only* imputed by thought in the sense that the horns of a rabbit or permanent sound — which utterly do not exist — are mere conceptual fabrications.

Non-exist*ents* such as the horns of a rabbit in turn must not be confused with non-exist*ence* such as the non-existence or absence of a pot in a particular place. The non-existence of a pot does exist because, in Pur-bu-jok's words, "with regard to whatever is selfless [i.e., all existents and non-existents] there are places where there are no pots."[6] In other words, the lack of pot does occur. Therefore, the non-existence or lack of pot's existence does not exist because, pots being existent phenomena, the non-existence of pots in general cannot be asserted. (The non-existence of the non-existence of the existence of pot is an affirming negative because it implicitly suggests the existence of pot.) The point, again, is that non-affirming negatives, being a division of phenomena, do exist.

Although non-affirming negatives exist, the explicit object negated by the term expressing such a negative may or may not exist. For example, in the statement "non-existence of the horns of a rabbit" (*ri bong rva med pa*) or "selflessness", the objects negated — horns of a rabbit, and in Sautrāntika, a substantially existent self — do not exist. Thus, non-affirming negatives are divided into two types; those whose negated objects do and do not exist. More technically, these categories are known as:

1. non-affirming negatives whose objects of negation occur among objects of knowledge (*rang gi dgag bya shes bya la srid pa'i med dgag*) and

2. non-affirming negatives whose objects of negation do not occur among objects of knowledge (*rang gi dgag bya shes bya la mi srid pa'i med dgag*).[7]

The absence of a pot (*bum pa med pa*) is an example of the first type; it is a non-affirming negative whose object of negation does exist. For, 'the absence of a pot' is a phrase that explicitly negates pot and thereby explicitly expresses the absence of pot. This absence is, in general, an existent and does not imply anything in its place. Examples of the second type of non-affirming negatives are the lack of a self-sufficient self of persons or, from the viewpoint of Prāsaṅgika-Mādhyamika, the lack of an inherently existent self of persons or of other phenomena. The term 'selflessness of persons' or 'selflessness of phenomena' explicitly negates a self (that is, substantial existence) and no such self or ontological status exists. The fact that substantial existence does not exist is significant for if it did the thought conceiving of it could not be the ignorance that is the source of suffering. The self or substantial existence of persons is neither a negative nor positive phenomenon because it does not exist, and we have observed that the classification into negative and positive is a categorization of existent phenomena only. The *lack of* such a self does exist; that absence is the non-affirming negative which is the emptiness or lack of a substantially existent self.

FURTHER IMPLICATIONS

The division of non-affirming negatives into those expressed by terms that negate existent or non-existent things contrasts with Tripathi's Indian-based observation, also analyzed from another perspective above, that:

> For Buddhists, negation is a subjective idea which denotes the non-existence of a thing at a particular place and time. The object which is not present at one place is present at another place.[8]

It has already been noted that for Gelukba scholars such as Pur-bu-jok, Jang-gya, and Gön-chok-jik-may-wang-bo, exclusions are phenomena; among affirming negatives, only mental exclusions such as meaning-generalities could remotely be considered 'ideas.' Beyond this, the second class of non-affirming negatives which negate something that does not exist stands in contrast to Tripathi's explanation that negative statements take as their objects of negation only phenomena which exist somewhere else. A substantially existent or inherently existent person does not exist anywhere; there is only the mistaken conception that such exists.

The ability of a negative statement *not* to suggest another positive phenomenon or even an affirming negative in place of the negated object is central to Buddhist logic and to Gelukba methods for realizing emptiness. From a Gelukba perspective therefore, a number of modern writers understand negatives in such a way as to preclude the possibility of cognizing emptiness. For example, D.N. Shastri explains a non-affirming negative as "a negation of something positive."[9] In the definition of non-affirming negatives given above, it is not the object of negation that determines status as a non-affirming negative, but the fact that no positive phenomenon or affirming negative is suggested in place of what is negated. A non-affirming negative can negate or exclude positive, negative, or non-existent phenomena. In Gelukba terms, therefore, Shastri's explanation is either confusing the object negated with the object suggested, or overlooking the fact that the terms expressing negative phenomena *may* both eliminate one thing and suggest another. The difference between affirming and non-affirming negatives in terms of suggestion is that the latter can suggest only another non-affirming negative in place of what is negated.

The view that Buddhism denies the existence of permanent phenomena such as non-affirming negatives is fairly common among modern scholars working from Indian traditions. Although it is not possible here to trace the history of Indian and Tibetan scholarship on this issue, it is worth noting that from the Gelukba standpoint a denial of non-affirming negatives would contribute to the misapprehension of Buddhism as nihilistic and anti-intellectual. Again, the denial of permanent phenomena is linked to what Gelukba would see as an overemphasis on the ubiquity of impermanent phenomena. The renowned scholar of Indian philosophy Karl Potter also sees a problem here:

> A ... difficulty we noticed in *apohavāda* [the theory of exclusions] was its tendency to reduce to anti-conceptualization; insight seemed to require giving up conceptual thinking altogether. But the Buddhist was forced to this because he refused to admit universals, and absences,

> [non-affirming negatives] into the external world. This conclusion is only necessary for someone like the Buddhist who believes in the momentariness of everything which exists.[10]

In this Gelukba framework, the explanation of negative phenomena — especially with respect to mental exclusions or meaning-generalities — is an integral part of the method set forth for cultivating and understanding subtle impermanence and selflessness. Far from being 'anti-conceptual' it signifies that conceptual thought has an important part to play in the path to liberating knowledge. The mental images used in this process are permanent in that they do not disintegrate from one moment to the next, but they do exist. Although the Gelukbas would corroborate the position Potter describes, namely, that universals are not asserted to exist in the external world in the sense that no universal pot, for example, exists apart from the instances of pot, it does not follow that they deny the existence of permanent phenomena as a class. In their presentations of the two truths, Gelukba writers clearly maintain that external negative and permanent phenomena such as uncaused space do exist. This tenet is a vital pillar of the proposition that emptinesses, which are themselves permanent, exist as phenomena to be known. This point in turn bolsters another central tenet: that cognition of emptiness or selflessness is not a mere drifting into nothingness — nihilism — but an actual cognition of a phenomenon which is a very specific type of absence. For example, when a meditator cognizes the selflessness of persons, it is said that he or she is not left merely with a vague sense of 'no-self;' this would indeed be nihilistic in its utter denial that persons and phenomena have any type of existence whatever. Rather, after having carefully conceptualized exactly what is to be negated — not persons and phenomena altogether, but some quality mistakenly imagined to inhere in them — the practitioner cultivates a cognition of the lack of that particular quality or type of existence. In Sautrāntika this means realizing that a substantially existent person does not exist; in Prāsangika-Mādhyamika, it means gaining direct realization of the lack of inherent existence.[11]

Potter is by no means the only well-known scholar to indicate, mainly on the basis of Indian material, that Buddhists in general deny the existence of permanent phenomena. Stcherbatsky also speaks of the concomitance of 'existence' and 'impermanent phenomena':

> Existence for them [the Buddhists] ... refers to the ultimate reality of the point-instant ... A non-existent or absent thing is imagination, it can produce no sensation directly.[12]

This position was well known in the post-Dharmakīrti Indian commentarial tradition. As M. Nagatomi notes, Ratnakîrti began his *Establishing the Category of Momentary Phenomena* (*Kṣaṇabhaṅgasiddhi*) with a reference to the "momentariness of all things":[13]

> ... being capable of (*arthakriyā*) [the] (ability to perform a function) is [a definition] known to everyone and is the only one framed to fit the word 'existence' that is amenable to proof.

Hattori points out that though Dignāga was unfamiliar with the concept of "the ability to perform a function" this became, with Dharmakîrti, a major factor in distinguishing specifically from generally characterized phenomena.[14] For the Gelukbas also, the capacity to function was considered the distinguishing feature of specifically characterized phenomena. However, the use of the word existent (*sattva*) as applying only to momentary or impermanent phenomena is foreign to them. In the Gelukba enumeration of phenomena[15] impermanent things are just one category among existents since this word (in Tibetan *yod pa*) includes permanent phenomena such as non-obstructive space or emptiness. Again, their intention to display a system in which the object of wisdom, emptiness, can be classified as a *phenomenon* (*dharma*, *chos*) necessitates that the capacity for functioning be applied only to certain existents, not to the category of existent phenomena itself. As mentioned in chapter one, according to the Gelukba formulation Sautrāntikas maintain that only impermanent phenomena are known to direct perception in the manner of casting an aspect toward the perceiving consciousness. The Gelukbas do not conclude from this that permanent phenomena in general do not exist or cannot be cognized. Moreover, although Sautrāntikas maintain that permanent phenomena cannot be cognized directly by a non-Buddha, this is not an assertion common to all Buddhist systems of tenets. In the Gelukba presentation of Cittamātra and Mādhyamika, emptiness — a non-affirming negative which is, therefore, a permanent phenomenon — can be cognized directly. Although Gelukbas would indeed agree with Stcherbatsky's statement that an absent thing such as a pot cannot act as a cause for direct sense perception, in the higher systems, a phenomenon such as emptiness — which itself *is* the lack of a specific type of self — can be directly cognized.

Summary

The goal set forth in all Buddhist systems of tenets is to go beyond an ordinary, ignorant and unduly binding perception of the world to an enlightened and liberating view. This entails the cognition of certain phenomena such as subtle impermanence and selflessness because understanding and direct perception of these phenomena act as an antidote which overcomes ignorance. Because these subtle phenomena are at present inaccessible to direct perception, the only recourse for a practitioner is to turn to thought, which is seen as able to develop and cultivate mental images of subtle impermanence and selflessness. These mental images are mental exclusions. The mental image of a table, for example, as impermanent involves a conceptual picture of momentary disintegration, the evocation of which serves to eliminate non-disintegration or permanence for thought. From this point of view such an image is most accurately described to be an appearance as opposite from non-permanence or opposite from non-disintegration. Through cultivating a mental image of subtle impermanence or emptiness, through making it more and more vivid, one can eventually realize the actual fact of impermanence or (in the higher systems) of emptiness in direct experience, no longer needing the medium of the conceptual image.

In order to build up a correct mental image of such subtle phenomena, it is necessary to rely on verbal description and analysis. It is essential to the Gelubka presentation of the path that words and reasoned contemplation be able to elicit correct mental images, and that the conceptual thought which has these as appearing objects does actually get at existent phenomena. Therefore, in order to investigate more fully the Gelukba claim that words and conceptual thought both relate to actual phenomena and that if properly used they can lead to direct perception — vivid experience — of such phenomena, it is necessary to grasp in more detail exactly how one learns to connect words or names with certain phenomena and the way in which words and thoughts relate to existent objects. In the following chapter, the relationship between words, thought, and external phenomena is investigated in light of the Gelukba interpretation of positive and negative phenomena.

8 Naming

Although direct perception and conceptual thought operate separately in their own spheres, most types of experience involve some collusion between the two and, moreover, most conceptuality derives from previous direct perception. The interconnection of these is discussed in the Gelukba presentation of how naming works, which details how thought makes possible a conceptual identification of what is seen in direct perception. This serves to indicate from a different viewpoint what the assertions on the two truths, on direct perception and conceptual thought, and on positive and negative phenomena also underscore: that interaction between conceptuality and non-conceptuality is such that the former, far from being antithetical to the latter, can enhance it in scope and subtlety.

How is it that, if a child learns to identify a '55 green Chevrolet as a car, he or she will also be able to recognize an '81 blue Oldsmobile as a car? What enables a person to generalize from one to the other? According to this presentation, such is possible because the generic image of a car that was formed in the child's mind during the original identification applies equally to all types of cars. This generic image will be mixed with a mental image of a specific car — perhaps the '55 Chevy that was originally identified. Although the image is mixed with that of a specific car, because it also represents a factor which all cars possess, it serves as a means of identifying all instances of cars.

Moreover, when one originally learned the name, the term 'car' was affixed not to the specific Chevrolet of the moment, but to the mental image of a car which then allowed one to distinguish car from non-car. The generic image itself is an appearance as opposite from non-car, whereby it can serve to represent everything that is not a non-car — in other words, everything that is a car. Every car is an instance of opposite-from-non-car, and just as there are individual instances of cars, so there are individual instances of opposite-from-non-car. It is not that there is a single entity of opposite-from-non-car which pervades all individual cars.

The overall Buddhist position on the relation of a mental image to particular objects is closely linked to the formulation of the relation between generalities and their instances. The Buddhist discussion of these issues, especially in Gelukba, is cast in part as a rebuttal to the non-Buddhist Indian Sāṃkhya school. The Sāṃkhya system asserts that a name is applied, not to a mental image, but to a partless generality which is present in every instance of, for example, a car. Thus, Sāṃkhya would maintain that through initially identifying the presence of the generality in one instance, a person is able later to identify all the various types of cars as 'cars.'

The Buddhist position, taking account of this earlier Sāṃkhya doctrine, contends that there is no car-generality which is a separate entity from its instances and which then pervades those instances. However, all cars are the same in not being non-car, or technically, in being opposite from all that is non-car. It is this factor which, upon being recognized, enables one to identify all cars of whatever size, shape, color, or condition as cars, and not confuse these with, for example, trucks. This presentation of naming and how it works is intended to establish that there is no need to posit a separate generality pervading its instances in order to account for the ability to apply the name learned with respect to one instance to other instances.

NAMES, CONVENTIONS, AND APPELLATIONS

Words or expressive terms,[1] as differentiated from meaningless sounds, have three distinct functions. Any word, depending on which function it performs at a given time, can be designated as a name, convention, or appellation. The term 'pot,' for example, is a name (*nāma*, *ming*) from the viewpoint that it leads or directs the mind to its object, a bulbous thing capable of holding fluid. The term 'pot' also has the function of bringing to mind the fact that because a pot is able to hold fluid, it is useful in pouring water, tea and so forth, and is not useful for other purposes such as holding up rafters (this being the function of a pillar). Thus, from the point of view that the term 'pot' not only directs the mind to an object but conveys a sense of that object's function, this term is known as a convention (*vyavahāra, tha snyad*).

A term such as 'pot' can only direct the mind to a certain object or impart a sense of a pot's function after one has learned to connect the name 'pot' with the correct object. This is something that must be taught. A baby or a non-English speaker would not, on hearing the word 'pot', either be led to think about a bulbous thing able to hold fluids or understand its uses. In order for conceptual thought to understand the meaning of words it is necessary for someone else to make the initial connection between a word and the object to which it refers. When such a term is connected to an object due to the namer's wish to teach another how the word is used, that term is called an appellation (*saṃketa, brda'*).

Because the single term 'pot' has all three of these functions, it is a name, a convention, and an appellation. However, it does not perform all three functions every time it is used; indeed, until the word is connected with an object, it does not perform any functions. Moreover, the word 'pot' only performs the function of an appellation the first time it is connected to an appropriate object for a person newly learning the term. In subsequent usage by a person familiar with the term it does not perform an appellation's unique function of making the initial connection between word and object, although it does function as a name and a convention because it directs the mind to the object and conveys a sense of that object's function.

Once the appellation has been connected — that is, once the name has been learned — one is able to use the convention to say or understand such things as "Bring me a pot." This is possible because the relationship between the name 'pot' and its meaning has been ascertained. Thus, a thought consciousness which has become capable of connecting a name with its appropriate object associates the name learned when the object was first identified with the object subsequently observed while using the convention. The word functions as a verbal convention, that is, it operates in conventional usage, only after the initial connection has been made.[2]

REASONS FOR APPLYING THE APPELLATION TO A GENERALITY

It is an observable fact that once a specific object has been connected with its name, the person who has learned the name will, in most cases, be able to recognize other objects of the same type as suitable to be designated by the same name. A child who has learned that a specific grey cat is called a 'cat' will understand that a black or calico feline is also called 'cat.' This ability to generalize is taken as a sign that when the name 'cat' was learned it was not understood to apply only to the grey cat present at that time. If it had been, the learner later would not be able to identify cats of different color or size as suitable to be called 'cat.' In the Buddhist view, such generalization is made possible by the fact that the name was initially applied, not to the specific grey cat, but to opposite-from-non-cat. All cats of whatever color or size are similarly opposite from non-cat and, therefore, can be recognized as suitable to be called 'cat.'

Thus, when learning the name, the word 'cat' is applied to a mental image that is an appearance to thought as opposite from non-cat. Nevertheless, the base of applying the name is an actual external cat. A mental image cannot perform the functions of a cat and would not be suitable as a basis for the name 'cat.' However, the meaning-generality which is an appearance as opposite from non-cat is the actual object of expression (*dngos kyi brjod bya*) of the term 'cat,' and the name is connected to that internal image.

Learning to identify a cat also means that one learns what a cat is not. When the name 'cat' is initially connected to the object, there is an elimination of what is not cat, and the name is applied, in a sense, to what is left over.[3] If that elimination is not done correctly, future usage of the term will be faulty. If a child who is told "That is a horse" takes the characteristics of a horse to be the possession of four legs, a mane, a tail, and a long face, the same child might later see a zebra and think it was a striped horse. This could come about because 'black and white stripes' were not among the characteristics eliminated at the time of learning the name horse. In order for the naming process to lead to correct usage of the convention learned, it must initially be applied to a mental image that correctly represents what is to be eliminated as *not* the thing so named.

Therefore, although the person explaining the name points to a specific grey cat in making the identification that "This is a cat," the name is *not* applied or connected to that specific grey cat, nor to the composite of grey cat and opposite-from-non-cat. Rather, it is connected to the image or meaning-generality (*artha-sāmānya, don spyi*) which is a conceptual appearance as opposite from non-cat.[4] However, it is the actual cat and not the image that is identified as a cat (*see table below*):

Table 5

NAME	OBJECT TO WHICH THE NAME IS APPLIED	OBJECT IDENTIFIED
cat	meaning-generality;here, a mental image of a cat	specifically characterized cat which is the basis of the name, i.e., the (impermanent) opposite from non-cat

Thus, although the grey cat is the basis of the process of naming, it is not the thing to which the name 'cat' is affixed. This is because the designator says, "This is a cat," and does not say, "This is a grey cat."

In order for the initial identification to be applied correctly, the learner must develop a general mental image which will apply equally to all instances of the thing being named. Otherwise, there will be error in subsequent use of the convention. The story is told that when the great Indian pandit Atīśa was travelling in Tibet he, not knowing Tibetan, pointed to a massive stone and asked its Tibetan name. He was told it was called a boulder. Sometime later a small pebble found its way into Atīśa's boot, and he told the group, "I have a boulder in my shoe." This error arose because when the appellation was initially given, Atīśa mistakenly connected the name 'boulder' with opposite from non-stone instead of opposite from non-*large* stone. Thus, he concluded that even a very small stone was suitable to be "called a boulder". The distinction between stone and boulder should have been made at the time of identification: "This is a stone; because it is a very large stone it is also called a boulder."[5]

An identification made with respect to a single instance allows one to recognize other instances of the same type because (1) an identification of, for example, 'cat' is made in connection with the opposite from non-cat and (2) because opposite-from-non-cat itself is a generality that applies to all instances of cat. Thus, identification by way of a single instance is sufficient. It will be possible for the learner to use the convention 'cat' with respect to calico cats even though calico cats are not present when the convention is learned. This possibility comes because the term 'cat' is connected to an appearance or mental image that represents the elimination of non-cat; that is, to a mental appearance as opposite from non-cat. Any particular cat is an instance of opposite-from-non-cat, and is therefore suitable to be recognized as a cat on the basis of such a mental image. Although the image of cat in general can be mixed with the appearance of a specific cat, the mental image does not depict a particular cat such as a grey cat but cat in general. Similarly, because the general name 'cat' and not the more limiting name 'grey cat' is applied to this image, it can function as a generality allowing one to identify correctly all instances of opposite-from-non-cat, whether they be white, black, calico, large or small.

The generality by which instances are understood is the meaning-generality — for example, the appearance to the thought consciousness as opposite from non-cat. This is explained by Den-dar-hla-ram-ba, using the example of a pot:

> ... when the appellation is [originally] connected, [as in] "This golden bulbous thing is a pot," one is connecting the terminology to the appearance as opposite from non-pot [which appears] to the thought consciousness apprehending pot.[6]

The Gelukba interpreters of Sautrāntika assert that when an identification is made connecting the term 'pot' with a bulbous thing, the appearance or image produced in the hearer's mental continuum is the appearance as opposite from non-pot or, to describe the same image from another point of view, an appearance as pot. In any case, this appearance is an image of a factor common to all pots, namely, their not being non-pots. A thing's being bulbous, flat-based, capable of holding fluids, and so forth is the sign of its being a pot; similarly, the debate texts state that an animal's being a composite of a hump, dewlap, and so forth is the sign of its being an ox; heat and burning is the sign that an entity is fire. In dependence on such a sign, a person connects the name with the object, thinking, "This bulbous thing is a pot." She or he thus becomes capable of using the convention 'pot.' This capability or knowledge is said to be a realization of pot. In this way, terms originally connected with mental images do relate to actual external objects.

Although it is the actual pot and not the image that is designated as a 'pot,' the impermanent pot is not the isolated explicit object of expression (*dngos kyi brjod bya 'i rang ldog*) of the term pot. An actual pot consists of the present shape, color, and so forth of the spout, handle, belly and other parts of a pot as these appear to the eye consciousness that perceives pot directly. The word 'pot' refers only to the composite of these parts, not to the specific elements that make up a pot. Like conceptual thought, a name gets at only one feature of a specifically characterized phenomenon. To say 'pot' implicitly eliminates non-pot and calls to mind non-non-pot. It evokes a generic image of a pot. It does not, however, evoke an image of the impermanence of a pot, nor of the handle, spout, color, specific size, and so forth of a pot. Therefore, it is impossible for a word to express or refer to a pot just as it exists.

Moreover, since pots are impermanent, subtly disintegrating from one moment to the next, by the time one comes to use the word 'pot' the *specific* moment of color and shape being referred to has already ceased. The fact that the Mongolian Gelukba scholar Den-dar-hla-ram-ba points this out is an indication that in terms of wholes such as pots — which are ultimate truths and specifically characterized phenomena in the system under discussion — 'whole' refers to the continuum of the momentary pot rather than to some gross extension of its continuum over time. Nevertheless, in dependence on terms one *can* realize specifically characterized phenomena. Den-dar-hla-ram-ba explains that only the meaning-generality is explicitly expressed by a term (*see table, p.195*): however, the object itself, such as a pot, is also expressed in the sense that Pur-bu-jok calls it the "object of expression," omitting the qualification "explicit." The meaning-generality itself — the appearance to thought as opposite from non-pot, for example — is the means by which one can recognize external things as pots, for a pot itself is opposite from non-pot. Because all pots regardless of shape, size, or material are opposite from non-pot, a person who has properly learned the name 'pot' can apply this name correctly to all of them.

HOW SIMILARITY OF TYPE IS PERCEIVED

A meaning-generality such as the image of a pot is a generality in the sense that its appearance as opposite from non-pot represents a factor which is present in every instance of pot. Such an image is *not* however a generality in the sense of being concomitant with the instances of that which it represents because an actual impermanent pot is not an image. Therefore, a mental image does not fit Pur-bu-jok's definition of a generality as "that which is concomitant with its instances"[7] in the sense that it does not apply to the various instances of the object it depicts. An instance, in turn, is defined as "a phenomenon having the [same] type of that which engages it as a pervader" [i.e., which is concomitant with it].[8] For example, a pot is a generality concomitant with all instances of silver, gold, and copper pot, for a silver pot is also a pot. From this point of view, a pot is a type-generality (*rigs spyi*) which is defined as "a phenomenon that is concomitant with many [phenomena] of its own type."[9] Roughly speaking, in order to use a term such as 'pot' or 'cat' or 'ox' correctly, it is not only necessary to apply this name to the proper mental image or meaning-generality, but to be able to recognize other phenomena of the same type to which the same name also can refer.

A proper understanding of a name and of the class comprised by the phenomena of similar type to which that name can later be applied requires understanding the typology implicit at the time of initially applying the name. For this reason, only persons adequately trained in the use of language can be the measure of whether or not any two or more phenomena are to be classified as belonging to the same type. A brief story illustrates why.

A clever man was having difficulty marrying off his daughter because she was considered uncommonly dull. In order to dispell this opinion, the father took her into the forest where there grew a rare tree known as a *pavonine tamāla*.[10] He taught her the name, which few others knew, intending that she would later identify it before a large group and thereby prove she was not dull. His daughter performed this successfully, but before the group could disperse, a dog ran up to her and the girl pointed to it saying, "This is a *pavonine tamāla*." Although she had learned the name, she had not learned to delimit the base to which it could be applied.[11] Not being trained in terminology, she was unable to identify correctly phenomena of the same type. She did not know what was excluded by the term.

DIFFERENCES BETWEEN SPECIFIC AND GENERAL TYPOLOGIES

It is commonly acknowledged that maple, oak, and fir trees, for example, are the same 'type' in that all are commonly recognized as trees, whereas pots and trees are not commonly seen to be of the same type despite both being products and forms. What is the basis for understanding types in this way? A maple and an oak tree are different substantial entities, just as a pot and a maple are different substantial entities. Yet, a mind of similar type commonly occurs with respect to the first pair but not the second. Therefore, the two trees are phenomena of similar type in general; the tree and pot are not, despite being the same type in that both are products. Den-dar-hla-ram-ba gives the following reason for positing certain phenomena as of similar type:

> Two phenomena are posited as one type [if] those trained in terminology *naturally* develop a mental conception of them as similar due to merely perceiving them by way of turning the mind [to them].[12]

Also, Pur-bu-jok speaks of phenomena similar in type as "appearing similar to the innate awareness of persons trained in terminology through their merely seeing them." Thus, even though pots and trees are both instances of impermanent phenomena and are products, they are not phenomena of similar type *in general* because one does not naturally conceive them to be so. The fact that they are of similar type in the sense of both being products and impermanent, therefore, does not make them of similar type in the broader sense.

If the fact of being opposite from the same thing, such as being opposite from non-product, were sufficient reason to consider the phenomena in question to be of one type, then all objects of knowledge — everything that exists — would be of one type. For, they are all equally opposite from non-object-of-knowledge. In the same way, all impermanent things from the coarsest forms up to and including the most subtle omniscient consciousness would be one type — for all are equally opposite from non-impermanent-thing. Therefore, the fact that a single exclusion can apply to a group of phenomena does not mean that a mind of similar type necessarily arises with respect to them. Although all existent phenomena are indeed one type from the viewpoint of being objects of knowledge, and although all products are the same type from the viewpoint of being impermanent things, this does not prove them to be one type in general because one does not naturally think of them as one type.[13]

WHY OBJECTS APPEAR SIMILAR IN TYPE

There are both internal and external reasons for certain objects appearing to be similar in type. The internal causes, in the Buddhist view, are a person's having been accustomed since beginningless time in countless past rebirths to applying a single word to designate oxen, for example, as a single type common to black, spotted, and other oxen.[14] Therefore, one is strongly predisposed to continue doing the same. Conversely, there is no such predisposition to consider ox and pot to be of similar type even though both are opposite from non-functioning-thing, opposite from non-object-of-knowledge, opposite from non-product, opposite from non-impermanent thing and so forth. Although both are the same type in being a functioning thing, object of knowledge, product, and so forth, they are not of the same type in general because one does not naturally think of them as the same type, there being no predispositions from the past to do so. This type of 'reasoning' tends to the circular, even if one grants the doctrine of rebirth. The second explanation of similarity is somewhat more compelling.

The external condition for perceiving similarity of type is said to be the visible similarity of shape shared by all oxen. Furthermore, black, spotted, and so forth oxen are the same in that all are equally the opposite of non-ox; that is, they are the same type of reverse or isolate (*ldog pa rigs gcig*). This is why the same type of mind arises with respect to them. This is colloquially analogized to the fact that whatever a human being's skin color — black, white, yellow, red, and so forth — the color of the shadow is always the same. There is no such thing as a yellow or red shadow. All shadows, just like all entities that are opposite from non-ox, are of the same type.[15]

The ability to understand correctly which phenomena are or are not of similar type, and in which contexts, is essential to the naming process. The correct designation of type relates to naming because the appellation is originally connected to a generality that applies to all phenomena of similar type; later use of the convention depends on being able to recognize other instances of that type, whether such discrimination comes naturally or not. For example, in order to apply the name 'ox' correctly it is only necessary to accord with what this system considers the natural inclination to see oxen as being the same type. However, in order to apply the name 'impermanent thing' correctly it is necessary to pass beyond natural impulse and distinguish phenomena that are in general of different type as the same type in the context of being impermanent.

In the case of oxen, the reason for applying the name is the presence of the various signs of being an ox — having a hump, dewlap, and so forth. These characteristics are said naturally to lead one to consider all animals possessing them to be of one type. Due to their being characteristic of all oxen, a person who has been taught to use the name 'ox' through initially connecting that name with a white ox as the basis is then capable of recognizing oxen of whatever color as belonging to the same category or type without needing to rely on any further reasoning or explanation.

NAME AND OBJECT

All names, like terms in general, are partial engagers (*sel 'jug*). Like thought, they do not operate in relation to all the factors which are of one entity of establishment and abiding with the object being designated. When the name 'cat' or 'pot' is spoken, for example, the object with respect to which that name operates — known more technically as the term's object of expression (*brod bya*) — is the actual cat or pot. An object of expression such as a pot has many features: spout, handle, colorful design and so forth. It is also characterized as being a product, impermanent thing, ultimate truth, specifically characterized phenomenon, and existent phenomenon. However, the term 'pot' does not refer to all these things individually, it refers only to the object which is a collection of these characteristics. The image of this is the word's *explicitly* expressed object. No one word could refer to all the specific qualities or aspects of any specifically characterized phenomenon.

Thus, a term such as 'cat' or 'ox' has two objects of expression, the actual chair or ox and the mental image that arises in the mind upon hearing that term. This is mentioned in Kay-drup's *Clearing Away Mental Darkness with Respect to (Dharmakīrti's) 'Seven Treatises'*:

> When the appellation 'ox' is connected taking a white ox as the basis, the two main objects of that appellation are (1) ox and (2) the [objective] exclusion opposite-from-non-ox. [These two, although different for thought, are one substantial entity.] Even though the meaning-of-the-term consists of the appearance of white ox *as* opposite from non-ox,

> [this] is the mere object of the appellation [and not the main one].[16]

This emphasizes Den-dar-hla-ram-ba's point, mentioned above, that it is the actual animal which is identified as, for example, an ox, even though the name is applied or connected to a mental image of that object on the basis of some specific ox. From this point of view, ox is the main object of expression of the term 'ox.' The other object of the term is the appearance as opposite from non-ox.

Table 6

NAME	EXPLICIT OBJECT OF EXPRESSION	MAIN OBJECT	BASIS
ox	the meaning-generality or mental image which is an appearance to thought as opposite from non-ox	ox opposite from non-ox	white ox
white ox	the meaning-generality or mental image which is an appearance to thought as opposite from non-white-ox	white ox opposite from non-white-ox	Sam's white ox

Thus, when the name of a phenomenon is initially learned, both thought and direct perception are involved. In the case of identifying an ox, one directly perceives the color and shape of a specific ox. The composite of hump and dewlap fully appears to direct perception. The terminological connection is made conceptually. Later, in dependence on seeing these limbs (*yan lag*) or segments of the ox, one recognizes the presence of an ox. (Since the ox is a being or person, it is not form and thus is not an object of apprehension of the eye consciousness, but there is no contradiction in an ox or another person's being directly seen by the eye consciousness because it is possible to see phenomena which are not technically objects of apprehension; if it were otherwise, it could not be said that persons can be seen directly.)

In the context of the Gelukba presentation of a path that uses verbal reasoning to refine conceptual thought as a means of generating deep understanding, it is essential to maintain that although words cannot conjure up all the richness of direct experience, words do express actual objects and do not just relate to internal images of them. This is the philosophical equivalent of having your cake and eating it too. Various Gelukba writers have slightly different ways of doing this.

According to Den-dar-hla-ram-ba the meaning-generality is explicitly expressed, whereas the actual object is not explicitly expressed, except in the sense that an actual pot can be obtained in dependence on the internal image. He says that *in this sense* it can be asserted that the actual object is explicitly expressed. According to Jang-gya, the meaning-generality is the self-isolate — the unspecified entity — of the explicit object of a thought consciousness though the actual object can be an explicit object of thought. He also says that the meaning-generality is the self-isolate of the basis of engagement of a verbal convention whereas the object itself is an illustration-isolate, or particular instance, of the basis to which the verbal convention becomes affixed. The following chart illustrates how these two Gelukbas describe the relationship of the term 'pot' to the meaning-generality of pot and an actual pot:

Table 7

	MEANING-GENERALITY OF POT	ACTUAL POT
Den-dar-hla-ram-ba	explicitly expressed (*dngos su brjod pa*)[17]	not explicitly expressed (*dngos su ma brjod pa*), in a sense explicitly expressed (*dngos su brjod pa*), and not able to be explicitly expressed (*dngos su brjod mi nus pa*)[18]
Jang-gya	self-isolate of the explicit object of a thought consciousness (*rtog pa'i dngos yul gyi rang ldog*[19]	explicit object of thought (*rtog pa'i dngos yul*)[20]
	self-isolate of the basis of the verbal convention (*sgra'i tha snyad 'jug pa'i gzhi'i rang ldog*)[21]	illustration-isolate of the basis of engagement of the verbal convention (*sgra'i tha snyad 'jug pa'i gzhi'i gzhi ldog*)[22]

In this manner, these two scholars retain the cake of the Sautrāntika assertion that the explicit objects of expression of terms are meaning-generalities and at the same time enjoy preservation of a meaningful connection between impermanent objects on the one hand and words and thought on the other. (In a similar vein, Bel-den-chö-jay [41.1-3] says that although specifically characterized phenomena actually appear to thought, their entities do not fully appear.)

Den-dar-hla-ram-ba explains that the thought apprehending pot does not explicitly apprehend pot; it explicitly apprehends the meaning-generality. Yet it is necessary to assert that thought explicitly *realizes* pot since, as stated above, a specifically characterized pot is undeniably obtainable in dependence on such a consciousness.[23] A different way of expressing this same point — that thought does actually get at impermanent phenomena even though, technically, these cannot be appearing objects of thought — is to say that the term 'pot' has two explicit objects. The two are the meaning-generality of pot and pot. However, it is still not the *specifically characterized* pot that is an explicit object of expression, but pot's self-isolate.[24] In the same vein, Jang-gya quotes Kamalaśīla[25] as saying that a thought consciousness is indirectly related with the actual thing but is incontrovertible with respect to the meaning. All these explanations preserve the basic ability of terms and thought consciousnesses to engage with impermanent phenomena in a significant and — in terms of the path — potentially constructive manner.

GENERALITIES AND THE NAMING PROCESS

The presentation of generalities and instances specifically takes issue with the non-Buddhist Sāṃkhya school of Indian thought. In both systems, the explanation of how different instances are recognized as the same type and therefore suitable to receive the same name has to do with the relationship of these instances to their generality.

Buddhists and Sāṃkhyas agree that naming works because one recognizes as suitable to receive a certain name not merely the specific instance at hand, but a generality of that instance. (This type of naming is a case of learning the meaning of a name; for example, learning the type of entity that the word 'table' or 'ox' refers to; it is not a case of learning to apply the name 'Sarah' to a particular individual.) As Jang-gya writes, Buddhists and Sāṃkhyas agree that:

1. a base such as a spotted ox is a basis for [initially] connecting the appellation

2. having taken one basis as an instance and made the terminological connection, all [instances] are recognized
3. the connecting of an appellation is for the sake of [later] conventional [usage].[26]

Both have to solve the problem of how, despite the fact that a name is learned with respect to a particular instance such as a green '55 Chevrolet, a person who learns the name can later apply it, without further instruction, to other very different instances of the same class. If the name 'car' had been applied *only* to the specific Chevy then, because that particular car is no longer present when the convention is used, one would be unable to designate old Volvos or brand new Buick convertibles as 'cars.' Both Buddhists and Sāṃkhyas assert that making a terminological connection to a specific item such as a car allows one to recognize all instances of cars because the generality 'car' applies in the same manner to each of its instances. The Buddhists and Sāṃkhyas have different views, however, on the manner in which a generality applies to or is concomitant with its instances.

Buddhist View on Generality and Instances

The relationship between a generality and its instances is something imputed by thought; there is no physical or metaphysical pervasion of instances by a generality. Thus, the general appearance to thought as being opposite from non-pot which applies to all instances of pots is a mental imputation; there is no general pot one can point to, there are only the specific instances of gold, silver, and so forth pots. This factor of being a pot that applies to all instances is permanent, which in this system means that it does not disintegrate from moment to moment. When the eye consciousness observes a pot, it sees only the impermanent factors that are one substantial entity of establishment and abiding with pot; it does not perceive the permanent factors that are the same entity as pot; nor does it perceive the permanent generality factor, for direct perception takes as its appearing object only impermanent phenomena.

Generalities can be either permanent or impermanent. A pot is a generality, as is uncaused space which is concomitant with all instances of uncaused space in the west, east, and so forth. Whether the phenomenon which is a generality is permanent or impermanent, the factor applying to or concomitant with its instances is permanent.

In the case of a pot, this factor is an appearance as opposite from non-pot; it is an appearance representing the exclusion of everything that is not pot. When the name 'pot' is initially learned, that name is applied to this appearance. Because all instances of pot are also opposite from non-pot, one can recognize them all as suitable to be called 'pot' even though the *specific* feature of being opposite from non-pot that is present in one pot is not present in another. If the name had not been connected with something broader than just the specific instance of the pot present at the time of learning the name, then it would be impossible to use the verbal convention later. Sagya Paṇḍita states in his *Treasury of Reasoning*:

> Because individual specifically characterized phenomena
> Are limitless, an appellation cannot be [connected with each].
> Also, at the time of using the convention
> It is difficult to find the original specifically characterized phenomenon.[27]

If the appellation 'pot' explicitly expressed only a single specifically characterized golden pot, for example, then because the number and variety of pots are limitless it would be impossible to connect all of them with names.

In this way, the Buddhists can posit an explanation of naming and object-identification without positing a generality that is a separate entity from the instances with which it is concomitant. In their view, a generality is not a Platonic ideal separate from its instances; there is only a factor of similarity, imputed by thought, that corresponds to the specific characteristic of, for example, being opposite from non-pot, present in all instances of pots. There is no general or abstract pot existing apart from the specific instances of pots and no separate nature of potness that is somehow shared by all pots.

Sāṃkhya Views on Generality and Instances

The Sāṃkhyas posit a generality known as the nature (*prakṛti, rang bzhin*) or principal (*pradhāna, gtso bo*) that pervades all its instances. The pervasion is not, as with the Buddhists, said to be merely imputed by thought; it is the actual nature of things that, for example, the general tree-nature pervades all instances of trees. In this system, instances are seen as evolutes (*parināma, rnam 'gyur*) of that nature. Accordingly, oxen, for example, are said to evolve or arise from the ox-generality which in turn is a manifestation of the fundamental nature.

Buddhists maintain that the relationship between a generality and its instances is merely imputed by thought and, like Sāṃkhya considers a generality and its manifestations to be one entity, but in Sāṃkhya, this relationship is not merely imputed by thought. However, the ox-generality which is one substantial entity with all instances of oxen can also exist even if no instances exist. Thus, even if there were no oxen there could be an ox-generality containing the non-manifest-yet-to-be-evolved oxen within it.

The fact that oxen are evolutes of the ox-generality means that according to Sāṃkhya the identification or naming of 'ox' does not involve eliminating all that is not ox. Exclusion is not part of the process; all that is necessary is to identify the positive ox-nature present in all oxen. By contrast, the Buddhists consider that an identification of oxen is made through excluding all that is non-oxen; oxen are only known in relation to what are not oxen. Thus, unlike the Buddhists, the Sāṃkhyas do not posit a theory of exclusion in order to explain the naming process.

Buddhist Critique of Sāṃkhya

Sāṃkhya asserts that the general principal is partless and yet is fully concomitant with each of its instances. The fact that this generality is partless seems to signify that all of it pervades each and every instance; it is not a case of part of the pot-generality, for example, existing with one pot and part with another.

The Buddhist position is that a generality having parts does pervade its instances, it being merely imputed by thought to do so. In this way they avoid a difficulty for which Sāṃkhya is criticized, namely, that if the same partless generality pervades two separate instances, those instances must share an identical nature. The Sāṃkhyas would in fact agree that an oak and a cedar tree share the same tree nature. The Buddhists take this position to its absurd conclusion by maintaining that then it would follow that the nature of a cedar exists in an oak. This is untenable because, as the Buddhists emphasize, all impermanent phenomena abide as unmixed with other phenomena in terms of place, time, and nature. Mixture of place, time and nature is erroneously imputed by thought according to the Buddhists; Sāṃkhya, however, maintains that this is how things actually exist. Dharmakīrti in the first chapter of his *Commen-*

tary on (Dignāga's) 'Compendium on Valid Cognition' rejects this assertion in order to refute the Sāṃkhya tenet of a partless general principal that pervades all its instances:

> That entity possessed by a spotted [ox]
> Does not exist in a white one.[28]

In the Gelukba presentation of Sautrāntika, it would be unsuitable to consider that the nature or entity of one phenomenon exists in another phenomenon. In this view (1) there is no pervasive generality which exists apart from its instances and (2) the nature of phenomena is to be unmixed with any other phenomena. In other words, the specific characteristic of being a pot that exists in relation to a silver pot is not mixed with the specific characteristic of being a pot which exists in relation to a golden pot or another silver pot.

The Buddhists have another criticism of the Sāṃkhya view that a partless generality pervades its instances. Not only do they find this position difficult to posit in terms of the natures of the individual instances being mixed, but also in terms of the generality itself. The Buddhists ask, how can a single partless generality, such as Sāṃkhya asserts, be fully present in each and every instance? Either the generality would be many or the instances would be subsumed into a single, partless object. This would follow, they say, because Sāṃkhya considers it impossible to assert that only part of the generality inheres in any of its instances and in this sense holds that the generality is partless. Sāṃkhya maintains that the entire partless ox-generality, for example, inheres in each and every diverse instance of ox.

In the Buddhist view, Sāṃkhyas are correct to posit that generality and instance are one entity, but at fault in being unable to posit any difference between them at all. The Buddhists posit difference within sameness on the basis of their theory of exclusion. Although the generality pot and an instance of pot are one entity, they are different isolates — pot being opposite from non-pot and gold pot being opposite from non-gold pot. They are different opposites of the negative, or even more technically, opposite from not being one with pot and opposite from not being one with gold pot, respectively. These two are *not* separate for direct perception — one simply sees a pot which is gold. They *are* different for thought because thought can isolate a particular factor in relation to pot and focus only on it; thus one can think 'generality' or 'instance' with respect to a single pot. In the Buddhist view, these categories are merely verbal or mental designations; thus, it is not necessary to have different ultimate entities that correspond to each designation. In the Buddhist view, the Sāṃkhyas are unable to posit difference within sameness because they have no theory of exclusion and thus no assertions regarding the ability of thought to isolate certain factors contained within the same entity; they therefore consider generality and instance to exist in a single entity in the sense that the instances are evolved from the general nature.

Because Sāṃkhyas consider that the relationship between a generality and its instances is not merely posited by thought but exists by the power of those phenomena themselves, they maintain that the entire, partless generality is actually present in each of its instances. Indeed, this generality, as noted above, is partless precisely because it exists in its entirety wherever it is found. It is not that part of it is in one place and part in another. In the Buddhist view, the generality-factor of, for example, a pot is merely imputed by thought. Generalities are not necessarily partless because gross impermanent objects such as chairs or tables are also generalities. In any case, the Buddhist meaning of 'partless' differs from the Sāṃkhya usage. In the view of the former, to be partless does not mean to be partless in every respect. For example, minute particles of matter are spatially partless in Sautrāntika, but they do have parts in the sense of possessing the various factors of being a product, being impermanent, being a functioning thing and so forth. Thus, the Buddhists can posit even a spatially partless particle as a generality because its factor of being opposite from non-partless particle is concomitant with all other instances of spatially partless particles. This concomitance, however, is merely imputed by thought; it does not, as in Sāṃkhya, exist from its own side or by its own power. In this way, the Buddhist position claims to avoid the difficulties involved in positing that a single generality exists in all its instances.

Sāṃkhya View on Similarity of Type

Based on their different presentations of generalities, the Buddhists and Sāṃkhyas also have different explanations as to why minds of similar type arise with respect to, for example, maple and oak trees. As noted above, the Buddhists maintain that because both maple and oak are trees — that is, both are opposite from non-tree — and because of predispositions formed by earlier naming, a mind conceiving of 'tree' arises with respect to each. Sāṃkhyas, however, would say that oak and maple are recognized as being of similar type because the tree generality which is a positive phenomenon dwells in or is present in both. A pot and a tree are not naturally seen as similar in type because the tree-generality is not present in both. However, since there are some generalities such as impermanence and productness that are present in both pots and trees, it would seem that according to Sāṃkhya one would necessarily generate a mind seeing these as the same type, provided the initial identification of impermanence or productness had been made.

Sāṃkhyas further say that the fact of a single generality dwelling in both maple and oak trees proves the existence of the partless generality. For, they argue that there must be some cause for understanding the individually separate entities of maple and oak as being of one type, since, if there were no such cause, this type of understanding would not arise. Consequently, they hold that there exists a single cause which is the agent for the production of various individual effects of similar type such as different types of trees. Moreover, in the Sāṃkhya view it is unsuitable to posit anything other than the tree-generality as such a cohesive cause of its instances. The maple and oak are manifestations of that tree-generality. Prior to their manifest production both trees existed in non-manifest form within the tree generality. At that time they were one substantial entity with the tree-generality and after production they continue to be one substantial entity with that generality. Production, according to Sāṃkhya, is not a case of creating a new, separate substantial entity but rather a manifestation of an entity that previously existed in non-manifest form within the general nature. Although the tree-generality can exist separately from manifest trees because it is theoretically possible for all such trees to dissolve back into the tree-generality, that tree-generality is never separate from the potential for manifesting trees. In other words, it is always one substantial entity with non-manifest trees. Moreover, when the manifest tree appears to direct perception, the tree-generality also appears.

This markedly contrasts with the Buddhist view that the factor which applies to individual trees — the tree-generality or factor of being opposite from non-tree — may be imputed by thought and thus not appear to direct perception. Thus, Sāṃkhyas describe the naming process as a matter of identifying the single nature — a positive phenomenon — which pervades all instances. For Buddhists, naming involves eliminating all that is not the thing being named — for example eliminating non-ox — and connecting the name with a mental image — the appearance as opposite from non-ox — that corresponds to a negative phenomenon which exists with every instance of oxen; that is, to opposite-from-non-ox. The theory of exclusion and the ability to posit negative phenomena thus allows the Buddhists to describe the naming process without positing a positive generality that even in theory could exist separately from its manifest instances. In this way, they avoid the difficulties mentioned above.

The theory of exclusions also enables the Buddhists to posit difference within sameness; to assert that a single substantial entity can contain qualities or factors which are isolatable by thought.

PHENOMENA AS INEXPRESSIBLE

According to Gelukba, the Sautrāntikas consider all impermanent phenomena such as trees or oxen to be ultimate truths. Such phenomena can appear in all their richness of detail only to direct perception. Thought can realize these phenomena but cannot apprehend all the specifics that characterize them. Similarly, words cannot fully express impermanent phenomena, cannot evoke all the constituent aspects of, for example, a table.[29] An image of a table is the explicit object of expression of the term 'table' according to Den-dar-hla-ram-ba. It is to this image that the name 'table' was applied when one initially learned the term. However, it was not the *image* which was being identified as a table but an external object with four legs, a flat top, and so forth. Similarly, at the time of using the convention 'table', although the explicit object of expression is the image evoked by that term, the object to which the name refers and which is the main object of expression of that term is an actual table. Thus, ultimate truths — impermanent phenomena — though they cannot be *fully* expressed by words, are expressed by words. The inexpressibility of such phenomena simply means that words cannot evoke an understanding of any impermanent phenomenon, however ordinary, in all its detail. When we say 'table' we do not refer to 'product', 'impermanent thing', or 'specifically characterized phenomenon.' The name 'table' refers only to the collection-generality table. It does not refer to or operate with respect to these other factors even though they are all necessarily present together in one substantial entity.[30] Thus, a term is a partial engager (*sel 'jug*) that refers to only some of the factors coalesced in any one object. When direct perception sees a table, for example, it sees all the factors involved with it: the factors of impermanence, its momentary disintegration, its productness and so forth. Thus, direct perception is a collective or complete engager (*sgrub 'jug*) that operates with respect to all the factors which are of one entity of establishment and abiding with the observed object.

Terms or names can never be complete engagers. Therefore, even though a person may directly perceive the object named, the name itself operates with respect to only the collection-generality — in this case, the table itself — and not with respect to a table as an ultimate truth, specifically characterized phenomenon, and so forth. Thus, words and thought pale in comparison with direct perception.

It should be noted that although it is considered essential and religiously significant to realize the coarse and subtle impermanence of phenomena, this is not, in the Buddhist view, the most profound fact that one can realize about them. It is even more helpful to understand things as empty; that is, in terms of the Sautrāntika path, to realize them as selfless in the sense of not being used by substantially existent persons; one comes to this understanding by realizing that substantially existent persons do not exist.

Sautrāntika emphasizes that although words cannot fully describe impermanent phenomena nor thought take them as appearing objects, words and thought do significantly get at such phenomena. Similarly, although words do not do full justice to a description of emptiness — whether the emptiness of a self-sufficient self taught in Sautrāntika, or the more subtle emptiness of inherent existence in Mādhyamika — they do point the way. Just as specifically characterized phenomena are inexpressible in Sautrāntika, the emptiness taught in Mādhyamika is inexpressible also. Yet, just as words can be used in the process of cultivating an understanding of subtle impermanent phenomena nor thought take them as appearing obemptiness. That words cannot evoke a conceptual realization of these phenomena that has all the clarity of direct perception is seen as less important than that through gaining familiarity with the meaning of those words one is actually taking the first steps along the road that culminates in full-fledged direct perception. The first time one hears an explanation of subtle impermanence or emptiness — and perhaps for many times thereafter — one may well be left with little more than a verbal echo in one's mind. The Gelukba structure of the path is based on the premise that the effects of words and of the thoughts they induce are by no means limited to such meager benefits. Like beginning with an outline on canvas and then coloring it in with various shades and variety of detail, one can start with a mere term-generality and cultivate a more and more refined and evocative mental image until, finally, the picture comes to life, as it were, when both the term and meaning-generalities fade away and conceptual thought itself evolves into direct cognition. Gelukba may be unique in its willingness to wed so closely a vigorous and extensive scholastic tradition with a highly refined meditative technique for the overall purpose of transformative realization. This welding of the conceptual and non-conceptual elements of the path to liberating knowledge is founded on the conviction that the inexpressible can be discussed sufficiently well to give rise to factually concordant conceptual consciousnesses that can then be enriched into direct perception.

Frederick Streng notes that "Nāgārjuna [whose systemizations of the *Perfection of Wisdom* sutras are the basis for Mādhyamika] used the term emptiness with a keen awareness of the problems involved in expressing the inexpressible ..."[31] Similarly, in terms of the Sautrāntika presentation, the inexpressible is expressible to a significant enough degree to make such expression worthwhile. At the same time, the limitations of words and thought must be understood. To use words for any specifically characterized phenomenon — never mind for emptiness — is to talk about 'the inexpressible.' The message from Gelukba is not to expect too much from words, that is, not to expect the full measure of direct insight to arise from them, but not to underrate them either. In this view it would be unfortunate to conclude that because a complex discussion of impermanence or emptiness initially calls forth only minimal understanding, all conceptuality will always remain at that level.

The Sautrāntika presentation of naming and the relationship posited between a generality and its instances, as given here, is also accepted by the Cittamātrins and Mādhyamikas according to Gelukba. Their presentation underscores the tenet that words and thought do indeed relate to actual phenomena. Existent phenomena such as tables or chairs, but more importantly impermanence and selflessness, *can* be expressed by words to a degree sufficient for paving the way to direct perception and non-dualistic understanding. Further evidence set out in Sautrāntika to emphasize this possibility is discussed in the following chapter.

9 *Conclusion: Conceptuality and Non-Dual Wisdom*

Gelukba written and oral traditions emphasize a collaboration between scholarship and meditative experience. These have the common purpose of enabling a scholar-practitioner to achieve a non-conceptual realization that, when accustomed to over a long period and combined with other factors, leads to liberating knowledge. Only such a vivid and direct cognition of impermanence and selflessness is capable of destroying the ignorance which Buddhists see as the source of cyclic existence and all its sufferings. Moreover, an analog to the liberating non-conceptual cognition of a yogi already exists in ordinary non-conceptual sense perception.

Progress toward such realization is said to have three broad phases: hearing, thinking, and meditating. Both hearing and thinking, as well as many stages within meditation, involve various levels of conceptuality. Whereas the earlier stages of hearing entail mainly term-generalities — words devoid of much meaning — and also include, in the Gelukba tradition, many years of sometimes dry debate, there are far more subtle forms of conceptuality. The shimmering mental image of, for example, momentary disintegration, that appears as if spontaneously to the accustomed mind in meditation, or a correct space-like image of emptiness, is also conceptual. These various modes of conceptual thought are stages on the way to direct perception, which is by definition non-conceptual and can even be, in the case of a direct cognition of emptiness, non-dualistic. Among religious philosophies of the world, it is not unusual to depict the human mind as capable of conceptual and non-conceptual experience; what is unusual, perhaps, is to harness the former in service of the latter. The Gelukba presentation of the two truths and the minds that cognize them, of the mental exclusions by which thought operates and, most importantly, their description of the method by which direct experience of impermanence and emptiness can be gained, are based on the principle that conceptuality and direct perception are not only compatible but mutually enhancing.

To carry this argument further, it is well to review some of the main Gelukba tenets on the workings of conceptuality. As elaborated in Sautrāntika, thought knows actual objects by way of an image that serves to exclude everything other than the represented object. This image may or may not be noted in the course of ordinary activity. A meaning-generality may be an identifiable mental picture or may even be a simple abstraction that serves to eliminate a class of objects. Because any meaning-generality, however abstract, serves the purpose of excluding everything other than the represented object, it is most accurate to describe the image of, for example, a table, as an appearance as opposite from non-table. This description of mental images takes account of the fact that, once familiarity with an object is gained, there is no need consciously to eliminate what is not that object in order to reflect on it; it is as if the thing itself simply appears to the mind. Nevertheless, if one investigates the manner in which this image — however abstract — operates, it is to eliminate all that it does not represent.

That an image of a table eliminates what is not a table may be insignificant given the ease with which ordinary persons can recognize or recall a table. However, to say that thought operates in the manner of excluding what is not its object becomes highly significant when it comes to a more subtle object of reflection such as selflessness. To use Sautrāntika terms in the context of cultivating the view of emptiness, the way that one becomes acquainted with the meaning of selflessness is by carefully building up a mental image — an understanding — of the 'self' which is to be negated. One must identify the object of negation before one can know the non-affirming negative selflessness which is nothing other than the absence of that misconceived 'self.' Selflessness or emptiness is difficult to realize because its metaphysical space is a hair's breadth between the two overriding tendencies of any ordinary conceptual thought grappling with this concept: either nihilistically to eliminate objects entirely or to reify them too strongly. In the context of Sautrāntika, one must be careful to delineate the substantially existent person negated from the insubstantial person which does exist. In other words, one must conceptually exclude the self-sufficient person without excluding the impermanent person that in Sautrāntika is an ultimate truth. In such a case, the significance of correctly eliminating all that is not the object — that is, all but the mere impermanent person qualified by lacking self-sufficiency — becomes a more complex procedure than merely eliminating, for example, non-table.

The technique of making an identification through eliminating all that is other than the object identified is an ancient one. The pre-Buddhist Indian Upanishads 'describe' the ineffable Brahman with the words "*neti, neti*"[1] — not this, not this, eliminating verbally all the things that Brahman is not. In Buddhist sutras, nirvana is frequently alluded to as what is not — namely, as unconditioned. The conceptual *via negativa* or negative route is a route to the unseen. Thought, operating along this route, is the branch of awareness by which one can learn to ascertain what is not apparent to direct perception. The ability to eliminate what is not the object may not be particularly significant when it is just a matter of learning to distinguish tables from chairs, but is absolutely essential in learning to understand the unseen, final nature of phenomena which, according to the highest tenet system, is unconditioned and empty of a specific object of negation. This nature is inaccessible not only to ordinary direct perception but to untutored thought which has not learned precisely what must be eliminated before this truth can be realized. In using reasoning to get at the subtle emptiness taught in Mādhyamika, one must first of all carefully identify in terms of one's own experience exactly what is negated by the view of selflessness. One must in fact cultivate one's own sense of self — for example, get a clear sense of the feeling of 'I' that arises when one is suddenly accused or harmed. This sense of an inherently existent 'I' is the self to be negated. Such an identification must be done very carefully and clearly; it is perhaps the most crucial and difficult step on the way to developing an inferential cognition of emptiness. In this case, the process of realizing emptiness is a kind of slow motion enactment of what goes on routinely in the course of identifying ordinary things. In coming to know anything one also — implicitly and simultaneously — identifies what that thing is not. To know a chair is to eliminate non-chair. Emptiness is so subtle a phenomenon that it is not immediately apparent just what is to be negated; therefore, this must be identified in a separate step that precedes cognition of emptiness itself.

Although the process of negation may be a necessary part of identifying or understanding both ordinary and very subtle phenomena, if it were not the case that words and thought involved in such a process are able, respectively, to express and realize actual phenomena — impermanence or emptiness — the Gelukba presentation of the path to liberating knowledge would fall apart. Therefore, a vital sub-topic of the presentation of positive and negative phenomena and how consciousnesses perceive them is the discussion of how a conceptuality engendered by words can actually realize phenomena and, with respect to impermanence in Sautrāntika and emptiness itself in Mādhyamika, yield to direct perception of these very entities. In order to uphold these assertions, it is emphasized that a word or phrase has both an internal image and an external phenomenon as its objects of expression.

The Gelukba position on Sautrāntika agrees with modern scholars who interpret Dharmakīrti to assert that the mental images elicited by terms are affirming negatives or mental exclusions and that these are the explicit objects of expression of a term (or at least explicitly expressed by a term — the latter distinction being made by Den-dar-hla-ram-ba). However, the Gelukba position does not agree with modern scholars who take the explicit object of expression to be a term's *only* object of expression. Mookerjee brings this idea to its logical extreme, concluding that "The Buddhist denies ... that words contain an objective reference."[2] This would indeed be the case if a mental image were a term's only object of expression but, according to Gelukba, it is not. Mookerjee says further that "The Buddhist maintains that words have no reference to reality in any sense. Words in their opinion deal with concepts [images] and these concepts are purely subjective constructions."[3]

Similarly, Barlingay writes, "The Buddhist theory of *Apoha* [exclusion] cannot point to the original thing."[4] Shastri takes this train of thought a step further:

> The external real [cow] ... and the thought image [cow] are absolutely different, and there is not the slightest similarity or affinity between them.[5]

This is not the Gelukba assertion. In their view, existent or 'real' objects can actually be apprehended through the medium of an image. As mentioned earlier, it is precisely because the image pertains to *both* the thought consciousness perceiving it and the external referent object that such an appearance is known as a meaning-*generality*. It thus partakes of both the thought consciousness and the represented object. Thus, words are indeed seen as referring to the original thing, that is, to actual impermanent objects, and not merely to mental constructs. Furthermore, Gelukbas point out that an actual pot and the term 'pot' have the relationship of actually expressed object (*dngos kyi brjod bya*) and agent of expression (*rjod byed*) and thus possess some sort of connection, albeit through common usage. In short, words do have objective referents.

Thus, terms have two objects of expression: the explicit object of expression being the mental image evoked by the term and the mere object of expression (*brjod bya*) being the actual object, for example, a pot. In this way it is asserted that words and thought do relate to objective reality. The Gelukbas note that an appearance of a pot to thought is not as clear as an appearance of a pot to direct perception, but they would not agree with Sharma and Mookerjee who use this reason to deny that words relate to external reality because they do not evoke the "full-blooded experience of the objects to which they refer."[6] In the Gelukba view, the fact that an experience evoked by a word or thought image is not as vivid as direct experience does not indicate a lack of relation between word and object. Rather, it is emblematic of the difference between thought and direct perception. Thought is general and less vivid. It gets at instances of specifically characterized phenomena only through taking as an appearing object a generality that partially mirrors those instances.

All thought (*kalpanā, rtog pa*) operates by means of an elimination of that which is discordant in type from its object. It is a mind of eliminative or partial engagement (*sel' jug gi blo*) whereas direct perception is a mind of collective engagement (*sgrub 'jug gi blo*) because it observes — even if it does not notice — all the features of a given object.

Thought engages its object in a partial manner because, for example, the word 'table' expresses only part of the composite of qualities that is a table; it does not express — nor does the thought it engenders cognize — the table's color, impermanence, material, specific shape and so forth. Also, when an image of table in general appears to thought, there is a blurring of area, time, and nature.

Thought takes these three aspects with respect to all tables as if they were identical; however, tables, like all specifically characterized phenomena, each have their own unique features of area, time, and place. On the other hand, when a particular table appears to direct perception, all its individual characteristics, even down to the tiny particles composing it, also appear. Even its momentary impermanence appears.

Though ordinary beings do not ascertain subtle momentary disintegration, it is considered possible for them to develop a mental image of momentary impermanence. By building up such an image and clarifying it, one can come to ascertain a direct perception of subtle impermanence. Such is possible in part because the words describing momentary disintegration and the thought apprehending a mental image of this do actually relate to the phenomenon of momentary disintegration. This relationship would be impossible if Gelukba posited an unbridgeable gulf between words and reality. It would also not be possible except for the fact, discussed in more detail below, that the nature of mind or awareness (*buddhi, blo*) is such that conceptuality can transform itself into direct perception. Furthermore, although the Sautrāntika presentation makes it clear that thought is unable to fully perceive specifically characterized phenomena, it also carefully points out that thought has an important place on the path. If one presumed that because thought is unclear and limited it is useless, or that because direct perception apprehends every aspect of its appearing objects it alone is sufficient, one would not appreciate the possibility of mental development espoused by this system. Direct perception is hampered by a lack of ascertainment — of noticing what appears to it — and thought, despite being obstructed with respect to a clear and vivid appearance of impermanent things, is the instrument whereby one can cultivate ascertainment of what appears unnoticed to direct perception.

The Gelukba presentation of Sautrāntika does not merely deny an unbridgeable chasm between thought and impermanent phenomena; on the positive side, it asserts that conceptual thought actually does realize such objects. Gyel-tsap, one of the two chief disciples of Tsong-ka-pa, founder of the Gelukba sect, makes the point that thought is mistaken because it cannot see the actual mode of abiding — the momentariness, productness and so forth — of specifically characterized phenomena[7] but that all thought is not equally mistaken. He draws the example that whether one mistakes the light of a jewel to be an actual jewel, or the light of a lamp to be so, one is mistaken in apprehending what is not a jewel to be a jewel; yet, through following the light of the jewel, one can eventually apprehend the jewel itself, whereas through following the lamplight, one cannot.[8]

The thought which mistakes the light of the jewel to be a jewel in this example is analagous to factually concordant thought (*rtog pa don mthun*). The thought which apprehends the body as impermanent is such a factually concordant thought. The thought which apprehends the body as permanent is not factually concordant and so is like mistaking lamplight for a jewel. Both thoughts are mistaken in that they take as their appearing object a general image which is irretrievably fused with the appearance of an impermanent phenomenon; thus, they are mistaken in confusing specifically and generally characterized phenomena as well as blurring the specific characteristics of place, time, and nature. However, the thought which apprehends the body as impermanent is a means for getting at actual impermanence and therefore is essential to the path. The thought apprehending the body as permanent is neither correct nor useful on the path.

Gyel-tsap examines the doubt that because the appearance to a thought consciousness cannot, in the case of a pot, perform the function of, for example, holding water, the thought observing it is necessarily utterly deceived with respect to the specifically characterized pot because it perceives only the general image, not the actual pot.[9] Gyel-tsap points out that it would then absurdly follow that the term expressing a 'pot' would give rise to a conceptual mind observing an image that does not correspond to any actual phenomenon. In other words, although correct thought is indeed mistaken (*bhrānti, 'khrul ba*) with respect to the image in terms of the specifics of place, time, and so forth, it is not also deceived (*slu ba*). This is because 'deceived' here means to be factually discordant which in turn signifies that the image appearing to thought does not correspond to any specifically characterized phenomenon. Thought, however, is a subject — a consciousness — that does get at specifically characterized phenomena (*rang mtshan thob byed kyi yul can*).[10] Moreover, although thought does not directly depend on a specifically characterized phenomenon in the manner of direct perception, it does depend on the object indirectly, because it derives from remembered direct perception.[11]

The Sautrāntika texts define awareness or mind as "clear and knowing."[11] The higher systems agree that this is the very entity, the nature, of all types of minds, conceptual and non-conceptual. Thus, conceptuality and direct perception are not merely compatible in terms of the potential of one to enhance the other, but their basic nature is the same. With this in mind, it is not surprising that Gelukbas should maintain with such vigor the possibility of conceptuality yielding to direct perception. This is not so much a case of making a leap over a chasm as of a shift from one mode to another.

The division of mental images into term-generalities and meaning-generalities indicates the great range of conceptual experience: gradations that approach closer and closer to direct perception. When one hears a word one does not know, the term-generality that appears to the mind is a mere echo of that name, conveying no sense of the meaning. If images evoked by words were always as dry as this, any system would be hard put to claim that hearing and thinking were an essential part of a path to liberation. However, once the meaning of words is understood, the image evoked by them increasingly takes on life and clarity. One progresses from the mere echoing in the mind of the words 'subtle impermanence' to a mental image — a meaning-generality — of subtle impermanence that is mixed with the term-generality; that is, one associates the actual meaning of momentary disintegration with the term 'subtle impermanence.' At this point, one has progressed from a conceptual consciousness apprehending only a term-generality to one apprehending both term and meaning-generalities.

In this way, the image that arises upon hearing the phrase 'subtle impermanence' for the first time will be meaningless compared to the meaning-generality that arises after one has investigated the reasonings and descriptions of subtle impermanence. On first hearing the term, one might think of subtle impermanence as merely some hard-to-find characteristic of finitude locked within an object. Then one learns it refers to the momentary disintegration of all impermanent phenomena. This is refined further by understanding that phenomena produced from causes are unable to last a second moment by their own power, that all products are impermanent because they are produced through the power of causes other than themselves. From the very first moment they lacked the ability to sustain themselves. Even though in Sautrāntika impermanent phenomena are said to have their own power in the sense of not being merely imputed by thought, they come about only through the force of other phenomena. They have no power to remain as they are.

Through such reflection the image of subtle impermanence becomes increasingly clear and correct. As familiarity develops, the sense of its being named 'subtle impermanence' drops away, and one is left only with an image of momentary disintegration. At this time, the mental chattering which says "Oh, this is impermanence, this is changing, this can never stay the same," and so on has ceased. Only the meaning-generality — the mental exclusion of non-momentary disintegration — is there. This is still conceptuality, however, because the mind is not operating on the basis of an aspect cast toward it, but apprehends a mental image that has been coaxed forth from one's own mind. Nevertheless, as the image becomes clearer and clearer, the conceptual mechanism maintaining it operates less and less, until it is no longer a case of the mind throwing out an image but of impermanence itself fully appearing in all its aspects. This is direct perception.

If one has cultivated a stable and heightened mind and then uses this mind to take subtle impermanence as an object of thought, then when the image component fades away, one has a yogic direct perceiver that directly cognizes subtle impermanence. Whereas a conceptual consciousness does not take on the aspect of its object but issues up an image of that object, a direct perceiver has the feature of taking on or being generated in the aspect of its object. In this case, the yogic direct perceiver takes on the aspect of impermanence. However, whereas in sensory direct perception the eye consciousness, for example, depends on the aspects of color and shape that are cast toward it, the yogic direct perceiver does not depend on or have as its base the aspect of subtle impermanence. Such a yogic perceiver does take on the aspect of impermanence, but its base is calm abiding (*śamatha, zhi gnas*) and special insight (*vipaśyanā, lhag mthong*), that is, meditative stability and penetrative understanding.[13]

Selflessness or emptiness, being permanent, cannot be directly cognized according to Sautrāntika. In the higher systems such a permanent phenomenon can be cognized directly, and the final antidote to ignorance is in fact said to be a direct cognition of what these systems describe as the ultimate truth, emptiness. The Mādhyamika system describes a yogic direct perceiver's direct and non-dualistic cognition of emptiness as being like fresh water poured into fresh water; subject and object — the mind and emptiness — are fused as if one. This description epitomizes the very antithesis of conceptuality. Yet, Gelukba stresses again and again that a correct non-conceptual realization of emptiness begins with a factually concordant conceptual consciousness. In the stages preceding this direct cognition, one learns what is to be negated and studies the reasonings by which the inherently existent self, the innate conception of which is asserted to be the root cause of cyclic existence and its attendant sufferings, is refuted. Emphatically, in this system, an understanding of emptiness is not seen as merely a matter of divorcing oneself from conceptuality. It requires patient cultivation of a specific understanding which is then brought to the level of direct experience. As in the case of realizing impermanence, one progresses from a mere term-generality — dry words — to an apprehension of term and meaning-generalities as mixed, to an apprehension of only the meaning-generality of emptiness itself.

Emptiness is a non-affirming negative, a mere absence of an inherently existent self that never did exist but, until its absence is actually cognized, is deeply conceived to exist. To realize emptiness is to realize the lack of such a self. For the sake of attaining this understanding, one investigates, in prior stages of study and practice, the hypothetical characteristics of this self to be negated. When the mind has attained sufficient stability and clarity, this non-affirming negative — selflessness or emptiness — can be perceived directly. At that time, one has a yogic direct perceiver which non-dualistically, like fresh water poured into fresh water, is mixed with this emptiness. As in the case of a direct perception of impermanence, the uncommon dominant condition of this special mind realizing emptiness is a union of calm abiding and special insight.

Emptiness cannot be realized directly unless the mind is extremely sharp and steady. When cultivation of calm abiding and special insight has ripened the mind sufficiently, the fading away of the last residues of the meaning-generality or image of emptiness is simultaneous with the onset of direct perception. At this time, the yogic direct perceiver, a non-conceptual mind and a positive phenomenon, takes on the aspect of emptiness, a non-affirming negative. One may speculate that just as the eye consciousness takes on the image of its object in such a way that it is impossible to separate that consciousness from the aspect in which it is generated, so in the case of yogic direct perception it is impossible to distinguish the mind from the aspect of emptiness into which it has been generated. One important difference is, perhaps, that because the eye consciousness actually depends on the aspect being cast to the object and is in that sense an effect of that objective aspect, the relationship of object and consciousness as cause and effect necessitates that sensory perception be dualistic. In the case of yogic direct perception, however, the aspect of emptiness is not a cause of the yogic direct perceiver, even though yogic direct perception does take on the aspect of emptiness in observing it. In the absence of a cause and effect relationship between this very special object and subject, there is no theoretical difficulty in positing an experiential union of subtle emptiness and the mind that cognizes it.

The fact that the Gelukba presentation of tenets sees both conceptual and direct minds as having an important role in the attainment of liberating knowledge means that a considerable variety of techniques can be employed. All the intelligence, resourcefulness, scope, and agility which conceptuality encompasses can be brought to bear on the religious endeavor. Conceptuality — from rigorous scholastic debate to the cultivation of subtle mental images — is seen not as an impediment but as a necessary auxilliary to non-dualistic experience. By understanding the profound compatibility between thought and insight, one can have confidence that what begins as a mere echo of sound in the mind can progress to actual direct experience. The starting point is precisely the ordinary type of conceptuality and direct perception one now has. Thus, the main import of Sautrāntika is its articulation of the structure of the mind and its potential for development. Understanding this, one whose main goal is a non-dual experience or a liberating realization can become willing to persevere through the stages of highly refined conceptualization on which that experience is based.

SARVA MAṄGALAM

Notes

After the first notation abbreviations are used for several books. In alphabetical order, with the number of the note bearing the full entry, they are:

Annotations	Chapter I, note 56
Den-dar-hla-ram-ba	I, 19
Dharmakīrti	Introduction, 30
Dignāga	Introduction, 12
Gomang	I, 22
Gön (Gön-chok-jik-may-wang-bo)	I, 5
Gyel-tsap	I, 25
Jam-yang-shay-ba	I, 56
Jang-gya	I, 4
Knowing, Naming, and Negation	Introduction, 11
Meditation on Emptiness	Introduction, 11
Mind	Introduction, 15
Practice and Theory	I, 4
Pur-bu-jok	I, 24
Ra-dö	I, 33
Vasubandhu	I, 2

Entries in the Tibetan Tripitaka Research Foundation publication of the Tibetan Tripitaka [Tokyo-Kyoto, 1956] are followed by the entry number. See Bibliography for full Sanskrit and Tibetan titles.

NOTES

INTRODUCTION

1. Stephen Katz, ed., *Mysticism and Philosophical Analysis* (New York: Oxford University Press, 1972) See especially Katz, "Language, Epistemology, and Mysticism," pp. 25-26.
2. Frederick J. Streng, *Emptiness, A Study in Religious Meaning* (New York/Nashville: Abingdon Press 1967), p. 149.
3. For a discussion of the differences between meditation and mystical experience see Robert Gimello, "Mysticism and Meditation" in *Mysticism and Philosophical Analysis*, p. 170 ff.
4. H. H. Tenzin Gyatso, the Fourteenth Dalai Lama, audience, July, 1977.
5. For a discussion of specific symbols of the ultimate, see Anne Klein, "Non-Dualism and the Great Bliss Queen" in *Journal of Feminist Studies in Religion*, Vol. 1, January 1985. See also Klein, "Primordial Purity and Everyday Life: Exalted Female Symbols and the Women of Tibet" in Atkinson, Buchanan and Miles, eds., *Immaculate and Powerful: The Female in Sacred Image and Social Reality* (Boston: Beacon Press, Harvard Women's Studies in Religion Series, 1985), especially pp. 124-135.
6. Katz, p. 26.
7. More specifically, these dualistic patterns are named, in the Mādhyamika system, as the dualistic appearance of:

1) inherent existence	(*bden grub kyi gnyis snang*)
2) subject and object	(*yul yul can gyi gnyis snang*)
3) conventionalities	(*kun rdzob kyi gnyis snang*)
4) mental images	(*don spyi 'i gnyis snang*)
5) difference	(*tha dad kyi gnyis snang*)

These five, listed by Kensur Yeshay Tupden in oral commentary, are some of the facets of ordinary consciousnesses that are dissipated through the complementary implementation of analysis and concentration that characterizes Gelukba religious practice. All five vanish during direct perception of emptiness within meditative equipoise. At the stage of Buddhahood, when emptiness and conventional phenomena are for the first time cognized simultaneously and directly, the 2nd, 3rd, and 5th appearances are retained, although corresponding *conceptions* of dualism are absent.

The first and third types of dualistic appearances above are also mentioned in the Svātantrika chapter of Jang-gya's *Presentation of Tenets* (356.9). For a translation of this chapter see Donald S. Lopez, Jr., *The Svātantrika Mādhyamika School of Mahāyāna* (Ithaca, New York: Snow Lion Publications, forthcoming). Jang-gya also mentions a sixth type, "the dualistic appearance of something different from itself" (*rang las gzhan ba'i gnyis snang*).

8. "Mysticism and Meditation" in Katz, ed., *Mysticism and Philosophical Analysis*, p. 176.

9. See Tsong-ka-pa, *Tantra in Tibet*, tr. Jeffrey Hopkins, (London: George Allen & Unwin, 1977), pp. 189-200.

10. Chronology here as reported in A.K. Warder, *Indian Buddhism*, (Delhi: Motilal Banarsidass, 1970), p. 43.

11. The translation "true suffering" is here preferred over the more common translation of *duḥkha-satya/sdug bsngal bden pa* as "truth of suffering." The translation of this term as "true sufferings" is meant to emphasize that the four noble truths, like the two truths — ultimate and conventional — are not abstractions or principles, but *objects*. For the same reason the remaining three truths, origins, cessations, and paths, are similarly translated. For discussion of the two and four truths as objects, see Jeffrey Hopkins, *Meditation on Emptiness* (London: Wisdom Publications, 1983). For Jang-gya's discussion of the four truths see Anne C. Klein, *Knowing, Naming, and Negation* (Ithaca, New York: Snow Lion Publications, forthcoming).

12. Hattori, Masaaki, translator and annotator, *Dignāga on Perception*, Harvard Oriental Series ed. by Daniel H. H. Ingalls (Cambridge: Harvard University Press, 1968), p. 2-3. The teacher-student relationship between Vasubandhu and Dignāga cannot be definitively documented on the basis of Sanskrit sources; it is however a viable hypothesis. (See also Hattori, Section 2, n. 2.4. and Warder, p. 446).

13. For discussion of the relationship of Dharmakīrti's *Pramāṇavārttika*/*'Commentary on (Dignāga's) 'Compendium on Valid Cognition'* to Dignāga's *Pramāṇasamuccaya*, see Masatoshi Nagatomi, "The Framework of the Pramāṇavārttika, Book I" *Journal of the American Oriental Society*, Vol. 79, No. 4, Oct-Dec, 1959.

14. This date was suggested by E. Frauwallner in "Landmarks in the History of Indian Logic," *Wiener Zeitschrift für die Kunde des Süd-und Ost Asiens*, Vienna, BD. V (1961), pp. 125-128.

See also Hattori, *Dignāga*, p. 4. Hattori quotes Frauwallner and uses his dates, although elsewhere he opines the dates as 470-530 for reasons discussed in his article "Dignāga to sono Shūhen no Nendai" (the Dates of Dignāga and his Milieu), *Essays on the History of Buddhism presented to Professor Zenryu Tsukamoto on his Retirement from The Research Institute for Humanistic Studies*, Kyoto University, pp. 79-96.

15. In the Gomang College of Drebung Monastery, "The Collected Topics" are studied for four years; students then study "Signs and Reasoning" and "Awareness and Knowledge" for one year each. In Loseling College of Drebung Monastery, only one year is devoted to "The Collected Topics" and, as at Gomang, a year each is spent on "Awareness and Knowledge" and "Signs and Reasonings." Elizabeth Napper, *Mind in Tibetan Buddhism*, (Ithaca, New York: Snow Lion Publications, 1980), p. 161. It should be clear that the term "Gelukba" as it occurs throughout this text is not used in any divisive sectarian sense but to indicate that the sources under discussion were written by scholars who trained in Gelukba institutions, and in many cases are still used as textbooks in Gelukba Monastic Colleges. I also use "Gelukba" to signify oral commentary from contemporary teachers in Gelukba Colleges. Inasmuch as I work here almost entirely with texts written long after the founding of Gelukba institutions, there is little ambiguity. However, use of the term is not necessarily exclusive. Many tenets are shared in common with other orders but major distinctive features of Gelukba are of course noted. A thorough chronicling of shades of interpretation which are uniquely Gelukba — a fascinating topic for future study — is outside the scope of this book. For a discussion of some of the issues involved in considering Gelukba or any other Tibetan Buddhist order as a unit of discourse, see Leonard van der Kuijp, "Miscellanea Apropos of the Philosophy of Mind in Tibet: Mind in Tibetan Buddhism" *The Tibet Journal*, Spring 1985, Vol. X, No. 1, pp. 32-43.

16. See Nagatomi, "Framework", p. 1. See also Obermiller, "The Sublime Science of the Great Vehicle of Salvation, being a Manual of Buddhist Monism" *Acta Orientalia*, 9 (1931), p. 99.

17. No less an authority than Daniel H. H. Ingalls has bluntly stated, "the *Pramāṇasamuccaya* [of Dignāga] exhibits in exaggerated form the elliptical style that characterizes Sanskrit texts of philosophy ... [a style which is in part] resulting from the social cohesion of the Indian circles in which philosophy was discussed." Foreword to

Dignāga on Perception, translated and annotated by Masaaki Hattori, *Harvard Oriental Series* ed. by Daniel H. H. Ingalls (Cambridge: Harvard University Press. 1968) p. vi.

18. This is a commonly accepted view among scholars of Tibet. However, in a lecture at the American Institute of Buddhist Studies in Amherst, Massachusetts (July 22, 1985), Prof. Namkhai Norbu of the Instituto Orientale, University of Naples, Italy, made a forceful case for the existence of a written language known as Zhang Zhung prior to the time of the 8th century Buddhist king Song-tsen-gam-po. In Prof. Norbu's view, the Bön culture of Shang Shung was seen as a political threat by Song-tsen-gam-po and thus this early Tibetan king adopted Buddhism and attempted to eliminate all traces of Bön, an effort which included a reshaping of the language and a re-writing of history. This, Prof. Norbu suggests, is the origin of the idea that Song-tsen-gam-po and scholars working under his auspices originated writing in Tibet.

19. The name "Sautrāntika" is rendered in Tibetan as *mDo sde pa*. In Sanskrit, *mDo sde* is *sūtrānta* which it would seem does not refer just to the *sūtrānta-piṭaka* but to sutras in general.

20. Kensur Yeshay Tupden, oral commentary.

21. They are thus sometimes known as proponents of Sautrāntika-Cittamātra. See Stcherbatsky, *Buddhist Logic*, Vol. 2, p. 370, n. 3.

22. See Nagatomi, *Framework* p. 264 and n. 14.

23. For a further explanation of yogic direct perception, see Napper, *Mind*, especially pp. 19-20; 63-64.

24. The word 'phenomenon' here is not used in the technical sense of Western philosophy or phenomenology. The Kantian distinction between objects and events as they appear in experience versus objects and events as they are in themselves is not intended. This type of distinction is of course important in Buddhist thought but does not in any way center around use of the word *dharma* or *chos* here being translated as 'phenomenon.' This word is also not intended here in its post-Hegelian synonymity with 'fact' inasmuch as the erroneously presumed facticity of the ontological status of ordinary and extraordinary phenomena is a major focus of Buddhist analysis. The word 'object' would be a reasonable equivalent of this meaning of *dharma*; however, 'object' is being used throughout to render *viṣaya* or *yul* which more particularly signifies phenomena in the context of their relationship to a perceiving consciousness.

25. See Dhirendra Sharma, *The Differentiation Theory of Meaning in Indian Logic*, (The Hague: Mouton, 1969), p. 27: "... it is this conceptualized world that is referred to by words ... since the word cannot refer to the *external* object, it refers to a concept which is formed by observation of similar and dissimilar cases." See also, Satkari Mookerjee, *The Buddhist Philosophy of Universal Flux*, (Delhi: Motilal Banarsidass, 1975) [First edition published by University of Calcutta, 1935] p. 108: "Words ... deal with concepts and these concepts are purely subjective constructions."

26. Mookerjee, *Ibid.*, pp. 107-108.

27. F. Th. Stcherbatsky, *Buddhist Logic*, 2 Vols. (New York: Dover Publications, Inc., 1962) I: 181-182.

28. *Ibid.*, p. 181.

29. Sharma, *Differentiation Theory*, pp. 10-11.

30. Dharmakīrti, *Commentary on (Dignāga's) 'Compendium on Valid Cognition'* (*Pramāṇavārttika*), P5709, Vol. 130, 88-3-5 [Chapter III. verse 3].

31. Dharmakīrti, P5709, Vol. 103, 78-5-6.

CHAPTER ONE

1. Tibetan tradition does not explicitly distinguish the Vasubandhu who authored the *Treasury of Knowledge* (*Abhidharmakośa*) from the Vasubandhu known as the author of *The Thirty* (*Triṃśikā*) and *The Twenty* (*Viṃśikā*). Western scholars however are familiar with the two-Vasubandhu theory especially as elaborated by Erich Frauwallner, *On the Date of the Buddhist Master of the Law Vasubandhu*, Rome: Istituto Italiano per il Medio ed Estremo Oriente, 1951. Frauwallner concluded that Vasubandhu the elder brother of Asaṅga, lived in the 4th century A.D. (p. 46) whereas Vasubandhu the younger, author of the *Abhidharmakośa*, lived in the 5th century A.D. (p. 53). For a comprehensive summary of other literature on this topic, see Sukomal Chaudhuri, *Analytical Study of the Abhidharmakośa* (Calcutta: Calcutta Sanskrit College Research Series No. CXIV), pp. 21-25.

2. Vasubandhu, *Explanation of the Treasury of Knowledge*, (*Abhidharmkośabhāṣya*), P5591, Vol 115, [Chapter VI, verse 4].

3. Dharmakīrti, P5709. Vol 130, 88-3-5 [Chapter III, verse 3]. Nagatomi translates the last sentence of this segment as follows: "These two [objects] are respectively the 'particular' and the 'universal.' The terms 'particular' (*svalakṣaṇa*, *rang mtshan*) and 'universal'

(*sāmānyalakṣaṇa, spyi mtshan*) are here rendered as "specifically characterized phenomenon" and "generally characterized phenomenon." Neither the Sanskrit nor the Tibetan term contains the adverb "specifically"; this is incorporated into the present translation equivalent based on the Gelukba explication of these terms. For example see Den-dar-hla-ram-ba, *Presentation of Specifically and Generally Characterized Phenomena* (*Rang mtshan spyi mtshan gyi rnam gzhag*) 158.3 (cited in note I. 19). He states that *svalakṣaṇa* or specifically characterized phenomena are so-called because "when they appear to the direct perceiver which directly perceives them they have [specific] characteristics which appear without depending on the appearance of other phenomena."

Jang-gya in "The Sautrāntika Tenet System" section of his *Presentation of Tenets* (*Grub mtha' rnam bzhag*) 98.16 ff (cited note I.4) defines an ultimate truth, which he explicitly takes to be synonymous with specifically characterized phenomena, as "that which is able to bear reasoned analysis by way of its own mode of subsistence without depending on imputation by terminology or thought." Denma Lochö Rinbochay expresses a typical Gelukba position in glossing "able to bear analysis" as meaning that the object casts its aspect — that is, the aspects of its various particular or specific characteristics — toward the perceiving consciousness. See "Jang-gya: The Two Truths" in Klein, *Knowing, Naming, and Negation*.

4. Jang-gya, *Grub pa'i mtha'i rnam bzhag*, (Sarnath, Varanasi: Pleasure of Elegant Sayings Press, 1970) p. 98.17; Gön p. 31-32; Sopa and Hopkins *Practice and Theory of Tibetan Buddhism* (London: Rider and Co., 1976), p. 94.

5. See "Jang-gya: The Two Truths" in Klein, *Knowing, Naming, and Negation* (This and other texts translated in Klein, *Knowing, Naming, and Negation* appear correlated with Tibetan numbering given here; the book's own pagination is not available as this volume goes to press); see also Sopa and Hopkins, *Practice and Theory*, p. 93, Gön-chok-jik-may-wang-bo (*dKon-mchog-'jigs-med-dbang-po*), (*Grub pa'i mtha'i rin po che'i phreng ba*) *Precious Garland of Tenets* (Mundgod, India: Dre-Gomang Buddhist Cultural Association, 1980); Gön p. 32.

6. *Practice and Theory* p. 94, Gön p. 33; see also "Jang-gya: The Two Truths" in Klein, *Knowing, Naming, and Negation*; Jang p. 98 and 99.

7. That consciousnesses are ultimate truths in the Gelukba for-

mulation of Sautrāntikas Following Reasoning is explicit in the Gomang *Collected Topics* and implicit in the *Collected Topics* of Ra-dö and Pur-bu-jok respectively. In the context of establishing that coarse or continuous entities are specifically characterized phenomena, it is argued that consciousnesses which are a continuum of former and latter moments are specifically characterized "because they are ultimate truths." It is further established that consciousnesses are ultimate truths "because they are actually comprehended (*dngos gzhal*) by direct valid cognizers." Gomang, p. 405.5-15.

8. *Mind*, p. 28; p. 163, note 24.

9. Dignāga, *Compendium on Valid Cognition* (*Pramāṇ-samuccaya*) v. 3c. See also Hattori, *Dignāga*, p. 25 and pp. 82-83, n. 1.25 and 1.27.

10. Kensur Yeshay Tupden, oral commentary.

11. When Prāsaṅgika uses the term *pratyakṣa* or *mngon sum* to refer to a consciousness (as opposed to referencing an object which is "before the eyes") a direct perceiver simply signifies a cognizer that does not depend on a sign.

12. In Cittamātra, where external objects are denied altogether, things are empty of existing as they appear in another sense. Gön, 51.3 states that "form is empty of being established by way of its own character as the referent basis of a thought which apprehends form" (*gzugs gzugs 'dzin rtog ba'i zhen zhir rang gi mtshan nyid kyis grub pas stong pa*). See also *Practice and Theory*, p. 117.

13. Stcherbatsky, "Every existence without exception is represented by the focus of efficiency, the point-instant ... Every stability, every duration is, on the contrary a[n unreal] construction ..." (Vol. I, p. 121). Also, Mookerjee, "All reals are momentary point-instances ..." p. 285. Also, Sharma, *Differentiation*, "In the Dignāga-Dharmakīrti school ... *svalakṣaṇa* [specifically characterized phenomenon] ... is the extreme point-instant ... it is the ultimate real, for it alone is efficient." p. 37.

14. See Hattori, *Dignāga*. p. 25(3c).

15. Hattori, *Dignāga* pp. 26-27 (verse 4cd); for the Tibetan, see pp. 178-79, and for the Sanskrit, p. 3 of Sanskrit appendix (verse Daa-1). See also Hattori, *Dignāga*, pp. 89-90, n. 39 and n. 40.

16. For example, Hattori and Nagatomi, in their work on Dharmakīrti use 'particular'; Stcherbatsky and Sharma use "point-instant."

17. Stcherbatsky, Vol. II, p. 35, (Dharmottara 13.6).

18. Stcherbatsky, Vol. II, p. 7, *Buddhist Logic*, commenting on Dharmottara's statement, apparently in support of external objects, that "... right knowledge is knowledge which points to reality, (a reality which) is capable of experiencing purposive action. (4.1.).

19. Den-dar-hla-ram-ba (*bsTan-dar-lha-ram-pa*) b. 1759, *Presentation of Generally and Specifically Characterized Phenomena* (*Rang mtshan spyi mtshan gyi rnam gzhag*), *Collected gSung 'bum of Bstan-dar-Lha-ram of A-lag-sha*, Vol. 1, (New Delhi: Lama Guru Deva, 1971) 158.3 ff. Translated by Anne C. Klein in *Knowing, Naming, and Negation*, (Ithaca, New York: Snow Lion Publications, forthcoming).

20. Treasury (*Abhidharmakośa*), VI. 4; *Compendium* (*Pramāṇa-samuccaya*) v. 4cd, "*Pratyakṣa*" chapter.

21. Hattori, *Dignāga*, pp. 79-80.

22. Nga-wang-dra-shi (*Ngag-dbang-bkra-shis*), *The Collected Topics by a Spiritual Son of Jam-yang-shay-ba* (*Sras bsdus grva*), (n.p. n.d.) p. 404. 9-405.2 [Available at PL 480 Libraries].

23. Tsong-ka-pa, *Door of Entry to the Seven Treatises*, (*sDe bdun la 'jug pa'i sgo*) (Sarnath, Varanasi: Pleasure of Elegant Sayings Press, 1972), p. 8.8.

24. See Pur-bu-jok, "The Lesser Path of Reasoning" from *The Presentation of the Collected Topics of Logic* (Buxador: n.p., 1965), p. 19. 1-4. Four types of isolates are mentioned: meaning-isolate (*don ldog*), illustration-isolate (*gzhi ldog*), generality-isolate (*spyi ldog*), and self-isolate (*rang ldog*). The meaning-isolate of a thing is its definition; the illustration-isolate, an illustrative instance of that thing. For example, the meaning-isolate of functioning thing is "that which is able to perform a function"; an illustration-isolate of a functioning thing is a particular pot. Generality-isolate and self-isolate are synonymous and refer to, for example, the mere pot focused on by a thought consciousness that does not conceive of any particular pot or even of the meaning of pot.

25. Gyel-tsap, *Explanation of (Dharmakīrti's) "Commentary on (Dignāga's)* 'Treatise on Valid Cognition'" (Sarnath, Varanasi: Pleasure of Elegant Sayings Press, 1974) Vol. I, p. 78.7.

26. Dharmakīrti, P5709, Vol. 130, 78-5-6 (Chp. I, v. 40).

27. See Pur-bu-jok, *Collected Topics*, 8.6-9.3. The debate presented here centers on disproving that whatever is an existent (*yod pa*) is necessarily impermanent because the subject of the debate,

unproduced space, does exist and is permanent. See also *Meditation on Emptiness* for charts on the divisions of phenomena.

28. I am indebted to Prof. Nagatomi for this observation. See *Treasury of Knowledge* (*Abhidharmakośa*) Chapt. I. 4-6 for discussion of space as permanent.

29. See *Treasury*, Chapter 9 for refutation of eternal deity; also *Meditation on Emptiness*, p. 326-7; also Dharmakīrti, *Pramāṇasiddhi* Chapter II. 10-11 for argument against an eternal valid cognizer; also, v. 25-26 for refutation of a causeless (and eternal) God acting as a cause.

30. See Jang-gya *Tenets* on impermanent phenomena, 105. 17 ff. Translated in Klein, *Knowing, Naming, and Negation.*

31. Dharmakīrti states: "Because all things naturally abide in their own entity/They possess dependence on reversal from other things" (P5709, Vol. 130. 78-5-6; I. 40). In commenting on this, Lati Rinbochay made the connection between "abiding in its own entity" and being "not mixed." However, although permanent phenomena are said to *abide* unmixed, they, unlike impermanent phenomena, *appear* as mixed.

32. For example, Pur-bu-jok 14. 1-2 defines a specifically characterized phenomenon as "that phenomenon which is established by way of its own nature without being merely imputed by terms or thought" (*sgra rtog gis btags tsam ma yin par rang gi mtshan nyid kyis grub pa'i chos*). See also Den-dar-hla-ram-ba 158.2 for a similar definition (both tr. Klein, *Knowing, Naming, and Negation.*

33. Jam-yang-chok-hla-ö-ser (*'Jam-dbyangs-phyogs-lha-od-zer*) 15th-century, *Collected Topics of Ra-dö* (*Rva stod bsdus grva*) (Dharamsala, India: Damchoe Sangpo, Library of Tibetan Works and Archives [printed at Jayyed Press, Ballimaran, Delhi], 1980) p. 10.3.

34. *Ra-dö*, 9.3-4.

35. Pur-bu-jok, "The Lesser Path of Reasoning" in *Collected Topics*, 12.3.

36. *Ibid.* 11.6.

37. *Ibid.* 11.5.

38. *Collected Topics of a Spiritual Son*, 405.15 ff.

39. *Practice and Theory* p. 94; Gön p. 33.

40. "Jang-gya: The Two Truths" *Knowing, Naming, and Negation*; Jang-gya p. 99.

41. Den-dar-hla-ram-ba, 159.2ff.; "Den-dar: Specifically Characterized Phenomena" tr. in *Knowing, Naming, and Negation.*

42. Kensur Yeshay Tupden, oral commentary.

43. Kensur Yeshay Tupden, oral commentary.

44. Sāṃkhya itself does not claim *pradhāna* is indivisible; the Buddhists force them to this position in debate on the basis of the Sāṃkhya assertion that *pradhāna* is partless. Compare this argument with Plato's "Parmenides." For example, Parmenides tells Socrates, "You say you hold that there exist certain forms, of which these other things come to partake ... then each thing that partakes receives as its share either the form as a whole or a part of it? Or can there be any way of partaking besides this? ... Do you hold that the form as a whole, a single thing, is in each of the many, or how? [If form is in each of the many] a form which is one and the same will be at the same time, as a whole, in a number of things which are separate, and consequently, will be separate from itself." From the Buddhist perspective, the entire section of "Parmenides" offers a stimulating analysis of the relation of the generality and the particular, and of the nature of 'one' and 'many.' Plato, *The Collected Dialogues*, Edith Hamilton and Huntington Cairns, eds., (New York: Bollingen Foundation, 1966), Bollingen Series LXXI, p. 925 ff.

45. This requires some qualification. Gön-chok-jik-may-wang-bo says that the five Saṃmitīya sub-schools of Vaibhāṣika do assert a substantially existent or self-sufficient self. *See Practice and Theory*, p. 82. Jang-gya also mentions this fact and states that in terms of their view, the Saṃmitīya sub-schools are like non-Buddhists because they assert a substantially existent self. *See Presentation of Tenets*, (Sarnath, Varanasi: Pleasure of Elegant Sayings Press, 1970), p. 78.19.

46. Source for this and the following paragraph is the Gomang textbook by Nga-wang-dra-shi, *The Collected Topics by a Spiritual Son of Jam-yang-shay-ba*, pp. 217-24.

47. *rdzas chos* can also mean a "substantial phenomenon" in contrast to a "reverse phenomenon" (*ldog chos*). In this context Pur-bu-jok defines a substantial phenomenon as: that which is observed as a common locus of (1) being an established base, (2) being itself, (3) what is not itself not being it and (4) its own isolate not being contradictory with a substantial phenomenon. For presentation and debates on this topic, see Pur-bu-jok, "The Lesser Path of Reasoning," 41.3 ff.

48. Gomang, pp. 223-224.

49. See *Practice and Theory*, p. 104; Gön, p. 38.6. Also, "Jang-

gya: The Two Truths" tr. in Klein, *Knowing*; Jang-gya, *Tenets* 121.7 ff.

50. According to Gelukba presentations of tenets, Yogācāra-Svātantrika-Mādhyamikas also maintain that persons and phenomena are the bases of emptinesses. However, the object negated is different. The object negated in the selflessness of phenomena is true existence (*satyasiddhi, bden grub*); the objects negated in the coarse and subtle selflessness of persons accord with the Sautrāntika presentation respectively: the lack of a person's being permanent, partless, and independent (*rtag gcig rang dbang can*) and the lack or emptiness of a person's being substantially existent or self sufficient. (*rang rkya grub ba'i rdzas yod*). The Sautrāntika-Svātantrika-Mādhyamikas agree, except that according to them (as in Sautrāntika itself) those firm in the Hearer (*śrāvaka, nyan thos*) and Solitary Realizer (*pratyekabuddha, rang sangs rgyas*) lineages do not realize the selflessness of phenomena. See *Practice and Theory*, pp. 126-7 and 131; also, Gön, 59.1 and 63.15. Also, *Meditation on Emptiness* pp. 299 ff.

51. *dbU ma la 'jug pa'i rnam bshad dgongs par rab gsal* (Dharmasala: Tibetan Cultural Printing Press, n.d.) p. 75.14.

52. *Ibid.* 75.16.

53. Jang-gya, 98.17.

54. The terms "eye," "ear" and so forth are used for ease of expression; the consciousness is not considered to originate from a fleshy sense organ as such but arises due to three causal conditions: (1) a subtle internal form (*nang gi gzugs can dwrang ba*) which is the consciousness' uncommon dominant condition (*adhipati-pratyaya, bdag rkyen*), (2) an observed object condition (*ālaṃbana-pratyaya, migs rkyen*) that is to say, the sense object; (3) a previous moment of consciousness which is the immediately preceeding condition (*samanantara-pratyaya, de ma thag rkyen*).

55. Thanks to Prof. Nagatomi on this point.

56. Quoted and discussed by Jam-yang-shay-ba in *Great Exposition of Tenets* (*Grub mtha' chen mo*), Folio printing in India, n.p. n.d.) 308.3; see also p. 230, n. 7.

57. Bel-den-chö-jay, *Annotations for (Jam-yang-ṣhay-ba's) 'Great Exposition of Tenets' (Grub mtha' chen mo'i mchan 'grel)* (Sarnath, Varanasi: Pleasure of Elegant Sayings Press, 1964), *dngos* 73.8.

58. Jam-yang-shay-ba, 309.6.

59. Pur-bu-jok, "The Lesser Path of Reasoning" 38.6-39.1 defines a generality as "A phenomenon concomitant with its own

instances" (*rang gi gsal ba la rjes su 'gro ba'i chos*). (See also Daniel E. Perdue, *Debate in Tibetan Buddhist Education*: Doctoral dissertation, University of Virginia, 1982, p. 856). Pur-bu-jok notes that in terms of how they are expressed, generalities are of three kinds: type generality (*rigs spyi*), meaning generality (*don spyi*) and collection generality (*tshogs spyi*). The meaning-generality is a mental image, as discussed in chapters one and four. A type generality is defined by Pur-bu-jok (39.1) as: a phenomenon concomitant with many [other objects] of the same type (*rang gi rigs can du ma la rjes su 'gro ba'i chos*). A collection generality is defined (39.3) as "A coarse form which is an aggregate of its many parts" (*rang gi cha shas du ma 'dus ba'i gzugs rags ba chos can*).

60. Hattori, *Dignāga*, p. 24.

61. See Hattori p. 78, end of n. 1.11; also, n. 1.14 pp. 79-10 for how this statement counters the Nyāya position. See also Stcherbatsky, *Buddhist Logic* Vol. II, 301. ff.

62. Pur-bu-jok, "The Lesser Path of Reasoning", 14.1.

63. *Ibid.*, 14.2.

64. Geshe Belden Drakba, oral commentary.

65. Den-dar-hla-ram-ba, *Presentation of Specifically and Generally characterized Phenomena*, Vol. I. 159.4.

66. Lati Rinbochay, oral commentary.

CHAPTER TWO

1. Dharmakīrti, P5709, Vol. 130., 88-3-3. See also Dak-tsang 124.3 *Ocean* and 14.1 Root text to *Ocean*: The reason why water, pot, and so forth are conventionalities is [given in the root text where it says]: "Water, pot, and so forth are unable to perform functions as ultimate objects, for whereas that" which is an object ultimately able to perform a function from its own side must be "asserted as a self-characterized actual object which generates an unmistaken [mind] apprehending it, these "— pot and so forth —" are conventional things, mental phenomena which depend on internal factors such as nomenclature. (Tr. Hopkins, unpublished ms. "Dak-tsang" p. 2-3; quote marks indicate phrases excerpted from root text. See Bibliography for full entry.)

2. Jang-gya, 98.17.

3. Vasubandhu, P5591, Vol. 115., (Chapter VI. verse 4).

4. Thanks to Prof. Nagatomi for this observation.

5. Dak-tsang, *Ocean* 125.6.

6. Jam-yang-shay-ba, *Great Tenets* 308.3.

7. Jam-yang-shay-ba quotes the Tibetan thus in *Great Tenets*, 308.3:

[51] a) *don byed nus pa gang yin pa*
b) *de ni rang gi mtshan nyid 'dod*

He appears to be referring to the *Pratyakṣa* Chapter verse 51.ab. However the Tibetan (P5709 89-2-4) there reads [preceeding three lines added for context]:

[50] b) *don byed par yang mi rung ngo*
c) *de mi rung phyir rang bzhin med*
d) *de ni dngos med mtshan nyid yin*
[51] a) *ji skad bshad las bzlog gang yin*
b) *de ni rang gi mtshan nyid 'dod.*

Line 51.b above is identical to Jam-yang-shay-ba's; 51.a above is worded completely differently but has the same meaning as Jam-yang-shay-ba's 51a. It is striking that Jam-yang-shay-ba's highly observant commentator, Bel-den-chö-jay (in *Annotations* 73.5ff.) does not mention that Jam-yang-shay-ba is giving the *meaning*, rather than the actual reading, of this line.

It is also possible that Jam-yang-shay-ba simply means to condensedly indicate 51.a thru 57b, which latter is identical to Jam-yang-shay-ba's second line above: *de ni rang gi mtshan nyid 'dod* (P5709 89-2-4 thru 89-2-5). (Thanks to Gareth Sparham on this point.)

8. Dharmakīrti, P5709 Vol. 130, 88-3-5.

9. Dak-tsang, *Ocean of Good Explanations*, Jeffrey Hopkins, unpublished translation, p. 6-7; *Grub mtha' kun shes*, Tibetan text, 126.6.

10. Dak-tsang, Hopkins translation, p. 7; Tibetan text, 127.1.

11. Kensur Yeshay Tupden, oral commentary; Sagya Khen Rinbochay Jamyang Shayrab, in conversation in Mundgod, South India, 1980.

12. See Den-dar-hla-ram-ba 159.3 ff., tr. in Klein, *Knowing, Naming, and Negation.*

13. See Jam-yang-shay-ba, *Great Tenets* 309.3 ff.; Bel-den-chö-jay, *Annotations* 73.5. ff.

14. Bel-den-chö-jay, *Explanation of the Meaning of Conventional, and Ultimate in the Four Systems of Tenets* (*Grub mtha' bzhi'i lugs kyi kun rdzob dang don dam pa'i don rnam par bshad pa legs bshad dpyid*

kyi dpal mo'i glu dbyangs) (New Delhi: Guru Deva, 1972), p. 46.4 ff.

15. Dharmakīrti, P5709, 88-4-2; quoted by Bel-den-chö-jay, *Ibid.*, 46.2.

16. Bel-den-chö-jay, *Ibid.*, 46.3 ff; translation from Jeffrey Hopkins and John Buescher, unpublished manuscript.

17. Bel-den-chö-jay, *Ibid.*, 46.7 ff. *and* Nagatomi, "*Arthakryā*," 56.

18. Leonard Zwilling, "Saskya Paṇḍita's Version of *Pramāṇavārttikam* III. 3 — A Case Study on the Influence of Exegesis upon Translation in Tibet" in *Studies in Indian Philosophy*, L.D. Series 84, Dalsukh Malvania and Nagin J. Shah, eds., (Ahmedabad: L.D. Institute in Indology, 1981), pp. 306-307.

19. Zwilling, *Ibid.*, p. 307. See also his n. 8, p. 312, reference to Kay-drup's *rGyas pa'i bstar bcos tshad ma rnam 'grel gyi rgya cher bshad pa rigs pa'i rgya mtsho las mngon sum le'u rnam bshad*, Zhol edition, ff. 9a. 4-5, 11.1.

20. Dak-tsang, Hopkins translation, p. 6; Tibetan text, 126.6.

21. Quoted by Dak-tsang, Hopkins translation p. 2; Tibetan text, p. 123.6; Also quoted and discussed in *Great Tenets*, 2b.7.

22. Dak-tsang, Hopkins translation, p. 3; Tibetan text, 124.4 (*sogs* on 124.4 refers to Dak-tsang's root text, same volume, p. 13.6-14-1).

23. As further evidence in his favor, Dak-tsang notes that Vasubandhu's *Treasury of Knowledge* (source text for the Sautrāntikas Following Scripture who are renowned as agreeing with the Vaibhāṣika presentation on the two truths) specifically explains that the Cittamātra assertions on the two truths are distinct from those of the Vaibhāṣikas, but does not indicate any difference between Sautrāntikas in general and Vaibhāṣikas. See also *Great Tenets*, 309.1 ff.

In the Sanskrit edition of the *Abhidharmakośabhāṣya* edited by Swami Dwarikadas Shastri (Varanasi: Baudda Bharati, 1972) p. 891, Vasubandhu gives a discussion of the two truths. Yaśomitra (whose commentary is included in the same volume) says that for Yogacāra there are three types of existence — ultimate, conventional, and substantial. However, the word "Yogacāra" does not appear in this Sanskrit edition of the *Kośa* text itself, although the word is italicized in the Yaśomitra commentary, which should indicate that it *is* in the text. The Tibetan edition of the text P5591 Vol. 115, 243-5-3ff. does not contain the word "Yogacāra" either although the word does occur in the Tibetan translation of the Yaśomitra commentary P5591

Vol. 115, 274-2-8 to 274-3-1. (Thanks to Prof. Harvey Aronson on these points regarding Yaśomitra.)

24. Dak-tsang, 126.1; Dharmakīrti, P5709 88-3-7 (III. 5, *Pratyakṣa* chapter). Translation from Hopkins, unpublished ms. Prof. Nagatomi, in his privately circulated manuscript translation of Dharmakīrti's text, notes Dharmakīrti's point is that a cognition is "the final effect (*antyaṃ kāryam*) of all the factors that go to produce it. ... there is a positive and negative correlation between the cognition (an effect) and the patch of color, ... This concomitance is not found to subsist between the cognition of a universal [generally characterized phenomenon], e.g. the conceptualized color which we refer to by the word 'blue', and the universal [or generality] itself." Thus, here, the universal or generally characterized, as in the Gelukba position is *not* seen as producing the mind which cognizes it.

It is notable that Bel-den-chö-jay (*Two Truths*, 39.6-40.2) reports that Prajñākaragupta, Suryagupta, Śāntarakṣita, Kamalaśīla and Jetāri take Dharmakīrti's own system to be Mādhyamika. Jetāri specifically uses this line "If all are without capacity" as evidence of Dharmakīrti's Mādhyamika position. Dharmakīrti's work clearly admits of many interpretations (see Intro. n. 17).

25. Bel-den-chö-jay, *Two Truths*, 47.6 ff. Dak-tsang is not openly named as the opponent but the position elaborated on and refuted here is clearly his.

26. Bel-den-chö-jay, *Two Truths*, 47.7 ff.

27. *Annotations*, *dngos* 74.2-3.

28. Dharmakīrti P5709, 88-3-7; See also, Dak-tsang, Hopkins, translation p. 5; *Ocean* 126.2.

29. *Annotations*, *dngos* 74.2.

30. *Annotations*, *dngos* 73.8.

31. Kensur Yeshay Tupden, oral commentary.

32. *Dharmakīrti*, P5709, Vol. 130, 88-3-3.

33. Gyel-tsap, *Explanation*, Vol. 2, p. 1.11-12.

34. Contrast is made for the sake of clarifying a Gelukba position; there is no insinuation that other scholars are not accurately reporting another viewpoint.

35. Karl H. Potter, *Presuppositions of India's Philosophies*, (Englewood Cliffs, New Jersey: Prentice-Hall, Inc., 1963) p. 203.

36. Stcherbatsky, Vol. I p. 363.

37. Stcherbatsky, Vol. I p. 366.

38. Quoted by Jam-yang-shay-ba, *Final Analysis of (Dharmakīrti's 'Commentary on (Dignāga's) Compendium on Valid Cognition '(Tshad*

ma rnam 'grel gyi mtha' dpyod), *Collected Works of 'Jam-dbyangs-bzhad-pa Ṅag-dbang btson-'grus* (New Delhi: Ngawang Gelek Demo, 1972) 842.3; Dharmakīrti, P5709 89-2-7. For Dignāga's debate regarding the Mīmāṃsa analysis of *pratyakṣa*, see Hattori, *Dignāga*, 63-70.

39. Jam-yang-shay-ba, *Final Analysis*, 843.5.

40. Den-dar-hla-ram-ba, *Beginnings of an Explanation of the General Meaning* (*rnam 'grel spyi don rdzom 'phro*) 653.5-6; brackets from 655.5-6; Dharmakīrti, P5709 89-2-7 ff; the Tibetan of this verse reads: *de ni rang gzhan ngo bo yis rtogs phyir gzhal bya gnyis su bshad.*

41. See, for example, Nagatomi, "Arthakriyā," *The Adyar Library Bulletin* Vols. XXXI-XXXII, 1967-1968, pp. 52-72.

42. Den-dar-hla-ram-ba. *Ibid.*, 353.6-354.1; Dharmakīrti, P5709, Vol. 130, 89-3-5.

CHAPTER THREE

1. The religious dimension of phenomenalist issues has of course also been noted in the West, though more in the context of handling otherwise insuperable difficulties than specifically incorporating the discussion into religious practice. For example, Berkeley, wishing to consider objects as merely collections of ideas (and thus in harmony with much in Buddhist epistemology) felt compelled to introduce the idea of God in order to explain the continuity of objects in the absence of an idea-producing subject. His was a notable attempt to deal with a major problem in phenomenalism: how the continuity of objects that are actually merely sense-data can be explained given that objects are not continuously observed by human (or animal) sense perception. Russell's answer by contrast was to assign such unobserved phenomena the status of sense-data that were not objects of mind. In terms of an overall system, this may be seen as accomplishing the same thing as the Buddhist formulation, for which lack of cognition was never a problem. This is because Buddhism asserts the existence of many omniscient consciousnesses possessed by the countless persons who have already attained enlightenment or Buddhahood. All objects are always objects of cognition for them. Moreover, even without such an assertion Buddhists could assert continuity inasmuch as there is no place — even the famous empty forest — which is devoid of living beings, visible or invisible, who are cognizant of objects in their vicinity. Although Buddhist systems do not see continuity itself as a problem there is much discussion

regarding the nature of that continuity and the extent to which it and other phenomenal criteria are over-reified by the mind. Foundational to that elaborate area of inquiry is the analysis of how direct perception operates in ordinary persons. The difficulty of 'reducing' a perceived object to a perceived object-aspect is analagous to the problem in linguistic phenomenalism's claim that statements about material objects can be fully translated into statements about the senses, and are actually what is meant when we speak of material objects. This equivalence is difficult to establish systematically.

2. See Dignāga, *Pramāṇasamuccaya*, 6ab; Dharmakīrti, *Pramāṇvārttika*, III. 123a.See also Hattori, *Dignāga on Perception*, p. 25 and 82-83, n. 1.25, and 88, n. 35.

3. Hattori, *Dignāga*, pp. 86-87 n. 1.31 and 1.32. See also, *Ibid.*, pp. 32-35 and p. 76, n. 1.11.

4. Hattori, *Dignāga*, p. 67.

5. Pur-bu-jok, "Greater Path of Reasoning," ("Rigs lam che ba") in *Collected Topics* 36a.5 (definition of complete engager).

6. Kensur Yeshay Tupden, oral commentary in discussion of an issue raised to me earlier by Leonard van der Kuijp.

7. Kensur Yeshay Tupden, oral commentary.

8. Kensur Yeshay Tupden, oral commentary.

9. Kensur Yeshay Tupden, oral commentary.

10. Ven. Sangyay Samdrup, discussion.

11. *Mind*, p. 142; Geshe Jam-bel-sam-pel, *Presentation of Awareness and Knowledge*, modern blockprint, n.p., n.d., 11a.1-2.

12. Den-dar-hla-ram-ba, *Presentation of Generally and Specifically Characterized Phenomena* 161.4 ff.

13. Kensur Yeshay Tupden, oral commentary.

14. *Ibid.*

15. *Ibid.*

16. Pur-bu-jok, "The Lesser Path of Reasoning," 7.3.

17. Kensur Yeshay Tupden, oral commentary.

18. Source for this and the preceding paragraph is Lati Rinbochay, oral commentary.

19. Ven. Sangyay Samdrup, discussion. That a table's shape is not a tangible object is a widely accepted assertion but, according to Ven. Sangyay Samdrup, some scholars argue that a table's tangibility is *not* one entity with it.

20. Pur-bu-jok, "The Lesser Path of Reasoning," 13.2.

21. Geshe Belden Drakba, oral commentary.

22. Kensur Yeshay Tupden, oral commentary.
23. *Ibid.*
24. Bel-den-chö-jay, *Explanation of the Conventional and the Ultimate in the Four Systems of Tenets* (*Grub mtha' bzhi'i lugs kyi kun rdzob dang don dam pa'i don rnam par bshad pa*) (New Delhi: Guru Deva, 1972), 31a.2.
25. See *Practice and Theory* p. 79 for further discussion.
26. In the epistemology and physics of classical Greece there is a similar notion phrased in terms of the nature of light. For example, see Plato's "Republic," *The Collected Dialogues*, p. 742 ff.
27. Geshe Gedun Lodrö, oral commentary.
28. Kensur Yeshay Tupden, oral commentary.
29. Geshe Gedun Lodrö, oral commentary.
30. Geshe Gedun Lodrö, oral commentary.
31. Geshe Gedun Lodrö and Geshe Belden Drakba, oral commentary.
32. Geshe Gedun Lodrö, oral commentary.
33. The Tibetan uses the term *bzung rnam* — apprehension aspect — for both subject and object. For the sake of clarity this term has been translated as subjective apprehension aspect or objective apprehension aspect according to context.
34. Kensur Yeshay Tupden, oral commentary.
35. *Ibid.*
36. Geshe Belden Drakba, oral commentary.
37. Kensur Yeshay Tupden and Geshe Belden Drakba.
38. Kensur Yeshay Tupden and Geshe Belden Drakba. This is an argument put forth by the Vaibhāṣikas in the *Commentary on the Treasury of Knowledge* by Chim-jam-bel-yang (*mChims mdzod*), text from Gomang Library, Mundgod, from blocks available to them, p. 69: *de dag gis yul 'dzin pa ni yul gyi rnam pa ma shar bzhin du 'dzin pa yin gyi rnam pa dang bcas pa ni ma yin te snang ba 'di don ma yin na mi snang ba'i don yod pa la sgrub byed med pa'i phyir dang rags snang shes pa yin na rags pa rdul phran bsags pa ma yin par thal ba'i phyir ro*. For a discussion of the Sakyaba Cha-ba-chö-gyi-seng-gay's (Phya-pa-chos-kyi-seng-ge) partiality to Vaibhāṣika and his handling of the *Pramāṇavārttika*, see Leonard W.J. van der Kuijp, *Contributions to the Development of Tibetan Buddhist Epistemology* (Wiesbaden: Alt-und Neu-Indische Studien: Franz Steiner Verlag, 1983) pp. 63 ff.
39. Geshe Tsultrim Puntsok, oral commentary.
40. Geshe Gedun Lodrö, oral commentary.

41. Geshe Belden Drakba, oral commentary.
42. *Ibid.*
43. Kensur Yeshay Tupden, oral commentary.
44. Geshe Belden Drakba, oral commentary.
45. Kensur Yeshay Tupden, oral commentary.
46. *Ibid.*
47. Geshe Gedun Lodrö, oral commentary.
48. Quoted in *Great Tenets*, 336.4 ff.
49. Geshe Belden Drakba, oral commentary.
50. Geshe Gedun Lodrö used the word *bzung rnam* (*apprehension aspect*). I am inferring this to signify "objective apprehension aspect."
51. Geshe Gedun Lodrö, oral commentary.
52. Gyel-tsap, *Commentary on (Dharmakīrti's) 'Ascertainment of Valid Cognition'* (*rNam nges ṭik chen*), Tashi Lhunpo blockprint, n.d., p. 110-2-7.
53. Ven. Sangyay Samdrup, discussion.
54. Geshe Belden Drakba, oral commentary.
55. Geshe Tsultrim Puntsok, oral commentary.
56. Geshe Belden Drakba, oral commentary.

The difficulty of 'reducing' a perceived object to a perceived objective-aspect is analagous to the problem in linguistic phenomenalism's claim, as noted above, that material objects are fully expressible in terms of sense data. One problem is that sense data are simply too variable to be systematically expressed.

Indeed, the reframing of what is meant by 'objects' of any kind, and thus by 'direct perception' is a major task for phenomanlist and Buddhist theorticians. For the latter this is moreover integral to what for Buddhists is primarily the spiritual challenge of overcoming *all* perceptual and conceptual error regarding the existential status of things, an accomplishment understood as tantamount to liberation from all adventitious limitations on human potential.

57. Geshe Belden Drakba, oral commentary.
58. Geshe Gedun Lodrö, oral commentary. In either case, the position of the proponents of an equal number of subjects and objects is refuted in Śāntarakṣita's *Commentary on the 'Ornament to the Middle Way'* (*Madhyamakālaṃkara-vṛtti*).
59. Tsong-ka-pa and his chief disciples assert that the "own system" (*rang lugs*) of (Dharmakīrti's) Commentary on (Dignāga's) 'Treatise on Valid Cognition' is that of the sequential non-pluralists.

However, the system (*lugs*) of this text is that of the proponents of an equal number of subjects and objects. Source: Geshe Gedun Lodrö, oral commentary.

60. According to Gön-chok-jik-may-wang-bo, Half-Eggists are so called because they are half like Sautrāntika in that their assertion that an eye consciousness and its object are different entities accords with Sautrāntika, and half like Cittamātra because of their assertion that an eye consciousness and its object are both of the nature of the mind. See *Practice and Theory*, p. 109-110. According to the present-day Nyingma scholar and *sNgags pa*, Ven. Khetsun Sangbo Rinbochay, the name reflects the Half-Eggist assertion that subject and object are like two halves of an egg.

61. Śāntarakṣita, *Commentary on the 'Ornament'* (*Madhyamakālaṃkāravṛtti*), P5285, Vol. 101, 4-5-4.

62. Jang-gya, p. 98.1; see translation in Klein, *Knowing, Naming, and Negation.*

63. It would be an interesting project to set up a controlled laboratory experiment by which these theories could be investigated and perhaps definitively established or rejected. For an example of a particularly relevant Western discussion of issues raised here see the chapter on "Perception" in A.J. Ayer, *The Problem of Knowledge* (Middlesex, England: Penguin Books, 1984) [reprinted from 1956].

64. Hattori, *Dignāga*, p. 30; see also n. 1.75 & 1.76.

65. Kensur Yeshay Tupden, oral commentary.

66. Ven. Sangyay Samdrup, discussion.

67. *Jam-yang-shay-ba, Great Tenets*, 335.6 ff.

68. That is, the mind that apprehends them. For more on Cittamātra, see *Practice and Theory*, pp. 107-121; also Jeffrey Hopkins, *Meditation on Emptiness* (London: Wisdom Publications, 1983) pp. 364-397.

CHAPTER FOUR

1. Kensur Yeshay Tupden, oral commentary.

2. *Ibid.*

3. Geshe Gedun Lodrö in oral commentary as reported by Jeffrey Hopkins.

4. Jang-gya, 100.15; translated in Klein, *Knowing, Naming, and Negation.*

5. Translated in Napper, *Mind*, p. 130; Tibetan text p. 9b.4.

6. *Great Tenets* p. 344.2-3. See also Hattori *Dignāga*, p. 14 n. 71. Jinendrabuddhi, commenting on Dignāga's definition of thought (*kalpanā*) says that even a cognition which is not associated with a word should be regarded as *kalpanā* inasmuch as it is capable of being designated by words.

7. Kensur Yeshay Tupden, oral commentary.

8. *Annotations*, *dngos*, 51a. 7-10.

9. A Sanskrit compound phrase in which there is a case relationship between the two components. Here the relationship is genitive, meaning that the second part of the compound is modified by the first.

10. Jang-gya, 102.17, translated in Klein, *Knowing, Naming, and Negation*.

11. Gomang Kensur Ngawang Nyima and Loseling Geshe Belden Drakba, oral commentary.

12. Tsong-ka-pa, *Door of Entry to the Seven Treatises*, 24.2-4.

13. Kay-drup, *Collected Works*, n.p., n.d., Vol. *nya* p. 141; in collection of Tibet House Library, Lodi Road, New Delhi.

14. Geshe Belden Drakba, oral commentary.

15. Pur-bu-jok, "The Lesser Path of Reasoning," 39.1-2.

16. Śāntarakṣita gives four reasons why the "image of an object" (*arthapratibimba* — *arthasāmānya* in this context) is called *apoha*. See *Tattvasaṃgraha* and *Tattvasaṃgrahapañjikā* 1006-1008. See also Hattori, pp. 72-3, n. 26.

17. Geshe Belden Drakba, Jambel Shenpen Rinboche, oral commentary. When a term such as *bum pa ma yin pa las log pa* is in the subject position its translation will be hyphenated as in "opposite-from-non-pot is a negative phenomenon." When such a term appears in the predicate position as a modifier, hyphens are not used. For example, "A mental image of pot is an appearance as opposite from non-pot" or "It is not opposite-from-non-pot which appears to direct perception according to Gomang; rather, the pot which is opposite from non-pot appears." See Perdue, "Debate in Tibetan Buddhist Education," Part III (forthcoming from Wisdom Publications).

18. Jambel Shenpen Rinboche, oral commentary.

19. Geshe Belden Drakba, oral commentary.

20. Gomang Kensur Ngawang Nyima, oral commentary.

21. Reported by Geshe Belden Drakba, oral commentary.

22. Gaekwad Vol. 80. See also Hattori, "*Apoha and Pratibhā*," in

Sanskrit and Indian Studies, ed. by M. Nagatomi, B.K. Matilal, J.M. Masson, and E.C. Dimock (Boston: D. Reidel Publishing Company, 1980) p. 73, n. 26.

23. Den-dar-hla-ram-ba, 180.1-2; translated in Klein, *Knowing, Naming, and Negation*. Most thought consciousnesses are mistaken in all three ways, but a thought consciousness apprehending an object of knowledge is free of the first type of mistake because the meaning-generality — which is perceived as an object of knowledge — actually *is* an object of knowledge. Yet, this thought consciousness is mistaken in that the image of object of knowledge appears to be *one with* the referent object, object of knowledge itself. Once the image appears to be one with the object, it also necessarily appears to be opposite from all that is not that object. See note IV. 26.

24. Jambel Shenpen Rinboche, oral commentary.

25. This clearly derives from the Indian logicians. Hattori observes that according to Dignāga, "individual trees are totally different from each other, but the 'differentiation from non-trees' is common to them all." Although the universal or generality is in many ways similar to this 'differentiation from non-trees,' the latter "is not a positive entity like the universal. It is simply attributed to the object through mental construction and as such it has no objective reality". See Hattori, *Apoha* p. 62.

26. Bel-den-chö-jay, *Annotations, dngos*, 75.6.

27. Kensur Yeshay Tupden, oral commentary.

28. Den-dar-hla-ram-ba, 180.5 ff; translated in Klein, *Knowing, Naming, and Negation*.

29. Geshe Belden Drakba, oral commentary.

30. For a discussion of problems in defining mental direct perception, see M. Nagatomi, "*Mānasa Pratyakṣa*: A Conundrum in the Buddhist Pramāṇa System" in *Sanskrit and Indian Studies*, (Nagatomi et. al. eds). See also Hattori, *Dignāga*, 9. 27, Gabff.

31. *Ibid*. This is one way in which the category of a subconscious that imperceptibly affects the conscious state fits into Buddhist discussions of mind.

32. Kensur Yeshay Tupden, oral commentary.

33. Ven. Sangyay Samdrup, discussion.

34. Kensur Yeshay Tupden, oral commentary.

35. Jambel Shenpen Rinboche, oral commentary.

36. Kensur Yeshay Tupden, oral commentary.

37. *Ibid*.

38. See *Practice and Theory*, Cittamātra chapter.

39. See M. Nagatomi, "*Arthakriyā*" p. 62; he notes that direct perception itself, being bereft of all mental construction, is never judgemental and thus, in terms of our example, would never make the mistake of conceiving a snow mountain to be blue.

40. For a presentation of all 23 types of non-associated compositional factors, see Hopkins, *Meditation on Emptiness* pp. 268-271.

41. Kensur Yeshay Tupden, oral commentary.

42. Geshe Jam-bel-sam-pel, 26.1; See also *Mind* p. 52.

43. Kensur Yeshay Tupden, oral commentary.

44. Jam-yang-shay-ba, *Presentation of Awareness and Knowledge*, *The Collected Works of 'Jam-dbyaṅs-bźad-pa'i-rdo-rje*, (New Delhi: Ngawang Gelek Demo, 1973) 308.4 ff.

45. According to Den-dar-hla-ram-ba, an actual pot explicitly (*dngos su*) appears to the thought consciousness apprehending a pot. According to Jambel Shenpen Rinboche, appearances are not discussed in terms of being implicit or explicit; there is, however, discussion of implicit and explicit realization. The only reason to state that pot appears *implicitly* to the thought consciousness realizing pot is to emphasize that such is appearing through the medium of an image. However, in order to make the point that an inferential thought consciousness does not implicitly realize its referent object — for example, impermanence — it must be noted that even a thought consciousness realizing a pot does so explicitly.

46. Kensur Yeshay Tupden, oral commentary.

47. Bel-den-chö-jay, *Explanation of the Conventional and the Ultimate*, 40.3.

48. Ven. Sangyay Samdrup, discussion.

49. Bel-den-chö-jay, *Explanation of the Conventional and the Ultimate*, 40.5-7.

50. Den-dar-hla-ram-ba, 177.5; see Klein, *Knowing, Naming, and Negation*.

51. Geshe Belden Drakba, oral commentary.

52. Bel-den-chö-jay, *Explanation of the Conventional and the Ultimate*, 41.2 ff.

53. This description of the process of realizing impermanence is from the oral commentary of Geshe Belden Drakba. Compare with Gilbert Ryle's description of building theories: "If a farmer has made a path, he is able to saunter easily up and down it. That is what the path was made for. But the work of making the path was not one

of sauntering easily, but one of marking the ground, digging, fetching loads of gravel, rolling and draining. ... Similarly a person who has a theory can, among other things, expound to himself, or the world ... he can, so to speak saunter in prose from any part to any other part of it. But the work of building the theory was a job of making paths where as yet there were none. ... There is a stage at which a thinker has his theory, but has not yet got it perfectly. He is not yet completely at home in it. There are places where he stumbles, slips, hesitates, ... As the farmer is both half-sauntering and still preparing [his path], so the thinker is both using his near-mastery of his theory, and still schooling himself to master it perfectly." pp. 289-290 in the *Concept of Mind* (New York: Barnes & Noble, 1949).

It is important to note that at the time of cultivating a mental image of subtle impermanence, the scholar-practitioner has already heard and correctly understood the Buddhist theory of momentary disintegration. The early phases of developing a mental image belong to the thinking phase of the practitioner's triad of hearing, thinking, and meditating. Still more significant, and in greatest contrast to Ryle's metaphor above, is the claim that one is gaining more than mere theoretical facility, is in fact moving toward an actual, direct understanding or mental *cognition* of factual data — namely, momentary disintegration. In this sense, the theory comes *before* the work of making the path of practice, but the full impact of the theory and actual experience of its correctness, comes only later.

54. Gyel-tsap, Vol. I. p. 107.16.

55. Kensur Yeshay Tupden, oral commentary.

CHAPTER FIVE

1. For discussion of the 108 phenomena in a classic Buddhist presentation of the world, see Hopkins, *Meditation on Emptiness*, pp. 201 ff.

2. Lati Rinbochay, oral commentary, based on Pur-bu-jok's discussion of negative phenomena. Neither Jang-gya in his chapter on "Exclusions," nor the Gomang or Pur-bu-jok *Collected Topics* give a definition of positive phenomenon. Nor does Ra-dö define this in discussing negatives and exclusions.

3. See p. 221, note 24.

4. Pur-bu-jok, "The Lesser Path of Reasoning," 10.6.

5. Except in the Gomang interpretation.
6. *Practice and Theory* pp. 96-97.
7. A.B. Keith, *Indian Logic and Atomism*, (New York: Greenwood Press, 1968) p. 106.
8. *Ibid.*
9. Hattori, *Dignāga on Perception* (Cambridge, Mass.: Harvard University Press, 1968), p. 3.
10. Hattori, "*Apoha* and *Pratibhā*" p. 62. More specifically, Hattori notes that Dignāga argued elaborately "against opponents who held that the word had direct reference to the individual (*vyakti*), the universal (*jāti*), the relation between the two (*sambandha*), or the possessor of the universal (*jātimat*), ..."
11. *Ibid.*, see also his note 4, p. 71.
12. Lecture by Prof. Jaganath Upadhyaya, South Asian Seminar Series, University of Virginia, April 1982.
13. Hattori, *Dignāga*, p. 62.
14. *Ibid.*, p. 69. These are seen as synonymous by Śāntarakṣita. For more on Bhartṛhari's discussion of *pratibhā* see also Harold G. Coward, *The Sphoṭa Theory of Language* (*Delhi: Motilal Banarsidas, 1980*) p. 121 ff. Also Subramania Iyer, *Bhartṛhari* (Poona: Deccan College, 1969); see also H.R.R. Iyengar "Bhartṛhari and Dignāga," *Journal of the British Royal Asiatic Society*, new series, 26 (1950).
15. Dignāga quotes Bhartṛhari's *Vākyapadīya* II, 160 and 157 in the fifth chapter — that on *apoha* — of the Pramāṇasamuccaya. See Hattori, *Dignāga*, p. 6; also, n. 3, p. 6.
16. Hattori, *Apoha* p. 63 ff.
17. *Ibid.*, p. 69.
18. *Ibid.*, p. 68.
19. *Tattvasaṃgraha* 1003; see also Hattori n. 73.
20. Pur-bu-jok, "The Greater Path of Reasoning," 31b.5-6.
21. See *Tattvasaṃgraha* 1003-1004 (Gaekwad Vol. 80, p. 533).
22. Sharma, *Differentiation*, p. 34. For a Sanskrit grammatical analysis pertinent to Mīmāṃsā styles of negation, see J.F. Staal, "Negation and the Law of Contradiction in Indian Thought" (London, *Bulletin of the School of Oriental and African Studies*, Vol. XXV: Part I, 1962, especially pp. 56-66).
23. Jam-yang-chok-hla-ö-ser, *Collected Topics of Ra-dö*, (Dharamsala, India: Damchoe Sangpo, c/o Library of Tibetan Works and Archives) [Printed at Jayyed Press, Ballimaran, Delhi], p. 345.6. For other Tibetan Gelukba discussions of the divisions of non-affirming negatives, see Jang-gya, 111.2; also, "Jang-gya: Ex-

clusions" tr. in Klein *Knowing, Naming, and Negation*, Gomang's *Collected Topics* pp. 463.1 ff; see Nga-wang-dra-shi, "Presentation of the author's own position" tr. in Klein, *Knowing, Naming, and Negation*.

24. *Ibid*. 345.7-8.

25. More precisely, *dravya-sat* is the Sanskrit equivalent of *rdzas yod* — substantially existent — in Tibetan. I have not found a Sanskrit equivalent for self-sufficient (*rang rkya ba*). However, in the Tibetan phrase *rang rkya grub pa rdzas yod*, "substantially existent" and "self-sufficient" are appositive; therefore, it is not unsuitable to consider *dravya-sat* an equivalent for the entire phrase.

CHAPTER SIX

1. Practice and Theory, p. 97; Tibetan text, p. 34.
2. Jambel Shenpen Rinboche, oral commentary.
3. Gomang's *Collected Topics*, 463.7.
4. Pur-bu-jok, "The Greater Path of Reasoning," 31b.3.
5. Jang-gya, 111.13, see "Jang-gya: Exclusions" tr. in Klein, *Knowing, Naming, and Negation*.
6. Jambel Shenpen Rinboche, oral commentary.
7. *Ibid*., Still, they must agree affirming negatives may be suggested, e.g. being a non-pot suggests being a non-gold pot.
8. *Ibid*., This topic merits further research with Gomang scholars.
9. Pur-bu-jok, "The Greater Path of Reasoning," 31b.6-32a.1.
10. Jang-gya, 112.4, see "Jang-gya: Exclusions" tr. in Klein, *Knowing, Naming, and Negation*.
11. Gomang's *Collected Topics*, 463-4.
12. All the Gelukba colleges agree that the existence of non-production from self or the existence of a pot's lack of a self of persons is an affirming negative. They also agree that the *existence* of any phenomenon, permanent or impermanent, does not disintegrate moment by moment and is therefore a permanent phenomenon. However, according to Gomang, whatever is permanent is a negative phenomenon. Therefore, in their view, the existence of even impermanent phenomena, such as tables, chairs, and so forth, is both permanent and a negative. Thus, form is considered a positive phenomenon, but its existence is a negative phenomenon.
13. C.L. Tripathi, *The Problem of Knowledge in Yogacāra Buddhism*, (Varanasi: Bharat-Bharati, 1972) p. 241.

14. Sharma, *Differentiation*, pp. 11-12.
15. Pur-bu-jok, "The Greater Path of Reasoning," 32a.3.
16. Keith, p. 102.
17. Dhirendra Sharma, "The Paradox of Negative Judgment and Indian Logic," *Vishveshvaranand Indological Journal*, Vol. 9 No., 4 (1966) p. 113.
18. Gomang's *Collected Topics*, 465-466.
19. Jambel Shenpen Rinboche, oral commentary.
20. *Ibid.*
21. Pur-bu-jok, "The Greater Path of Reasoning", 32a.1.
22. Gomang, *Collected Topics*, 466.9.
23. Pur-bu-jok adds this word.
24. Jambel Shenpen Rinboche, oral commentary.
25. Pur-bu-jok, "The Greater Path of Reasoning," 32a.1; Jang-gya, 112.7-9, see definitions in "Jang-gya: Exclusions": tr. in Klein *Knowing, Naming, and Negation.*
26. Gomang, *Collected Topics*, 467.7.
27. Jang-gya, 112.7-9; see "Jang-gya: Exclusions" in Klein, *Knowing, Naming, and Negation.*
28. This is also quoted by the Ra-dö text, 348.8-349.3. Arcata's *Hetubinduṭīkā* has an almost parallel passage: *yatra videḥ prādhānyam, pratiṣedho' rthagrhītaḥ, vidhibhākṣvapadena nocyate, ekāvakyatā ca tatra paryudāsavṛttitā* ..., quoted by Kajiyama in "Three Kinds of Affirmation and Two Kinds of Negation in Buddhist Philosophy," *Wiener Zeitschrift für Kunde Sudasiens und Archiv für Indische Philosophie*, 1973, p. 170.
29. Jang-gya, p. 112 (tr. in Klein); Ra-dö, p. 346 ff.
30. Kajiyama, "Three Kinds of Affirmation" p. 170.
31. Jang-gya, 111.18, in Klein *Knowing, Naming, and Negation.*
32. Pur-bu-jok, "The Greater Path of Reasoning", 31b.5-6.
33. Jang-gya, 112.17; see "Jang-gya: Exclusions" tr. in Klein, *Knowing, Naming, and Negation.*
34. Jang-gya, 112.20-113.2; see "Jang-gya: Exclusions" tr. in Klein, *Knowing, Naming, and Negation*; Dharmakīrti, P5709, Vol. 130, 78-5-6.
35. Kensur Yeshay Tupden, oral commentary.
36. Pur-bu-jok, "The Lesser Path of Reasoning," 11.5.
37. Tripathi, p. 240. The validity of Tripathi's and the other interpretations is not under examination at this time; I simply want to note the marked contrast between these and the Gelukba inter-

pretations.

38. Pur-bu-jok, "The Greater Path of Reasoning," 31b.6. Śāntarakṣita was probably the first to use this term, but does not define or explain it in detail. See *Tattvasaṃgraha* 1003. Kamalaśīla simply glosses the term *buddhātmapoha* as *buddhipratibhāso 'rtheṣvanugataikarūpa-tvenādhyavasti.*

39. Jang-gya, 111.17.

40. Jambel Shenpen Rinboche, Geshe Belden Drakba, oral commentary.

41. Jambel Shenpen Rinboche, oral commentary.

42. Pur-bu-jok, "The Lesser Path of Reasoning", 39.1-2.

43. Jambel Shenpen Rinboche, oral commentary.

44. Jambel Shenpen Rinboche, Geshe Belden Drakba, oral commentary.

45. Jambel Shenpen Rinboche, oral commentary.

46. Lati Rinbochay, oral commentary.

47. S.S. Barlingay, *A Modern Introduction to Indian Logic*, (Delhi: National Publishing House, 1965) p. 5.

48. C.L. Tripathi, p. 292.

49. Kensur Yeshay Tupden and Geshe Tsultrim Puntsok, oral commentary.

50. Ra-dö, 353.1.

51. *Ibid.*, 350.4.

CHAPTER SEVEN

1. Jang-gya, 111.13; tr. in Klein *Knowing, Naming and Negation.*
2. Gomang's *Collected Topics*, 467-8.
3. J.F. Staal, "Negation and the Law of Contradiction in Indian Thought," *Bulletin of the School of Oriental and African Studies*, Vol, 25, Part I (1962) pp. 56-57.
4. Pur-bu-jok, "The Greater Path of Reasoning," 32a.6.
5. Humorous perspective, Prof. Donald S. Lopez.
6. Pur-bu-jok, "The Lesser Path of Reasoning," 11.3.
7. Ra-dö, 347.6-348.1.
8. C.L. Tripathi, *Problem of Knowledge*, p. 250.
9. Dharmendra Nath Shastri, *Critique of Indian Realism: A Study of the Conflict Between the Nyāya-Vaiśeṣika and the Buddhist Dignāga School*, (Agra, India: Agra University, 1964) p. 357. Shastri draws this statement from a discussion (verses 1004-1015) in Śāntarakṣita's *Compendium on Suchness* and Kamalaśīla's *Commentary on the Diffi-*

cult Points of (Śāntarakṣita's) Compendium on Suchness [see Bibliography for full listings]. The relevant verses are translated in Stcherbatsky's *Buddhist Logic*, Vol. I., p. 471 ff.

10. Potter, p. 203.

11. For explanation of the meaning of the "self" negated in the theories of selflessness of Sautrāntika and Prāsaṅgika-Mādhyamika, see Hopkins, *Meditation on Emptiness*, chapter five.

12. Stcherbatshy, Vol. I, p. 363.

13. Nagatomi, "*Arthakriyā*" p. 52.

14. Hattori, *Dignāga*, p. 14. See also p. 79, n. 14.

15. See Hopkins, *Meditation on Emptiness* p. 215 ff.

CHAPTER EIGHT

1. *rjod byed kyi sgra*.

2. Den-dar-hla-ram-ba, 182.5 ff, see Den-dar: "Mode of Expression by Terms" tr. in Klein *Knowing, Naming, and Negation.*

3. Jambel Shenpen Rinboche, oral commentary.

4. Den-dar-hla-ram-ba, 192.4-5.

5. Denma Lochö Rinbochay, oral commentary.

6. Den-dar-hla-ram ba, 184.5.

7. Pur-bu-jok, "The Lesser Path of Reasoning," 38.6. Pur-bu-jok also mentions a third type of generality, a collection-generality (*tshogs spyi*), which he defines as a gross form that is an aggregation of many of its own parts (39.3); for example, a table or chair.

8. *Ibid.*, 39.5.

9. *Ibid.*, 39.1.

10. This name is contrived.

11. Entire story is from Lochö Rinbochay, oral commentary.

12. Den-dar-hla-ram-ba, 195.2; tr. in Klein, *Knowing, Naming, and Negation.*

13. *Ibid.*, 195.6-196.1. Also, as indicated in Den-dar-hla-ram-ba, 195.4-196.3, there are two kinds of sameness of types. (1) same type of reverse (*ldog pa gcig*) and (2) same substantial type (*rdzes rigs gcig*). A gold pot and a copper pot are both opposite from non-pot; thus, they are one type of reverse. An example of phenomena that are of the same substantial type are two barley grains grown from a single barley grain. Since these two share the same substantial cause — the original barley grain — they are one substantial type. They are not one substantial entity however because it is possible for one to be present and the other to be absent.

14. Quoted by Den-dar-hla-ram-ba, 195.3-5; see "Den-dar: Application of Names" tr. in Klein *Knowing, Naming, and Negation.*
15. *Ibid.*, 195.6 ff.
16. *Ibid.*, 197.5 ff. Translation of the title reflects the name by which this text is best known in Tibet, *sDe bdun yid kyi mun sel*; this is an abbreviation of the full title, *Tshad ma sde bdun gyi rgyan yid kyi mun sel (An Ornament of (Dharmakīrti's) 'Seven Treatises on Valid Cognition', Clearing Away Mental Darkness).*
17. *Ibid.*, 179.2 and 185.2; see "Den-dar: Mode of Perception by Thought" tr. in Klein *Knowing, Naming, and Negation.*
18. *Ibid.*
19. Jang-gya, 100.3 tr. in Klein, *Knowing, Naming, and Negation.*
20. *Ibid.*
21. Jang-gya, 101.11-12; see "Jang-gya: The Two Truths:" tr. in Klein *Knowing, Naming, and Negation.*
22. *Ibid.*
23. Den-dar-hla-ram-ba, 179.1-2; see "Den-dar: Mode of Perception by Thought" tr. in Klein *Knowing, Naming, and Negation.*
24. Jambel Shenpen Rinboche, oral commentary.
25. Jang-gya, 105.4 tr. in Klein, *Knowing, Naming and Negation.*
26. *Ibid.*, 103.6.
27. Quoted by Den-dar-hla-ram-ba, 199.3; see "Den-dar: Application of Names" tr. in Klein *Knowing, Naming, and Negation.*
28. Dharmakīrti, P5709, Vol. 130, 80-3-3.
29. This position was expressed clearly in India. See, for example, Hattori, "*Apoha*", p. 62; also, p. 70, n. 3 where Hattori cites Jinendrabuddhi in the *Viśālāmalavatī Pramāṇasamuccayaṭīkā*, Tibetan version Sde-dge ed., 237b.7-238a.2 (Peking ed. 269a.3-5) and Dignāga in the *Compendium on Valid Cognition* V. k. 12, cited in *Ślokavārittakaṭīkā*, ed. Kunhan Raja (Madras: n.p. 1946), p. 46.7-8: *bahudhāpy abhidheyasya na śabdāt sarvathā gatiḥ svasambandhānurupyeṇa vyavacchedrāthakāry asau.*
30. Kensur Yeshay Tupden, oral commentary.
31. Frederick J. Streng, *Emptiness: A Study in Religious Meaning*, (Nashville: Abingdon Press, 1967), p.21.

CHAPTER NINE

1. Śankarācārya, *The Bṛhadāraṇyaka Upanishad with the Commentary of Śankarācārya*, trans. by Swāmī Mādhvānanda, (Calcutta: Advaita Ashram, 1965), 2.3.6.

2. Mookerjee, p. 107.
3. *Ibid.*
4. S.S. Barlingay, *A Modern Introduction to Indian Logic*, p. 74.
5. D. N. Shastri, *Critique*, p. 346.
6. Mookerjee, p. 109; Sharma, *Differentiation*, p. 27.
7. Gyel-tsap, Vol. I, 107.14.
8. *Ibid.*
9. *Ibid.*, p. 124.
10. *Ibid.*, p. 107.
11. *Ibid.*, p. 124.
12. *gsal zhing rig pa* is the definition of a consciousness. Geshe Jam-bel-sam-pel, 1b.2-3.
13. For a discussion of yogic direct perception, see *Mind*, pp. 19-10; 61-65.

Bibliography of Works Cited

Abbreviations

P: *Tibetan Tripitaka* (Tokyo-Kyoto: Tibetan Tripitaka Research Foundation, 1956)

Toh: *A Complete Catalogue of the Tibetan Buddhist Canons*, ed. by Prof. Hakuji Ui, and *A Catalogue of the Tohoku University Collection of Tibetan Works on Buddhism*, ed. by Prof. Yensho Kanakura (Sendai, Japan, 1934 and 1953)

Bibliography

1. TIBETAN AND SANSKRIT SOURCES

Asaṅga (Thogs-med), 4th Century
Compendium of Knowledge
Abhidharmasamuccaya
mNgon pa kun btus
P550, Vol. 112

Avalokitavrata (sPyan-ras-gzigs-brtul-zhugs), probably 8th Century
Commentary on (Bhāvaviveka's) "Lamp for Nāgārjuna's 'Wisdom'"
Prajñāpradīpaṭīkā
Shes rab sgroṅ ma'i rgya cher 'grel pa
P5259, Vol. 96-97

Bel-den-chö-jay, *see* Nga-wang-bel-den
Bhāvaviveka (Legs-ldan-'byed), c. 400 A.D.
Blaze of Reasoning, Commentary on the 'Heart of the Middle Way'
Madhyamakahṛdayavṛttitarkajvālā
dbU ma'i snying po'i 'grel pa rtog ge 'bar ba
P5256, Vol 96
Bodhibhadra (Byang-chub-bzang-po) 16th Century
Explanation of (Āryadeva's) 'Compendium of Wisdom'
Jñānasārasamuccayanāmanibandhana
Ye shes snying po kun las btus pa shes bya ba'i bshad sbyar
P5252, Vol. 95
Chim-jam-bel-yang (mChims-'jam dpal-dbyangs)
Ornament of Knowledge, Commentary on the Chapters of (Vasubandhu's) 'Treasury of Knowledge'
Chos mngon pa'i mdzod kyi tshig le'ur byas pa'i grel pa mngon pa'i rgyan
Text from Gomang Library of Drebung Monastery, Mundgod, India, from blocks available to them.
Dak-tsang (sTag-tshang-lo-tsa-ba Shes-rab-rin-chen) b. 1405
Ocean of Good Explanations, Explanation of 'Freedom from Extremes Through Understanding All Tenets'
Grub mtha' kun shes nas mtha' bral grub pa zhes bya ba'i bstan bcos rnam par bshad pa legs bshad kyi rgya mtsho
Thim-phu: Kun-gzang-stobs-rgyal, 1976
Den-dar-hla-ram-ba (bsTan-dar-lha-ram-pa), b. 1759
Presentation of Generally and Specifically Characterized Phenomena
Rang mtshan spyi mtshan gyi rnam gzhag
Collected *gSung 'bum* of Bstan-dar Lha-ram of A-lag-sha, Vol. 1
New Delhi: Guru Deva, 1971
Introduction to the General Meaning of (Dharmakīrti's) "Commentary on (Dignāga's) 'Compendium on Valid Cognition' "
rNam 'grel spyi don rdzom 'phro
Collected *gSung 'bum* of Bstan-dar Lha-ram of A-lag-sha, Vol.1
New Delhi: Guru Deva, 1971
Devendrabuddhi (Lha-dbang-blo)
Commentary on (Dharmakīrti's) "Commentary on (Dignāga's) 'Compendium on Valid Cognition' "
Pramāṇavārttikapañjikā
Tshad ma rnam 'grel gyi dka' 'grel
P5709, Vol. 130

Dharmakīrti (Chos-kyi-grags-pa), 7th Century
Seven Treatises on Valid Cognition
Analysis of Relations
Saṃbandhaparīkṣāvṛtti
'Brel pa brtag pa'i rab tu byed pa
P5713, Vol. 130
Ascertainment of Valid Cognition
Pramāṇaviniścaya
Tshad ma rnam par nges pa
P5710, Vol. 130
Commentary on (Dignāga's) 'Compendium on Valid Cognition'
Pramāṇavārttikakārikā
Tshad ma rnam 'grel gyi tshig le'ur byas pa
P5709, Vol. 130
Drop of Reasoning
Nyāyabinduprakaraṇa
Rigs pa'i thigs pa zhes bya ba'i rab tu byed pa
P5711, Vol. 130
Drop of Reasons
Hetubindunāmaprakaraṇa
gTan tshigs kyi thigs pa zhes bya ba rab tu byed pa
P5712, Vol. 130
Proof of Other Continuums
Saṃtānāntarasiddhināmaprakaraṇa
rGyud bzhan grub pa zhes bya ba'i rab tu byed pa
P5716, Vol. 130
Reasoning for Debate
Vādanyāyanāmaprakaraṇa
rTsod pa'i rigs pa zhes bya ba'i rab tu byed pa
P5715, Vol. 130
Dignāga (Phyogs-glang), 5th Century
Commentary on "Examination of Objects"
Ālambanaparīkṣāvṛtti
dMigs pa brtag pa'i 'grel pa
P5704, Vol. 130
Compendium on Valid Cognition
Pramāṇasamuccaya
Tshad ma kun las btus pa
P5700, Vol. 130
Examination of Objects of Observation

Ālambanaparīkṣā
dMigs pa brtag pa
P5703, Vol. 130
Dharmottara (Chos-mchog)
Commentary on (Dharmakīrti's) 'Compendium on Valid Cognition'
Pramāṇviniścayaṭīka
Tshad ma rnam par nges pa'i 'grel bshad
P5727, Vol. 136
Gön-chok-jik-may-wang-bo (dKon-mchog-'jigs-med-dbang-po), 1728-1791
Precious Garland of Tenets/Presentation of Tenets, A Precious Garland
Grub pa'i mtha'i rnam par bzhag pa rin po che'i phreng ba
Mundgod, India: Dre-Gomang Buddhist Cultural Association (Printed by Dre-Loseling Press), 1980
Gyel-tsap (rGyal-tshab), 1364-1432
Commentary on (Dharmakīrti's) 'Ascertainment of Valid Cognition'
rNam nges ṭik chen
Tashi Lunpo blockprint, n.d.
Commentary on (Maitreya's) 'Sublime Science'/Commentary on (Maitreya's) 'Mahāyāna Treatise on the Sublime Science'
Thek pa chen po rgyud bla ma'i ṭīkkā
Toh. 5434
Commentary on (Śāntideva's) 'Engaging in the Bodhisattva Deeds'
Byang chub sems dpa'i spyod pa la 'jug pa'i rnam bshad rgyal sras 'jug ngogs
Toh. 5436
Explanation of (Dharmakīrti's) "Commentary on 'Compendium (Dignāga's) on Valid Cognition' "
Tshad ma rnam 'grel gyi tshig le'ur byas pa'i rnam bshad thar lam phyin ci ma log par gsal bar byed pa
Sarnath, Varanasi: Pleasure of Elegant Sayings Press, Vol. I, 1974, Vol. II, 1975
Toh. 5450
Eradication of Forgetfulness Regarding the Chapter on Direct Perception in (Dharmakīrti's) "Commentary on (Dignāga's) 'Compendium on Valid Cognition' "
mNgon sum le'u'i brjed byang
Toh. 5448
Great Eradication of Forgetfulness Regarding Valid Cognition

Tshad ma'i brjed byang chen mo
Toh. 5438
Illumination of the Thought, An Extensive Commentary on (Dharmakīrti's) 'Ascertainment of Valid Cognition'
bsTan bcos tshad ma rnam nges kyi tik chen dgongs pa rab gsal
Toh. 5453-4

'Jam-dpal-phrin-las
Compendium on the Meaning of the Collected Topics, a Good Explanation Indicating the Joy of Sages
bsDus grva'i don kun bsdus pa'i legs bshad mkhas pa'i dga' ston
Mundgod, India: Drepung Loseling Printing Press, 1978

Jam-bel-sam-pel, Geshe ('Jam-dpal-bsam-'phel, dGe-bshes), d. 1975
Presentation of Awareness and Knowledge, Composite of All the Important Points, Opener of the Eye of New Intelligence
Blo rig gi rnam bzhag nyer mkho kun 'dus blo gsar mig 'byed
Modern blockprint, n.p., n.d.

Jam-yang-chok-hla-ö-ser ('Jam-dbyangs-phyogs-lha-'od-zer), about 15th century
Collected Topics of Ra-dö
Rva stod bsdus grva
Dharamsala, India: Damchoe Sangpo, Library of Tibetan Works and Archives (Printed at Jayyed Press, Ballimaran, Delhi), 1980

Jam-yang-shay-ba ('Jam-dbyangs-bzhad-pa), 1648-1721
Final Analysis of (Dharmakīrti's) "Commentary on Dignāga's 'Compendium on Valid Cognition' "
Tshad ma rnam 'grel gyi mtha' dpyod
Collected Works of 'Jam-dbaṅs-bźad-pa
New Delhi: Ngawang Gelek Demo, 1972
Great Exposition of the Middle Way/Analysis of (Candrakīrti's) 'Supplement to the Middle Way', Treasury of Scripture and Reasoning, Thoroughly Illuminating the Profound Meaning [of Emptiness], Entrance for the Fortunate
dbU ma la 'jug pa'i mtha' dpyod lung rigs gter mdzod zab don kun gsal skal bzang 'jug ngogs
Buxador: Gomang, 1967
Presentation of Awareness and Knowledge
bLo rig gi rnam bzhag
The Collected Works of 'Jam-dbyaṅs-bźad-pa'i-rdo-rje

New Delhi: Ngawang Gelek Demo, 1973 Vol. 15
Great Exposition of Tenets
Grub mtha chen mo/Grub mtha'i rnam bshad gzhan grub mtha' kun dang zab don mchog tu gsal ba kun bzang zhing gi nyi ma lung rigs rgya mtsho skye dgu'i re ba kun skong
Mundgod: Gomang College (*bKra-shis-'khyil* edition), n.p., n.d.

Jang-gya (lCang-skya Rol-pa'i-rdo-rje), 1717-86
Presentation of Tenets/Clear Exposition of the Presentations of Tenets, Beautiful Ornament for the Meru of the Subduer's Teaching
Grub pa'i mtha'i rnam par bzhag pa gsal bar bshad pa thub bstan lhun po'i mdzes rgyan
Sarnath, Varanasi: Pleasure of Elegant Sayings Press, 1970

Jetāri (dGra-las-rgyal-ba)
Work on the Texts of the Sugata
Sugatamatvibhāṅgakārikā
bDer gshegs gzhung gi rab byed
P5867, Vol. 146

Jñānaśrīmitra
Arrayed Treatise of Jñānaśrīmitra
Jñānaśrīmitranibandhāvali
ed. with Introduction by Anantalal Thakur, Tibetan Sanskrit Series, Patna: Jayaswal Research Institute, 1961

Kamalaśīla, 8th Century
Commentary on the Difficult Points of Śāntarakṣita's *'Compendium on Suchness'*
Tattvasaṃgrahapañjikā
De kho na nyid bsdus pa'i dka' 'grel
P5765, Vol 138

Kay-drup (mKhas-grub), 1384-1438
Clearing Away Mental Darkness [with Respect to the Seven Treatises] An Ornament of Dharmakīrti's 'Seven Treatises on Valid Cognition', Clearing Away Mental Darkness
sDe bdun yid kyi mun sel/Tshad ma sde bdun gyi rgyan yid kyi mun sel
Toh. 5501

Nga-wang-bel-den (Ngag-dbang-dpal-ldan), b. 1797
Annotations for (Jam-yang-shay-ba's) 'Great Exposition of Tenets,' Freeing the Knots of the Difficult Points, Precious Jewel of Clear Thought
Grub mtha' chen mo'i mchan 'grel dka' gnad mdud grol blo gsal

bces nor
Sarnath, Varanasi: Pleasure of Elegant Sayings Press, 1964
Explanation of the Meaning of "Conventional" and "Ultimate" in the Four Tenet Systems
Grub mtha' gzhi'i lugs kyi kun rdzob dang don dam pa'i don rnam par bshad pa
New Delhi: Guru Deva, 1972

Nga-wang-dra-shi (Ngag-dbang-bkra-shis), 1648-1721
The Collected Topics by a Spiritual Son of Jam-yang-shay-ba
Sras bsdus grva
n.p., n.d.

Prajñākaragupta (Shes-rab-'byung-gnas-sbas-pa)
'Ornament' Commentary
Pramāṇavārttikālaṃkāra
Tshad ma rnam 'grel gyi rgyan
P5719, Vol. 132

Pur-bu-jok (Phur-bu-lcog Byams-pa-rgya-mtsho), 1825-1901
'Explanation of the Presentation of Objects and Object Possessors as well as Awareness and Knowledge' in *Magical Key to the Path of Reasoning, Presentation of the Collected Topics Revealing the Meaning of the Treatises on Valid Cognition*
Yul yul can dang blo rig gi rnam par bshad pa *in* Tshad ma'i gzhung don 'byed pa'i bsdus grva'i rnam bzhag rigs lam 'phrul gyi sde mig
Buxa: n.d., 1965
The Topic of Signs and Reasonings from the 'Great Path of Reasoning' in *The Magic Key to the Path of Reasoning, Presentation of the Collected Topics Revealing the Meaning of the Texts on Valid Cognition*
Tshad ma'i gzhung don 'byed ba'i bsdus grva'i rnam gzhag rigs lam 'phrul gyi sde mig
Buxa: n.d. 1965

Pūrṇavardhana (Gang-ba-spel-ba), about 8th Century
Commentary on Vasubandhu's 'Treasury of Knowledge,' An Investigation of the Characteristics
Abhidharmakośaṭīkālakṣaṇānusārininnāma
Chos mngon pa'i mdzod kyi 'brel bshad mtshan nyid kyi rjes su 'brang ba shes bya ba
P5594, Vol. 117

Sagya Paṇḍita (Sa-skya Paṇḍita Kun-dga'-rgyal-mtshan), 1182-1251

Treasury of Reasoning
Tshad ma rigs pa'i gter
The Complete Works of the Great Masters of the Sa-skya Sect of Tibetan Buddhism, Vol, 5, 155.1-1-167.2.1
Tokyo: Toyo Bunko, 1968
Śākyabuddhi/Śākyamati (Śākya-blo)
Explanation of (Dharmakīrti's) "Commentary on (Dignāga's) 'Compendium on Valid Cognition'"
Pramāṇavārttikaṭīkā
rNam 'grel shad
P5718, Vol. 131
Śāntideva (Zhi-ba-lha), 8th Century
Engaging in the Bodhisattva Deeds
Bodhisattvacaryāvatāra
Byang chub sems dpa'i spyod pa la 'jug pa
P5272, Vol. 99
Śāntarakṣita (Zhi-ba-'tsho), 8th Century
Commentary on the 'Ornament to the Middle Way'
Madhyamakālaṃkāravṛtti
dbU ma'i rgyan gyi grel ba
P5285, Vol. 101
Compendium on Suchness
Tattvasaṃgrahakārikā
De kho na nyid bsdus pa'i tshig le'ur byas pa
P5764, Vol, 138; See also Gaekward Oriental Series, ed. E. Krishnamacharya, 2 Vols. (Baroda, 1926); also, with *Pañjikā* of Kamalaśīla, ed. by Swami Dwarikadas Shastri in 2 vols, Varanasi: Bauddha Bharati, 1968
Ornament to the Middle Way
Madhyamakālaṃkāra
dbU ma rgyan gyi tshig le'ur byas pa
P5284, Vol. 101
Śāriputra
Aggregate of Phenomena
Dharmaskandha
Chos kyi phung po
Taisho 1537
Tsong-ka-pa (Tsong-kha-pa), 1357-1419
Door of Entry to the Seven Treatises
Sde bdun la 'jug pa'i sgo

Sarnath, Varanasi: Pleasure of Elegant Sayings Press, 1972
Essence of the Good Explanations, Treatise Discriminating What is to be Interpreted and the Definitive
Drang ba dang nges pa'i don rnam par phye ba'i bstan bcos legs bshad snying po
P6142, Vol. 153
Notes on (Śāntarakṣita's) Ornament to the Middle Way
dbU ma rgyan gyi zin bris
Blockprint, n.p., n.d.
Vasubandhu (dbYig-gnyen), 4th Century
Explanation of the 'Treasury of Knowledge'
Abhidharmakośabhāṣya
Chos mngon pa'i mdzod kyi bshad pa
P5591, Vol. 115; Skt. ed. by Swami Dwarikadas Shastri, Varanasi: Bauddha Bharati, 1972
Treasury of Knowledge
Abhidharmkośakārikā
Chos mngon pa'i mdzod kyi tshig le'ur byas pa
P5590, Vol. 115
Yaśomitra (rGyal-po'i-sras Grags-pa'i-shes-gnyen), probably 8th Century
Commentary to (Vasubandhu's) 'Treasury of Knowledge'
Chos mngon pa'i mdzod kyi 'grel bshad
P5593, Vol. 116

II. WORKS IN ENGLISH AND FRENCH

Ayer, Sir Alfred J.
The Problem of Knowledge
Middlesex, England: Penguin Books, 1984 [1956 reprint]
Bareau, André
Les sectes bouddhiques du Petit Véhicule
Saigon: Bulletin de l'Ecole Francaise d'Extrême Orient, 1955
Barlingay, S.S.
A Modern Introduction to Indian Logic
Delhi: National Publishing House, 1965
Chandra, Dr. Lokesh
Materials for a History of Tibetan Literature
New Delhi: International Academy of Indian Culture, 1963
Coward, Harold G.
Sphoṭa Theory of Language

Delhi: Motilal Banarsidass, 1980
Dasgupta, Surendranath
A History of Indian Philosophy, Vol. 1
Cambridge: University Press, 1957
Datta, D. M.
The Six Ways of Knowing
Calcutta: University of Calcutta Press, 1960 (originally published in 1932 in Great Britain)
Frauwallner, Erich
History of Indian Philosophy, Vol. II; tr. by V.M. Bedekar
Delhi: Motilal Banarsidass, 1973
"Landmarks": Landmarks in the History of Buddhist Logic
Wiener Zeitschrift für die Kunde des Sud-und Ost-Asiens, Bd. V [1961], pp. 125-148
Gön-chok-jik-may-wang-bo (dKon-mchog-'jigs-med-dbang-po), 1728-91
"Precious Garland of Tenets" translated in Sopa & Hopkins, trans., *Practice and Theory of Tibetan Buddhism*
London: Rider & Co., 1976
Hattori, Masaaki
"*Apoha* and *Pratibhā*"
Sanskrit and Indian Studies
Boston, MA: D. Reidel, 1979
Hiriyanna, M.
Outlines of Indian Philosophy
London: George Allen & Unwin, 1932
Hopkins, P. Jeffrey
Meditation on Emptiness
London: Wisdom Publications, 1983
Iida, Shotaro
Reason and Emptiness, A Study in Logic and Mysticism
Tokyo: The Hokuseido Press, 1980
"*Āgama* (Scripture) and *Yukti* (Reason) in Bhāvaviveka"
Kyoto: Heirakuji-shoten,
Kanakura Festschrift, October, 1966
Ingalls, D.H.H.
Materials for the Study of Navya-Nyāya Logic
Cambridge: Harvard Oriental Series, 1951, Vol. 40
Iyengar, H.H.R.

"Bhartṛhari and Diṅnāga"
Journal of the Bombay Branch, Royal Asiatic Society
New series 26 Bombay: 1950, pp. 147-149
Jam-bel-sam-pel, Geshe ('Jam-dpal-bsam-phel, dGe-gshes), d. 1975
Presentation of Awareness and Knowledge
trans., ed., Elizabeth Napper, with commentary by Lati Rinbochay in *Mind in Tibetan Buddhism*
London: Rider & Co., 1980
Jayatilleke, K.N.
Early Buddhist Theory of Knowledge
London: George Allen & Unwin, 1968
Jha, Ganganatha, tr.
"The Tattvasaṅgraha of Śāntarakṣita with the Commentary of Kamalaśīla"
Gaekwad Oriental Series Vols. 80 and 83
Baroda: Oriental Institute, 1937 and 1929
Kajiyama, Yuichi
An Introduction to Buddhist Philosophy: An Annotated Translation of the Tarkabhāsā of Mokśakāragupta
Kyoto, Memoirs of the Faculty of Letters, Kyoto University, No. 10, 1966
Kajiyama, Yuichi
"Three Kinds of Affirmation and Two Kinds of Negation in Buddhist Philosophy"
Wiener Zeitschrift für die Kunde Sudasiens und Archiv fur Indische Philosophie, 1973
Keith, Arthur Berriedale
Indian Logic and Atomism
New York: Greenwood Press, 1968
Matilal, Bimal K.
Epistemology, Logic, and Grammar in Indian Philosophical Analysis
The Hague and Paris: Mouton, 1971
Mookerjee, Satkari
The Buddhist Philosophy of Universal Flux
Delhi: Motilal Banarsidass, 1975 (First published 1935)
Mookerjee, S. and Nagasaki, Hojun, translators
The Pramāṇavārttikam of Dharmakīrti, An English Translation of the First Chapter with the Autocommentary and with Elaborate Comments, Kārikās I-LI

Nalanda: Nava Nālandā Mahāvihāra, 1964
Nagatomi, Masatoshi
A Study of Dharmakīrti's Pramāṇavārttika, An English Translation and Annotation of the Pramāṇavārttika, Book I (*Pramāṇasiddhi*); Doctoral Thesis, Harvard University, June, 1957
"Arthakriyā"
The Adyar Library Bulletin, Dr. V. Raghavan Felicitation Volume, 1967-68, XXXI-XXXII, (Adyar, Madras) p. 52-72
"The Framework of the Pramāṇavārttika, Book I"
Journal of the American Oriental Society, Vol. 79, No. 4. Oct-Dec., 1959, pp. 263-266
Mānasa-pratyakṣa: A Conundrum in the Buddhist Pramāṇa System"
Sanskrit and Indian Studies, M. Nagatomi, B.K. Matilal, J.M. Masson, and R. Dimock, eds.
Boston: D. Reidel, 1980
Potter, Karl H.
Presuppositions of Indian Philosophies
Englewood Cliffs, New Jersey: Prentice-Hall, Inc., 1963
Ryle, Gilbert
The Concept of Mind
New York: Barnes & Noble, 1949
Rogers, Katherine
Tibetan Logic: A Translation with Commentary of Pur-bu-jok's "The Topic of Signs and Reasonings from the 'Great Path of Reasoning' " in the *Magic Key to the Path of Reasoning, Explanation of the Collected Topics Revealing the Meaning of the Texts on Valid Cognition*
M.A., University of Virginia, 1980
Śankarācārya
The Bṛhadāranyaka Upaniṣad with the Commentary of Śankarācārya
trans. by Swāmī Madhvānanda,
Calcutta: Advaita Ashram, 1965
Sharma, Dhirendra
The Differentiation Theory of Meaning in Indian Logic
Paris and The Hague: Mouton, 1969
The Paradox of Negative Judgement and Indian Logic"
Vishveshvaranand Indological Journal, Vol. 9, No. 4, 1966
Shastri, Dharmendra Nath
Critique of Indian Realism: A Study of the Conflict Between the

Nyāya-Vaiśeṣika and the Buddhist Dignāga School
Agra, India: Agra University, 1964
Smart, Ninian
The Philosophy of Religion
New York: Oxford University Press, 1979
Sopa, Geshe Lhundup
Lectures in Tibetan Culture
2 Vol., Dharamsala: Library of Tibetan Works and Archives, 1983
Sopa and Hopkins
Practice and Theory of Tibetan Buddhism
London: Rider & Co., 1976
Staal, J.F.
"Negation and the Law of Contradiction in Indian Thought"
Bulletin of the School of Oriental and African Studies, Vol. 25, Part I, 1962
Stcherbatsky, F. Th.
Buddhist Logic
New York: Dover Publications, Inc., 1962 (First published 1930)
Streng, Federick J.
Emptiness: A Study in Religious Meaning
Nashville: Abingdon Press, 1967
Tripathi, C.L.
The Problem of Knowledge in Yogacāra Buddhism
Varanasi: Bharat-Bharati, 1972
Tsong-ka-pa
Tantra in Tibet
trans, and ed. Jeffrey Hopkins
London: George Allen & Unwin, 1977
van der Kuijp, Leonard W.J.
Contributions to the Development of Tibetan Buddhist Epistemology
Weisbaden: Franz Steiner Verlag, Alt-und Neu-Indische Studien herausgegeben vom Seminar für Kultur und Geschichte Indiens an der Universität Hamburg) 26, 1983
"Phya-Pa Chos-Kyi Seng-Ge's Impact on Tibetan Epistemological Theory"
Journal of Indian Philosophy, Vol. 5, 1978
Wayman, Alex
Calming the Mind and Discerning the Real, From Tsong-ka-pa's Lam Rim Chen Mo

New York: Columbia University Press, 1978; reprint New Delhi: Motilal Banarsidass, 1979

Warder, A.K.
Indian Buddhism
New Delhi: Motilal Banarsidass, 1970

Wylie, Turrell
"A Standard System of Tibetan Transcription"
HJAS, Vol. 22, 1959, 261-267

Yamaguchi, Susumu
"*Ālambanaparīkṣā* with *Vṛtti* of Dignāga, Tibetan version" in
Seshin Yuishiki no Genten Kaimei
Kyoto, 1953

Zwilling, Leonard
"Dharmakīrti on *Apoha*"
Ph.D. Dissertation, University of Wisconsin, 1976

"Saskya Paṇḍita's Version of *Pramāṇavārttikam* III. 3 — A Case Study on the Influence of Exegesis upon Translation in Tibet"
Studies in Indian Philosophy, A Memorial Volume in Honour of Pandit Sukhalalji Sanghvi
L.D. Series 84, Dalsukh Malvania and Nagin J. Shah general editors.
Ahmedbad: L.D. Institute of Indology, 1981

"Some Aspects of Dharmakīrti's Ontology Reconsidered"
KAILASH, A Journal of Himalayan Studies
Kathmandu: Ratna Pustak Bhandar, Vol. III, No. 3, 1975

Glossary

English	*Sanskrit*	*Tibetan*
abiding	sthāna	gnas pa
actual	sākṣāt	dngos
affirming negative	paryudāspratiṣedha	ma yin dgag
affixing the appellation		brda' sbyar ba
affliction	kleśha	nyon mongs
aggregate	skandha	phung po
aggregation		'dus pa
alternative	koṭi	mu
Amitayus	amitayus	tshe dpag med
analytical cessation	pratisaṃkhyānirodha	so sor brtags 'gog
antidote	pratipakṣa	gnyen po
appearance	pratibhāsa	snang ba
appearing object	pratibhāsaviṣaya	snang yul
appellation	saṃketa	brda
apprehend	grahaṇa	'dzin pa
apprehended object	*grahyaviṣaya	gzung yul, gzung don
apprehending aspect	grāhakākāra	'dzin rnam
apprehension aspect	grāhyākāra	bzung rnam

English	*Sanskrit*	*Tibetan*
Āryadeva	āryadeva	'phags-pa-lha
Asaṅga	asaṅga	thogs-med
aspect	ākāra	rnam pa
attribute	viśeṣa	khyad par
autonomous syllogism	svatantraprayoga	rang rgyud kyi sbyor ba
Avalokitavrata	avalokitavrata	spyan-ras-gzigs-brtul-zhugs
Avalokiteśvara	avalokiteśvara	sPyan-ras-gzigs
awareness	buddhi	blo
basal subject		rang rten gyi chos can
base	āśraya	rten
basis of affixing		'jug gzhi
Bhāvaviveka	bhāvaviveka	Legs-ldan-'byed
Blessed One	bhagavān	bCom ldan 'das
Bodhibhadra	bodhibhadra	byang-chub-bzang-po
Bodhisattva	bodhisattva	byang chub sems dpa'
causal condition	hetupratyaya	rgyu rkyen
calm abiding	śamatha	zhi gnas
cause	hetu	rgyu
challenger (in debate)		snga rgol
Cittamātra	cittamātra	sems tsam
collection		tshogs pa
collection generality		tshogs spyi
color	varṇa	kha dog
common	sādhārana	thun mong
common locus	samānādhikaraṇa	gzhi mthun
compassion	karuṇā	snying rje
complete engager	*vidhipravṛtti-buddhi	sgrub 'jug gi blo
composite		bsags pa

English	*Sanskrit*	*Tibetan*
compositional factor	saṃskāra	'du byed
conception of a self of phenomena	dharmātmagrāha	chos kyi bdag 'dzin
concordant example	sadṛṣṭānta	mthun dpe
condition	pratyaya	rkyen
consciousness	jñāna/vijñāna	shes pa/rnam par shes pa
consequence	prasaṅga	thal 'gyur
constituent	dhātu	khams
continuum	samtāna	rgyud
contradictory	virodha	'gal ba
convention	vyavahāra	tha snyad
conventional truth	saṃvṛtisatya	kun rdzob bden pa
conventionally existent	saṃvṛtisat	kun rdzob du yod pa/tha snyad du yod pa
cooperative condition	sahakāripratyaya	lhan cig byed rkyen
correct reason	*saṃyakliṅga	rtags yang dag
counter pervasion	vyatirekavyāpti	ldog khyab
definiendum	lakṣya	mtshon bya
definition	lakṣaṇa	mtshan nyid
designation		brda'
Devendrabuddhi	devendrabuddhi	lha-dbang-blo
Dharmakīrti	dharmakīrti	chos-kyi-grags-pa
Dignāga	dignāga	phyogs-glang
direct perceiver/direct perception	pratyakṣa	mngon sum
discipline	vinaya	'dul ba
discrimination	samjñā	'du shes
disintegration	vināśa	'jig pa
dissimilar class		mi mthun phyogs
effect	phala	'bras bu
effect sign proving a general cause		rgyu'i spyi sgrub kyi 'bras rtags

English	*Sanskrit*	*Tibetan*
effect sign proving a particular cause		rgyu'i khyad par sgrub kyi 'bras rtags
effect sign proving a preceding cause		rgyu sngon song sgrub kyi 'bras rtags
effect sign proving an actual cause		rgyu dngos sgrub kyi 'bras rtags
effect sign which is a means of inferring causal attributes		rgyu chos rjes dpog gi bras rtags
empowering condition	adhipatipratyaya	bdag rkyen
emptiness	śūnyatā	stong pa nyid
entity	vastu	ngo bo
established/proven	siddha	grub pa
established basis		gzhi grub
established through its own power	svairīsiddhi	rang dbang du grub pa
evolute	parināma/vikāra	rnam 'gyur
exclusion	apoha	sel ba
Exemplifiers	dārśṭāntika	dpes ston pa
existence	sat	yod pa
experience		myong ba
explicit	sākṣāt	dngos
explicit object of expression		dngos gyi brjod bya
explicit realization		dngos rtogs
explicitly suggest		dngos su 'phen pa
eye sense power	cakṣurindriya	mig dbang
factor	amṣa/bhāga	cha
factually concordant	anvartha	don mthun
factually other		don gzhan
feature	viśeṣa	khyad par
feeling	vedanā	tshor ba
Foe Destroyer	arhan	dGra bcom pa

English	*Sanskrit*	*Tibetan*
Followers of Reasoning	*nyāyānusārin	rigs pa'i rje su 'brangs pa
Followers of Scripture	*āgamānusārin	mDo sde'i rjes su 'brangs pa
form	rūpa	gzugs
form aggregate	rūpaskandha	gzugs gyi phung po
Four Noble Truths	catvaryāryasatyāni	bden pa bzhi
fruit	phala	'bras bu
functioning thing (that which is able to perform a function)	bhāva, *kriyāśakta, *kriyāsamarta, arthakriya-kāritva	don byed nus pa/ dngos po
generality	sāmānya	spyi
generally characterized thing		dngos por 'gyur ba'i spyi mtshan
generally characterized phenomenon	sāmānyalakṣaṇa	spyi mtshan
Half-Eggists		sgo nga phyed tshal ba
Hearer	śrāvaka	nyan thos
hidden phenomenon	parokṣa	lkog gyur
hue		tshon
illustration		mtshan gzhi
illustration-isolate		gzhi ldog
immediately preceding condition	samanantarapratya-ya	de ma thag rkyen
impermanent	anitya	mi rtag pa
impermanent thing	bhāva	dngos po
implicitly suggest		zhugs la 'phen pa
imputedly established	*prajñaptisiddhi	btags du sgrub pa
imputedly existent	*prajñaptisat	btags yod

English	*Sanskrit*	*Tibetan*
incontrovertible	avisaṃvādin	mi slu ba
inference	anumāna	rjes dpag
inference by the power of the fact	*vastu-bala-anumāna	dngos stobs rjes dpag
inference thru belief	*āpta-anumāna	yid ches rjes dpag
inference thru renown	*prasiddha-anumāna	grags pa'i rjes dpag
inherent existence	svabhāvasiddhi	rang bzhin gyis grub pa
instance, manifestation	vyākti	gsal ba
isolate	vivartana	ldog pa
Knowledge	abhidharma	chos mngon pa
latency	vāsanā	bag chags
liberation	mokṣa/vimokṣa	thar pa
Mādhyamika	mādhyamika	dbu ma pa
manifest phenomenon	abhimukhī	mngon gyur
matter	kanthā	bem po
meaning/object	artha	don
meaning-generality	arthasāmānya	don spyi
meaning isolate	*arthavivartana	don ldog
meaning-of-the-term	śabdārtha	sgra don
meditative absorption	samāpatti	snyoms 'jug
mental and physical aggregates	skandha	phung po
mental application	mānaskara	yid la byed pa
mental direct perceiver	mānasapratyakṣa	yid kyi mngon sum
mental exclusion	buddhyātmakānyā-poha	blo'i gzhan sel
mental factor	caitta	sems byung

English	*Sanskrit*	*Tibetan*
merely propounded subject, mere subject		chos can 'ba' zhig pa
method	upāya	thabs
mind of partial engagement	*apohapravṛtti-buddhi	sel 'jug gi blo
minute particle	paramāṇu	rdul phra rab
mistaken	bhrānta	'khrul ba
mix, associate		'dres pa
mode of abiding		gnas lugs
mode of subsistence		sdod lugs, gnas lugs
moment	kṣaṇa	skad cig
momentary	kṣaṇika	skad cig ma
mutual	anyonya	phan tshun
mutual exclusion	anyonyaparihara-virodha	phan tshun spangs 'gal
Nāgārjuna	nāgārjuna	klu-grub
name	nāma, saṃketa	ming, brda
natural existence	svalakṣaṇa-siddhi	rang gi mtshan nyid kyis grub pa
nature	prākṛti	rang bzhin
nature sign	*svabhāva-liṅga	rang bzhin kyi rtags
nature sign that is free of qualification		khyad par dag pa pa'i rang bzhin kyi rtags
nature sign that relates to a qualification		khyad par ltos pa pa'i rang bzhin kyi rtags
nature sign which implies [a qualification or agent which is another substantial entity]		khyad par kyi chos rdzas gzhan 'phen pa'i rang bzhin kyi rtags
nature sign which implies [a		rdzas gzhan ma yin pa 'phen pa'i rang

English	*Sanskrit*	*Tibetan*
qualification or agent which is not another substantial entity]		bzhin kyi rtags
negative/negative phenomenon	pratiṣedha	dgag pa
negative, affirming	paryudāsaprati-ṣedha	ma yin dgag
negative, non-affirming	prasajyaprati-ṣedha	med dgag
nine successive meditative absorptions	navānupūrvavihār-asamāpatti	mthar gyis gnas pa'i snyoms par 'jug pa dgu
nirvana without remainder	anupadhiśeṣa-nirvāṇa	lhag med myang ngan las 'das pa
noble/superior	ārya	'phags pa
non-affirming negative	prasajyapratiṣedha	med dgag
non-associated compositional factor	viprayukta-saṃskāra	ldan min 'du byed
non-conceptual	nirvikalpaka	rtog med
non-observation sign	*anupalabdaliṅga	ma dmigs pa'i rtags
non-observation sign of the non-appearing	*apratibhāsān-uplabdhiliṅga	mi snang ba ma dmigs pa'i rtags
non-obstructive	apratihata, apratigha	thogs pa med pa
non-mistaken	abhrānta	ma 'khrul ba
Non-Pluralists		sna tshogs gnyis med pa
non-revelatory form	avijñaptirūpa	rnam par rig byed ma yin pa'i gzugs
non-thing	abhāva	dngos med
object being proved	sādhya	bsgrub bya
object condition	ālambanapratyaya	dmigs rkyen

English	*Sanskrit*	*Tibetan*
object of comprehension	prameya	gzhal bya
object of engagement	*pravṛttiviṣaya	'jug yul
object of expression	abhidheya, vācyam	brjod bya
object of knowledge	jñeya	shes bya
object of negation	pratiṣedhya	dgag bya
object of operation		'jug yul
object of the mode of apprehension		'dzin stangs gyi yul
objective exclusion	arthātmaka-svalakṣaṇa-anyāpoha	don rang mtshan gyi gzhan sel
obscured	saṃvṛti	kun rdzob
observed object condition	ālambana-pratyaya	dmigs rkyen
odor	gandha	dri
one substantial entity	ekadravya	rdzas gcig
one substantial entity of establishment and abiding		grub bde rdzas gcig
opposite	vyatireka	log pa
other-exclusion	anyāpoha	gzhan sel
other-knower	*anyasaṃvedanā	gzhan rig
partial engager	*apohapravṛtti	sel 'jug
path	mārga	lam
path of seeing	darśanamārga	mthong lam
perfection	pāramitā	phar phyin
permanent	nitya	rtag pa
pervasion/positive pervasion	anvayavyāpti	rjes khyab
phenomenon imputed by thought		rtog pas btags tsam gyi chos
phenomenon-source	dharmāyatana	chos kyi skye mched
phrase/word	vacana	tshig
positive phenomenon	vidhi	sgrub pa
power of the thing	*vastubala	dngos stobs

English	*Sanskrit*	*Tibetan*
Prāsaṅgika	prāsaṅgika	thal 'gyur pa
predicate of the probandum	sādhyadharma	bsgrub bya'i chos
predicate of the negandum		dgag bya'i chos
prime cognizer/ valid cognizer	pramāṇa	tshad ma
principal	pradhāna	gtso bo
product	saṃskṛta	'dus byas
production	utpatti	skye ba
property of the subject	pakṣadharma	phyogs chos
proponents of an equal number of subjects & objects		gzung 'dzin grangs mnyam pa
pure thing	vastumātra	dngos po dag pa
reality	dharmatā	chos nyid
realize	adhigamana	rtogs pa
referent object	*adhyavasaya-viṣaya	zhen yul
reflection	pratibiṃba	gzugs brnyan
reverse	vivartana, vyatireka	ldog pa
Sāṃkhya	sāṃkhya	grangs can pa
Śāntarakṣita	śāntarakṣita	zhi-ba-'tsho
Sautrantika	sautrāntika	mdo sde pa
self-isolate		rang ldog
self-knower	svasaṃvedanā	rang rig
self of persons	pudgalātman	gang zag gi bdag
self of phenomenon	dharmātman	chos kyi bdag
selflessness	nairātyma	bdag med
selflessness of persons	pudgalanairātmya	gang zag gi bdag med
selflessness of phenomena	dharmanairātmya	chos kyi bdag med
self sufficient		rang rkya ba

English	*Sanskrit*	*Tibetan*
sense direct perceiver	*rūpagrahanendriyapratyakṣa	gzugs 'dzin dbang mngon
Sequential Non-Pluralists		rim gyis ba'i sna tshogs gnyis med pa
sets of discourses/ sets of sutras	sūtrānta	mdo sde
shape	samsthāna	dbyibs
sign	liṅga	rtags
sign of non-dependence		ltogs med kyi rtags
sign of observation of a contradictory object		'gal zla dmigs pa'i rtags
sign of sameness of entity	svabhāva-liṅga	rang bzhin gyi rtags
sign which is a non-observation of a related object		'brel zla ma dmigs pa'i rtags
sign which is a non-observation of the suitable to appear		snang rung ma dmigs pa'i rtags
similar aspect		'dra rnam
similar class		mthun phyogs
similar example	sadṛṣṭānta	mthun dpe
small particle		rdul phran
Solitary Realizer	pratyekabuddha	rang sangs rgyas
sound	śabda	sgra
source	āyatana	skye mched
space	ākāśa	nam mkha'
special insight	vipaśyanā	lhag mthong
specifically characterized phenomenon	svalakṣaṇa	rang mtshan
subject	dharmin	chos can
subsequent cognizer	*pariccinna-jñāna	bcad shed/dpyad shes

English	*Sanskrit*	*Tibetan*
substantial entity	dravya	rdzas
substantial entity of establishment and abiding		grub bde rdzas gcig
substantially established	dravyasiddha	rdzas su grub pa
substantially existent	dravyasat	rdzas yod
substratum		khyad gzhi
suggest		'phen
suitable to be mixed		'dres rung
superimposition	āropa	sgro btags
syllogism	prayoga	sbyor ba
tangible object/ object of touch	sprastavya	reg bya
tenet	siddhānta	grub mtha'
term	śabda	sgra
terminology	saṃketa	brda'
thesis	pratijñā	dam bca'
thing	bhāva	dngos po
thirty-seven harmonies with enlightenment		byang phyogs so bdun
thought/thought consciousness	kalpanā	rtog pa
three modes	trirūpa	tshul gsum
truly existent	*satyasat	bden par yod pa
type generality	*gotrasāmānya	rigs spyi
two truths	satyadvaya	bden pa gnyis
ultimate truth	paramārthasatya	don dam bden pa
ultimately established phenomenon	paramārtha-siddhidharma	don dam du grub ba'i chos
ultimately existent	paramārthasat	don dam par yod pa
uncommon	asādharaṇa	thun mong ma yin ba
uncommon cause	asādharaṇa-hetu	thun mong ma yin ba'i rgyu

English	*Sanskrit*	*Tibetan*
unconditioned	asaṃskṛta	'dus ma byas
undermining sign		gnod pa can gyi rtags
Vaibhāṣika	vaibhāṣika	bye brag smar ba
Vasubandhu	vasubandhu	dbyig-gnyen
valid cognizer/ prime cognizer	pramāṇa	tshad ma
Vinītadeva	vinītadeva	dul-ba-lha
yogic direct perceiver	yogipratyakṣa	rnal 'byor mngon sum

Index

explicit (*dngos gyi brjod bya*), 189, 195, 196, 203-210
Object of Knowledge (*jñeya, shes bya*), 142, 145, 152, 159, 191, 239 n.23
Object of negation (*pratiṣedhya, dgag bya*), 40, 65, 142, 143, 144, 207, 208
Object of operation (*'jug yul*), 38, 129, 193
Objective specifically characterized exclusions *see* exclusions
Objects, two types of, 83, 84
One substantial entity, 77, 78, 93, 105, 114, 133, 202, 203
One substantial entity of establishment and abiding (*grub bde rdzas gcig*), 92, 94, 95, 96, 97, 108, 109, 110, 124, 131, 197
Opposite-from-non-pot, 124, 160-161, 167, 168, 172, 173, 238 n.17
Opposite from non pot, appearance as, 169-170, 238 n.17
Ornament to the Middle Way (*Mādhyamakālaṃkāra*), 105-106, 109

Partial engager (*gsal 'jug gi blo*), 65, 156, 193, 203-204, 210, *see also* conceptual thought
Partless particles, 29, 30, 34-35, 41, 44, 49, 51, 69-70, 72, 74, 77-79, 80, 81, 95, 201
Parts and wholes, ontology of, 31-32, 34-35, 44, 49, 50-52, 75, 77-78, 84-88, 95, 189
Paryudāsa-pratiṣedha, see affirming negative
Path of preparation (*prayoga-mārga*), 16
Path of seeing, 16, 17, 152, 156
Person,
  ontology of, 52, 54-55, 56, 58, 85, 132, 151, 194
  selflessness of, 55, 56, 83, 151-152, 208-209, *see also* emptiness
Phenomena,
  existent, 45, 46, 82, 142, 180-181
  impermanent, 26, 36, 46, 53, 77-78, *see also* specifically characterized phenomena
  as mixed and unmixed, 26-27, 45-46, 47, 50-52, 72, 81, 116, 128-129, 167, 199-200, 226 n.31
  negative, *see* negative phenomena *and* exclusions
  permanent, 26, 36, 46-47, 53-54, 179, 181, 226 n.29; *see also* generally characterized phenomena
  positive, *see* positive phenomena
Phenomenon, 47, 142, 221 n.24
Phenomenalism, 89, 233 n.1
Plato, 50, 198, 227 n.44
Point-instant, 29, 30, 31, 43, 82, 181, 224 n.13, *see also* specifically characterized phenomena
Positive phenomena, 22, 124, 141-143, 167, 241 n.2
  definition of, 142
Potter, Karl, 82, 179-180
Prajñapti-sat, see imputedly existent
Prakṛti, see fundamental nature
Pramāṇasamuccaya, see *Compendium on Valid Cognition*
Pramāṇavārttika, see *Commentary on (Dignāga's) 'Compendium on Valid Cognition'*
Prāsaṅgika-Mādhyamika, 14, 17, 39-40, 49, 55-56, 64-65, 69, 73, 87-88, 89, 100, 105, 111, 113, 134, 144, 152, 174, 175-180, 224 n.11, *see also* Sautrāntika, relation to Mādhyamika
Prasajya-pratiṣedha see non-affirming negative
Pratibha, see sentence
Pratibimba, see sentence
Pratyakṣa, see direct perception
Projection, 89, *see also* imputation by thought *and* superimposition
Proponents of an Equal Number of Subjects and objects, 108, 110
Pur-bu-jok (Phur-bu-lcog), *see Col-*